Managing international construction projects:
An overview

International Construction Management Series No. 7

Managing international construction projects:
An overview

Edited by R. Neale

International Labour Office   Geneva

Neale, R.
Managing international construction projects: An overview
Geneva, International Labour Office, 1995 (International Construction Management Series No. 7)

/Management development/, /guide/, /construction/, /project management/, /civil engineering/, /construction industry/. 08.10.1
ISBN 92-2-108751-4
ISSN 1020-0142

ILO Cataloguing in Publication Data

ILO publications can be obtained through major booksellers or ILO local offices in many countries, or direct from ILO Publications, International Labour Office, CH-1211 Geneva 22, Switzerland. A catalogue or list of new publications will be sent free of charge from the above address.

PREFACE

The International Labour Office, through its Construction Management Programme, has a continuing interest in the development of construction enterprises throughout the world. Specifically, this interest stems from the dual role of construction not only as a significant source of direct employment but as a sector which contributes through its wide range of operations and projects to the growth and development of virtually all other economic sectors.

Many construction enterprises have chosen to limit their operations to the home market. Others appreciate the scope for diversifying into international projects, but are wary of the risks involved in venturing into an alien environment. Others still have suffered severe losses as a result of international ventures, and have resolved to avoid them in future. The caution regarding international contracting is well-founded, but the potential attractions remain. The world construction market is very large, and the projected demand for improved infrastructure and shelter suggests that it will continue to offer attractive opportunities to the discriminating bidder. Many national contractors could offer a competitive service in selected areas, provided they offer realistic bids based on a proper appreciation of resources and risks.

International Construction Management (ICM) books have been written for engineers and members of other construction professions who are working in such enterprises, and wish to fit themselves for a career in international project management. They are also suitable for undergraduate and postgraduate engineering students. Such readers are likely to have a technical background in civil engineering or a related discipline, but may have only a limited understanding of accounting, finance, strategic management, marketing and commercial topics. Whilst there are numerous books that tackle the latter topics in a national context, the ICM series seeks to provide an integrated introduction to international construction management as a basis for making informed investment and operating decisions so as to minimize risk and improve the profitability of the construction enterprise.

The ICM series is ideal both for individual study and group study, since relatively complex topics are carefully explained and the active participation of the reader is ensured by the extensive use of case-studies, worked examples and exercises. Although British practice is used as a frame of reference, the books encourage the reader to compare alternative approaches and adapt the application of techniques to suit local regulatory, contractual and tax regimes. This book provides an overview to the ICM series and the style is deliberately terse and factual, with a strong emphasis on the use of flowcharts, diagrams and checklists. The aim is to permit a competent manager to absorb the content quickly, and then refer back to specific sections and topics as the need arises. It also serves as a companion volume to A. D. Austen and Richard Neale (eds.): *Managing construction projects: A guide to processes and procedures* (Geneva, ILO), 1984, a general introduction to construction project management.

The overview is divided into eight chapters. The first three of these have been designed to provide the reader with an appreciation of the principles underlying contemporary project management, commencing in Chapter 1 with a general review of concepts and principles together with an explanation of the special characteristics of construction projects that differentiate them from practices in other industries. Chapter 2 explains how construction projects are organized and staffed, while the increasingly important topic of information technology is dealt with in Chapter 3.

The second part of the book summarizes the functional aspects of site management and the use of computer systems in planning and control. Chapter 4 reviews the principles and practice of quality assurance, explaining the procedures required to conform with international standard ISO 9000. Chapter 5 deals with site facilities and layout, including flowcharts and a series of checklists. Chapter 6 tackles the often neglected issues of health and safety, and is also liberally supported with flowcharts and checklists. Chapters 7 and 8 provide case-studies of construction planning and cost analysis, providing substantial illustrations of the use of computer systems. The information is provided in sufficient detail for it to be used as a basis for training exercises, or as comprehensive input data for the comparative evaluation of computer systems. Although the diagrams in Chapters 7 and 8 show some inconsistencies, they are **as used** by the planning engineers involved in these projects. Throughout the book all unsourced tables and figures are the original work of the authors concerned.

The overview has been edited by Richard Neale, Senior Lecturer and Leader of the Building Group in the Department of Civil and Building Engineering of the Loughborough University of Technology in the United Kingdom. The ICM series editor is Derek Miles, previously Director of the ILO Construction Management Programme and now Director of Overseas Activities and Leader of the Water, Engineering and Development Centre in the Department of Civil and Building Engineering of the Loughborough University of Technology.

ACKNOWLEDGEMENTS

This book in the International Construction Management (ICM) series was designed to assist the China International Contractors' Association (CHINCA) to meet the needs of its member corporations to build the broad management expertise needed to expand their operations on the international market. It was prepared within a technical cooperation project carried out by the ILO as executing agency under the United Nations Development Programme (UNDP). In view of the dearth of textbooks and training material that would be suitable for the needs of senior and middle level management staff of these enterprises, it was decided to commission a series of texts that would enable them to improve their understanding of the range of specialist management skills that are required to compete effectively in the international construction market.

We are grateful to the staff of CHINCA and its member corporations for their advice and assistance during the field testing of the material upon which this book is based, and the agreement of both CHINCA and UNDP that it should be made accessible to a wider audience.

The editors wish to acknowledge the contributions of Simon Barber (Managing Director, Claremont Controls Limited, United Kingdom), Alistair Gibb and William Sher (Loughborough University of Technology). The attribution of authorship by chapters is as follows:

Chapters 1 and 2: Richard Neale

Chapter 3: William Sher

Chapters 4, 5 and 6: Alistair Gibb

Chapters 7 and 8: Richard Neale and Simon Barber.

CONTENTS

Tables

INTRODUCTION

Aims and context

This guide is written for managers of major construction enterprises, and is one of a series of books on construction management published by the ILO. The main aim is to provide a companion volume to the successful *Managing construction projects: A guide to processes and procedures*, which was originally published in 1984, and has been reprinted several times, and in several languages. The aim of the original guide was to describe "the processes and procedures of construction project management, with emphasis on their use in developing countries", and "the general principles of construction project management". Readers of the guide will appreciate that this was a very broad aim. Consequently the depth of coverage had to be limited, and the book concentrates on fundamental principles, at a level of the widest applicability.

This new guide (the "overview") extends the content of the original guide, with specific focus on the management of major projects by those organizations which undertake the site construction work (usually called "contractors"). The overview is intended for construction managers who are responsible for substantial elements of major projects, and the more senior managers to whom they are responsible. There is, therefore, an emphasis on the organization of the project team, their functional responsibilities, and on the major aspects of their work-quality assurance, site layout, planning, cost control, and health and safety. With this readership in mind, the assumption has been made that construction managers will already be familiar with basic principles of project management, and also with the principles of planning and control. These are covered in the original ILO guide,[1] referred to above, in books listed in an ILO bibliography,[2] and also in such readily available texts as *Construction planning* by R. H. Neale and D. E. Neale.[3]

An additional consideration is that the ten years since the original guide was published have seen the extensive adoption of the tools of information technology for construction management, and this is emphasized in the overview wherever relevant. It has been recognized that it is only relatively recently that the use of information technology has become widespread, and so it is highly likely that it will not have been included in the education and training of senior managers. Therefore, some detailed case-studies of the practical application of computer systems have been included in the overview. The intention is that readers who are unfamiliar with this technology will be able to learn about it quickly, and in a way that is directly applicable.

A second assumption is that construction managers will be too busy to read long and complex expositions of project management theory. Thus the style of the overview is terse and factual, with a strong emphasis on flow charts, diagrams and check-lists. The aim is that a competent manager should be able to absorb the content quickly.

The overview begins with a general review of the concepts and principles of construction project management, together with an explanation of the special characteristics of construction projects that make managing them rather different from practices in other industries. The second chapter explains how construction projects are organized and staffed. Information technology is reviewed in Chapter 3. These three chapters establish a basis for contemporary construction project management, and are followed by three chapters summarizing the functional aspects of site management.

The final two chapters give detailed case-studies of construction planning and cost analysis, providing substantial illustrations of the use of computer systems. The information provided is in sufficient detail for it to be used as the basis for training exercises, or as comprehensive input data for the evaluation of computer systems that readers may be considering for acquisition.

The content of each chapter is summarized in the next section. This is followed by brief notes describing the authors.

Brief description of the contents of each chapter

Chapter 1: Construction project management
by Richard Neale
This chapter gives a strategic review of the subject of construction project management. It includes a discussion of the characteristics of construction projects, and the implications for management. General management functions, and the goals of construction project management are also explained. The increasing use of design-and-build forms of contract is discussed, and is illustrated by a short case-study of a prestigious national project.

Chapter 2: Project management organization
by Richard Neale
The way in which projects are organized and staffed is described, bearing in mind their essential characteristics An analysis is made in some detail of the functions necessary for the successful completion of a

construction project, and the allocation of these functions to parties to the contract and their professional staff. The chapter includes an explanation of the role and qualities of the project manager. Two case-studies illustrate some of the topics discussed.

Chapter 3:   Systems support for projects
by William Sher

International projects demand and generate enormous volumes of information, from design through estimating, planning, costing, and plant management to measurement of completed work and payment. Information is also a major element in personnel management, and of course procurement and accounting. This chapter summarizes the systems required, their form and the way in which they are used.

Chapter 4:   Control of quality and quality assurance
by Alistair Gibb

A review of the principles and practices of quality assurance, including systems and guidelines for managerial control. Conformity with International Standard 9000 is explained, and the process is illustrated by case material.

Chapter 5:   Site layout and facilities
by Alistair Gibb

The project site is the contractor's factory, so the planning of the facilities and layout will have a significant impact on productivity. This chapter explains the principles, and provides flowcharts for the planning process. Check-lists are given in an appendix.

Chapter 6:   Construction site safety
by Alistair Gibb

An issue that is often neglected. The importance of safety is emphasized in this chapter, and systems, flowcharts and check-lists are provided. Good, contemporary practices, and their management, are discussed.

Chapter 7:   Planning case-studies
by Richard Neale and Simon Barber

This chapter reviews the planning and control process briefly, emphasizing the need to operate simple systems that give timely information on which managers can base their decisions. The main text of the chapter comprises two planning case-studies, one from India and one from the United Kingdom, which are given as practical examples. The use of computer systems is explained in some detail. The application of spreadsheet software to perform line-of-balance calculations is illustrated by a brief case-study which originated from Richard Neale's involvement with an institute in India.

Chapter 8:   Cost analysis case-study
by Richard Neale and Simon Barber

An analysis of the crucial managerial activity of controlling the costs of a project, rather than simply monitoring them. The pace of construction work, and the inherent difficulty of predicting outputs with certainty, requires managers to make timely decisions to maintain progress and resolve problems. An efficient system for providing relevant cost information is required. The principles and practices are summarized in this case-study, which is an extension of the one used in the previous chapter, and shows how a project management system can form the basis of the control of time and cost for a project.

Contributors

Richard Neale BSc, MSc, CEng, MICE, FCIOB

Senior Lecturer and Leader, Building Group, Department of Civil and Building Engineering, Loughborough University of Technology

Richard joined the University in 1974 following a career in design and construction, in which he progressed to project manager. He is currently Course Director for the MEng degree in Civil and Building Engineering.

Research interests include an involvement over twenty years in the planning and scheduling of construction projects and the production of construction materials, including SERC grants for controlling contractors' costs, and computer applications in the design, draughting and materials scheduling of temporary works. He led the team that won the Chartered Institute of Building 1991 Research Award "Prefabricated modules and site productivity". Current research projects include PhD students funded by major UK companies, ECC Building Products and J. Sainsbury. Publications include *Construction planning*, published by Thomas Telford.

Internationally, Richard has been consultant to the International Labour Office since 1980, and this work has resulted in two books, a bibliography and seven training manuals. He has written a policy paper for the World Bank on the development of local design and construction firms in developing countries. Training assignments include the design and delivery of a professional development programme for the technical staff of the UN Relief and Works Agency for Palestine Refugees, and consultancy assignments to Botswana, Ethiopia, Kenya, Ghana, India, Iraq, Jordan, Syrian Arab Republic and the United Republic of Tanzania.

Simon Barber BSc, PhD

Managing Director, Claremont Controls Limited, England

Simon graduated with a first-class honours degree in civil engineering from the University of Newcastle upon Tyne in 1977. He followed this with a doctorate at the University, for research into the design and construction of heavy duty pavements, typically those constructed within the container handling areas of ports around the world. As part of this project he developed a simplified design tool suitable for use on medium-sized computers and developed a series of graphical design charts for heavily loaded flexible pavement structures. These design charts were later published by the British Ports Authority.

In 1981 Simon joined Claremont Controls Limited as a director and was responsible for the development of the company's project planning software package. This product, named Hornet, was first released in 1981 on the early personal computers used by industry, and has subsequently been upgraded several times to take advantage of the development of computers over the last 14 years. The software package has been adopted and used in a wide range of industries throughout the world, providing solutions to a range of project scheduling requirements. The Hornet system has established itself in several international construction companies as their core planning tool for major projects. Over the past five years, Claremont Controls has implemented a new planning package based on the Unix operating system, using commercial SQL database engines. This product has been adopted by a number of large organizations to provide the project scheduling functions for the control and scheduling of their larger projects. Simon maintains an active role in the design and implementation of the company's products, in addition to being Managing Director of the company.

Alistair Gibb BSc, CEng, MICE

Lecturer, Building Group, Department of Civil and Building Engineering, Loughborough University of Technology

Alistair joined Loughborough University in January 1993. Previously he has been employed by UK-based contractors Taylor Woodrow and Sir Robert McAlpine, but most recently by Laing Management on several large, technically complex buildings in London. The London contracts included management of design, fabrication, testing and installation of prefabricated toilet modules and systemised cladding units. Alistair was Construction Manager for Laing Management Ltd. on Vintners Place, London, a £75 million high-quality building, responsible for management of off-site and on-site activities from pre-tender to final account stage.

William Sher BSc, MSc, MCIOB, MSAIB

Lecturer, Building Group, Department of Civil and Building Engineering, Loughborough University of Technology

William is Course Director of the BSc Construction Engineering Management, a degree course sponsored by ten of the UK's largest construction companies. He has 20 years of experience of the building industry, both in the United Kingdom and in South Africa, working for contractors as an estimator, planner and site manager.

Prior to his present position he spent four years as Senior Lecturer in the Department of Building at the University of the Witwatersrand, South Africa. Before this he spent six years as a consultant and director of a construction computing company specializing in installing and training contractors in the use of computer-aided estimating, planning and cost control software.

Notes

[1] A. D. Austen and R. H. Neale (eds.): *Managing construction projects: A guide to processes and procedures.* ILO, Geneva, 1984. Reprinted 1986 and 1990. ISBN 92-2-103553-0. Reprinted by Dialogue Publications, New Delhi, India, 1985. Bahasa Indonesian edition 1991. There is also a Thai language edition of this book.

[2] R. H. Neale: *Construction management and technology: A bibliography.* 122 pp., Gower Press, Aldershot, United Kingdom, 1987, on behalf of the ILO, 1987. ISBN 0-566-053-79-9.

[3] R. H. Neale and D. E. Neale: *Construction planning*, Thomas Telford, London, Dec. 1989, 160 pp. ISBN 0-7277-1322-1.

CONSTRUCTION PROJECT MANAGEMENT

1

1.1 Construction projects

The most basic definition of a project is some form of human activity that has a beginning, a productive middle phase and an end, creating something that has not previously existed. In the construction business, the project will create a building or a work of civil engineering construction. The definition is important, because it emphasizes the transitory nature of the construction process – construction companies arrive on site, build, and leave for the next project. The project site may be far from the headquarters of the construction company, and in the case of major international construction projects, it may well be in another country, operating in a social, economic and physical environment that is quite different from that within which the construction company is based. No other industry sets up a new factory, in a new place, for every product it produces. Few make their products in the open air, adjusting their manufacturing methods to the climate and season.

This context gives construction project management its distinct body of knowledge and skills, and also its unique culture and traditions. These have a great influence on the management principles and processes of construction project management, as the following section explains.

1.2 Characteristics of construction projects and managerial implications

Built wherever required

International construction is a highly mobile business. Clients of its products are spread worldwide, it is one of the most basic industries, supporting the needs of the human race for shelter and mobility, and enclosing and facilitating all other industries. Construction firms have to seek out work wherever it is required.

Managerial implications:

1. Construction firms must seek new work continually. The range of potential work is very wide, so the marketing function – "indemnifying and satisfying a customer's need at the required level of profit" – of a construction company is of crucial importance. Marketing should

include answering the questions "What business are we in?" and "How can we best organize ourselves to succeed?"

2. Staff have to move from project to project, rather than have a job that is settled in one place, which makes recruitment and retention of good people very difficult. The personnel function has to manage this, and to look after employees who – in international construction – commonly work away from their home country. The human element of the company *is* the company, and all contemporary management concepts and principles emphasize the primary importance of managing people.

3. If the project is remote from headquarters, the people with the best understanding of the work are actually on the project site. Therefore, authority must be devolved to the site as far as realistically possible. "The best way to manage construction projects is to employ really good project managers and let them get on with it"; an old adage, but one that has stood the test of time.

Subject to local environmental conditions

Construction projects will almost always be constructed on the ground and exposed fully to the local environment. One of the most common causes of technical problems, and consequently of dispute between the parties to the contract, is unexpected ground or other site conditions. For example, one major contractor in the United Kingdom was rendered bankrupt because the excavation in rock in one major contract was far more difficult than had been anticipated, although within the contract specification. However, it is commonly the case that clients are unwilling to pay for site and other investigations of sufficient thoroughness to eliminate potential problems and conflict. Their solution is often to pass on this responsibility through the contract.

Managerial implications:

1. Major problems can be caused by inadequate investigation of the site and ground. All reasonable actions should be taken to avoid this.

2. The local climate and seasonal variations will have a very significant effect on productivity. These must be investigated fully, and the consequences assessed.

3. Both these managerial implications indicate the need for a competent and adequately resourced planning function.

Large, expensive, bulky product

Major international construction projects usually cost vast sums of money, have project durations measured in years, and most of the materials used are heavy, bulky and of relatively low value.

Managerial implications:

1. Even large companies have few "products" at a given time – ten major projects may be more than adequate for most companies. Consequently, identifying and winning suitable projects is crucially important, and so is getting them at the right price. One of the major fears of senior managers of construction companies is becoming committed to a seriously underpriced major contract; this could very easily destroy them. Again, this emphasizes the importance of good marketing, a management function which includes accurate estimating and good pricing.

2. It is extremely unlikely that a company will import all the resources and skills that are required for the project. Most materials will have to be obtained locally, and local people will, generally, best understand how to use them. Thus, a thorough survey must be made of local resources and skills, their availability, quality and cost. So, there is clearly a need for an effective management function for the acquisition of resources, or procurement as it is commonly known.

3. Managers are therefore faced with the task of bringing together a diverse selection of resources, of which many will be unfamiliar to them. The basic management functions of coordinating and communicating will have to be done well.

4. With a significant proportion of skills and resources being obtained locally, the earlier statement that the company's own staff members *are* the company is reinforced, and managing them effectively is of paramount importance.

Unique design

Most construction projects are unique – designed for a specific purpose in a specific location. "We specialize in building prototypes" is a common aphorism among construction personnel. Inevitably, therefore, things will go wrong, because it is almost impossible to foresee all the possible problems in the design, construction and commissioning process.

Managerial implications:

1. The design, together with the construction process, must be assessed very carefully and thoroughly, in an attempt to identify deficiencies and potential problems. This is part of the risk management function, which aims to identify and evaluate all the risks of each project.

2. The management staff on the project must be capable of dealing with unexpected problems. This requires innovative, problem-solving attitudes, and the ability to maintain control in difficult circumstances, and when plans do not work out.

3. Planning must allow for things to go wrong, so must not be too deterministic and rigid. Plans must "expect the best and prepare for

the worst". The role of the planning function is to provide a supportive basis for the work of the project, not to produce rigid plans which have to be made to work despite changing circumstances.

Fast-moving, intense level of resource demand

External forces dictate that most major projects are built to a fast time-scale. The enormous expense of major projects concentrates the minds of the client on getting the facility into service as fast as possible, so that the benefits – which may be economic, political, or social – can be realized.

Managerial implications:

1. On-site decision-making is of paramount importance. There is often not time to refer back to headquarters for decisions, or to undertake time-consuming analyses of alternative solutions to problems. The need to maintain progress is paramount, so decisions often have to made quickly. "The ship is moving, so we have to steer it" is a common expression among project managers. However well-planned the voyage, there is always a need for an occasional detour to avoid a problem, to achieve the same overall result.

2. Managers really have to concentrate on the most important aspects. Identifying exactly what the important aspects are is one of the prime skills of management.

The nature of construction activities changes during the project

All project organizations are dynamic, changing and developing throughout the project. For example, in a typical building project, the initial project organization will be for site works, drainage, and foundations. Later, this will be for structural frame, cladding and major services elements. Finally, there will be finishing and commissioning. The project may thus progress from the management of muddy holes, through the erection of heavy elements at height, to the fitting of marble baths with gold-plated taps.

Managerial implications:

1. The demands on management, workforce attitudes and complexity of the control process will be quite different in each of these phases, requiring a "rolling wave" approach to organization. Therefore many of the management systems and personnel will change during the project.

2. Clients tend to be more familiar with the finished facility, and may find it difficult to relate to the earlier phases.

1.3 General management functions

Fundamental management principles

The characteristics of construction projects discussed above, and the managerial implications, emphasize the principle that this industry has different managerial requirements from other industries. Nevertheless, at a very general level, the basic management functions are the same for all industries, so these will be briefly summarized as a starting-point for the development of the explanation of construction project management.

The following quotations are taken from one of the world's most successful management textbooks, *Management* by Koontz and Weihrich.

We define *management* as the process of designing and maintaining an environment in which individuals, working together in groups, accomplish efficiently selected aims.[1]

Considering this definition in the context of construction project management discussed in the previous section, it is clear that the main task of construction managers is to design a project organization, bring together a project team who really will work as a team, and to provide support to that team.

The functions of management provide a useful framework for organizing management knowledge. There have been no new ideas, research findings, or techniques that cannot be placed in the classifications of planning, organizing, staffing, leading and controlling.[2]

These functions are summarized in table 1, based on the descriptions of Koontz and Weihrich. In addition, the function of coordination has been added, although Koontz and Weihrich regard it as "the essence of managership" rather than as a separate function.[3] In this chapter, these terms are explained within the general management of an organization or enterprise. In Chapter 2, which describes the organization of a construction project, they are explained in more detail, and more specifically.

Table 1. The functions of management

Planning functions	Executive functions
Planning Selecting objectives, deciding upon future course of action	*Leading* Influencing people so that they will contribute to organization and group goals
Organizing Establishing an intentional structure of roles for people to fill in an organization	*Coordinating* "The essence of management", the achievement of harmony of individual efforts towards the accomplishment of group goals
Staffing Filling, and keeping filled, the positions in the organizational structure	*Controlling* Measuring and correcting the actions of subordinates

Planning functions

These three planning functions "bridge the gap between where we are to where we want to be in the desired future".[4] They are the crucial functions by which construction managers exercise vision and perceive opportunities, and initiate actions to exploit them.

Figure 1. Time spent on managerial functions

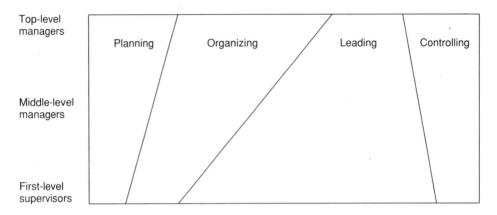

Source: Koontz and Weihrich, 1988.

Planning itself is the function of charting the course for the future, formulating a vision of some future state of the organization or project, and the decision-making processes involved in deciding on the methods by which this state will be achieved. Planning is a prime task of construction management, and managers must spend a larger proportion of their time planning as they become more senior. This principle is depicted in figure 1, which illustrates generally how the manager's role changes with career progression. At the more senior levels, managers experience an additional difficulty having to plan in a much more uncertain context, in which the information on which they base their plans may be sparse, imprecise and in many ways subjective.

Organizing is the function of analysing all the tasks that have to be performed in order to achieve the objectives set down in the plans, and creating a structure of tasks and relationships in which each task is delegated to an individual. These tasks are further divided into subtasks, and allocated to individuals, and so on until the whole of the actions in the plan are specified as team or individual tasks.

Staffing is the function which maintains the human structure of an organization. It requires managers to recruit and develop the careers of subordinates, and includes all the activities of selecting people for the right jobs, maintaining and extending their knowledge and skills through training, and developing career plans and succession policies which will ensure a supply of talent for senior positions.

Executive functions

These are the functions that turn plans into realizations, requiring drive and determination to lead colleagues through difficulties.

Leading is concerned predominantly with the human relations aspect of management. There is no doubt that the management of people is one of the most difficult managerial tasks, and it is primarily concerned with motivation, leadership styles and communication.

In terms commonly used by managers, *coordinating* is "the art of getting everyone pointing in the same direction". It requires managers "to reconcile differences in approach, timing, effort or interest, and to harmonize individual goals to contribute to organization goals". This function emphasizes the need for teamwork.

Controlling is the measurement of performance, and taking corrective action where necessary. Few plans will ever work out in practice exactly as intended, and the manager's role as a controller is to re-plan as necessary in the light of experience, and to take whatever action is necessary to achieve the set objectives. Controlling requires relentless monitoring, analysing, discussing and re-organizing to keep the pressure on people to produce results. It is the daily grind of management, spiced with occasional major, strategic decisions.

1.4   The goals of project management

Figure 2 illustrates what all clients require from a construction company: a project completed on time, within budget, and to the required technical performance and quality standards. Clients are increasingly demanding that all three of these aims are achieved, and are increasingly unwilling to accept the "management compromise", which was common practice until quite recently. Quality is an especially important requirement, and quality assurance procedures are now commonplace. If the construction contractors fail to manage the project effectively, the only "compromise" that they can make is to spend more of their own money to achieve the other two aims. This is not good project management, and it is not good business.

1.5   Scope of projects

Construction companies are commonly called "contractors", and the term will be adopted in this book. This traditional term has a long history, with its origins in a contractual system in which a client or employer engaged a designer, who then supervised the construction of the design by a company who had a direct contract with the client. This form of client-designer-contractor (CDC) process and relationship, illustrated by figure 3, was commonly adopted in the realization of international projects, including those supported by the World Bank and other major development agencies. In order to distinguish the main contractor from other contractors and subcontractors, we have capitalized the word "Contractor".

The contemporary international construction market demands far more of construction companies. Clients choose to adopt other methods of procuring construction products for a variety of reasons, some of which are discussed below.

Reduce their risk. The CDC relationship gave scope for Contractors to claim additional sums of money, extensions of time, or both from the client if the design or specification was incorrect or inadequate. CDC sets up adversarial relationships between the three parties involved. In some cases, this has caused arguments that continue for years after all work on site was completed.

More efficient design and construction. The CDC process is based on the principle that the Contractor will build whatever the designer has drawn or written in the contract documents. Thus, the Contractor's considerable experience of the process of construction is not used to influence the design, which in many cases can be made easier to construct.

More scope to direct the project during construction. The CDC process in its traditional form requires the design to be complete before the contract is let, and the whole project is let as one contract. This is a very rigid system, and some clients wish to "steer" the project as it

Figure 2. Project objectives and their relationship

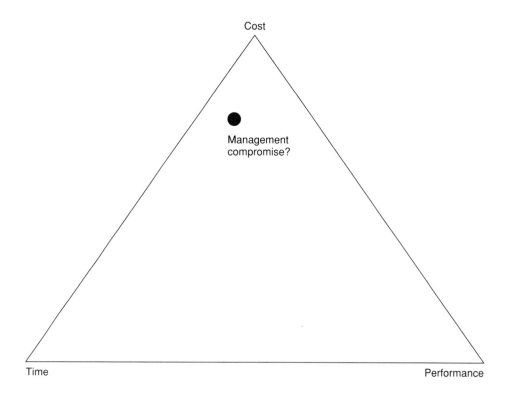

proceeds, making changes as appropriate. Alternatively, they may wish to make a start on some parts of the project while others are under consideration.

Quicker results. Design and construction need not be sequential, some overlap can reduce the overall project duration.

For these and other reasons clients of the international construction industry adopt a wide variety of procurement methods. The scope of the work for which construction companies bid has a profound effect upon the way in which it is managed, and the organization structure of the company. In order to facilitate discussion of the organization of major projects, the broad classification of client procurement methods under the three headings described below has been adopted in this book. The terms used are general and descriptive, and do not necessarily reflect any specific form of national or international contract form.

Client-designer-contractor (CDC)

This is the traditional method described above. The client lets the design for the whole project to a principal design company, which engages other specialists as required. All major designers and advisers (such as construction economists) have contracts directly with the client. The physical construction work is let in a single contract to a major, general Contractor, who will then provide the skills and resources, and engage other contractors as required. Some of the other contractors will have been nominated by the client or designers, and the Contractor has to adopt them.

The form of contract is usually based on a fully detailed design, with complete documentation. The price is usually based on a detailed schedule of items and quantities, and will normally be a fixed price. Sometimes the contract will allow for adjustments for inflation.

Figure 3. Traditional client-designer-contractor relationships

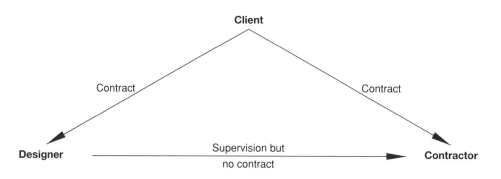

This form of procurement by the client has the advantages to the Contractor that prior to tender the whole project is fully designed and specified, and the payment system is developed in detail. It is still in common use throughout the world. Clients have, however, found it inflexible. There are many examples in developing countries where the client – usually a ministry or government agency – finds itself short of money, but is powerless to change the nature or reduce the scope of project to bring it within a more modest budget, without incurring substantial claims from its Contractors for making such major changes to the contract. As stated above, the Contractor can also claim for any costs caused by poor design, and for those arising from unforeseen circumstances, especially in the ground.

Design and construct (D&C)

The client lets the whole process of design and construction to a single Contractor. The client will prepare a comprehensive brief which describes the requirements of the project and the constraints, from which the Contractor produces a design. The Contractor has to deliver the whole project, and is wholly responsible for employing the required skills and resources, and for the work of all those so employed. When the design is approved, the Contractor proceeds with the construction work.

A common variation of this client procurement method is for the client to engage a consultant to make a preliminary design and cost estimate. This forms the basis of mobilizing the project: obtaining the necessary planning permissions for the project and the site, raising finance, and inviting tenders for the more detailed design and construction. A good example is the National Cycling Centre in the United Kingdom – the Velodrome – described as a case-study at the end of this chapter.

There are many arguments for and against D&C, but the client has the advantage of getting the complete project from one Contractor, who has to handle all the disputes between designers, subcontractors, and all the other people involved. There is an efficiency advantage also, because D&C teams have the opportunity to minimize the tender price by designing for their own special construction skills. However, as the Velodrome case shows, compared to CDC the Contractor's risk increases significantly.

Construction management (CM)

In this form of procurement, the client dispenses with the general Contractor completely, and instead engages a company skilled in the management of construction projects. The complete project is analysed, and all the work – including design – is "packaged" into discrete elements of work. Tenders are invited for each package from a select list of contractors who have satisfied a careful pre-selection process. The package often requires the successful tenderer to complete the detailed design, and also to liaise with other package contractors with whose work there are interrelationships.

This is an effective form of project management, because in many ways it simply reflects what general contractors do anyway. Few major contractors employ directly all the resources used in a major project, but engage a whole range of subcontractors and specialists to do the work on their behalf. The important advantage of CM is that it puts this core of project management function into the hands of a firm who is employed by the client to manage the client's interests. Many major contractors have formed separate divisions for this type of contract.

Other forms of procurement by clients

There is no doubt that many more variations exist, project procurement systems that are carefully developed blends of contract clauses and payment methods to suit specific circumstances. These include contract forms with very broad scope, in which the Contractor is required to raise the finance for the project, or to manage the facilities for some years after the project is complete. In this book, nevertheless, the broad classification given below will be sufficient to define the scope of projects, and to form a basis for the development of the principles and practices of construction project management.

1.6 Summary of main conclusions

> Each major project forms a significant part of the company's turnover, with a commitment for several years. Selection and pricing contracts is therefore of crucial importance.
>
> Each major project will operate within the physical, economic and social environment within which it is situated. There will be intense, fast-moving activity, constructing a unique product. Therefore, decision-making will usually be more effective and timely if the project organization has a substantial degree of autonomy from headquarters.
>
> Construction companies will draw significantly upon local resources, so the "company" may comprise just a small group of their permanent employees. They must be selected, trained and managed effectively.
>
> The scope of the project may include design as well as construction, or the company may be engaged solely to manage the project on behalf of the client.
>
> Contemporary construction projects may require contractors to take considerable risks across a wide range of project requirements, and beyond the normal risks associated with the construction of the works themselves.

Case-study A

DESIGN AND BUILD, LUMP SUM, FIXED PRICE

National Cycling Centre, Manchester, United Kingdom, The Velodrome Project

Brief description of the project

The project was for the construction of an indoor cycle track to Olympic standard. As shown in the photograph, the building is elliptical in shape, covered completely by a roof that curves in both directions. The maximum span of the roof is approximately 120 metres. It was fully insulated to comply with national energy-saving regulations, and to resist overheating on sunny days. Spectators are provided with a high quality view of the track from all seats, and have good and safe access and egress. The accommodation for athletes, officials, media and spectators is of a high quality.

The Velodrome was constructed on the site of an old power station in Manchester, United Kingdom. This is an urban area, and the site is constrained on one side by a canal.

Form of tender

This is a good example of a design-and-build project which demands considerable technical skill of the successful contractor, who is also required to take substantial risks. The tender was fixed price, lump-sum, design and build to a fairly tight time-scale. The tender was based on outline design by a specialist in the United States, which was used to obtain planning permission and as a basis for the design brief. This design, however, was very schematic, and gave only the broad outlines of the shape and nature of the building. The track itself was provided by a specialist firm of international repute, with whom the successful tenderer had to enter into a design-supply-erect contract.

Tenders were open to any European contractor who was deemed to have the necessary skills, experience, and resources. One hundred and fifty firms applied for selection. Fifteen received briefing documents on which to make presentations at an interview. Five were selected and invited to submit tenders.

The successful tenderer

The tender was won by AMEC Building, part of a major construction group in the United Kingdom. They believe that they won the tender for the reasons discussed in the following paragraphs.

Good design. The company put considerable effort into trying to get "competitive advantage" out of good design. For example, by careful analysis of the functional specification, they improved on the original design of the accommodation for competitors and officials, providing the required facilities in a slightly smaller space. This reduced the overall dimensions of the Velodrome, and because this is an expensive structure, made a significant cost-saving.

Figure 4.   Velodrome project. (*Photograph kindly supplied by AMEC Building Ltd.*)

Constructibility. The roof was designed to make construction as straightforward as possible. The original design required two large trusses to span the arena, as shown in the photograph. These trusses carried transverse beams which spanned to the edge walls of the arena, and also beams that spanned between the trusses, which also carried large roof-lights to give natural light to the track below. AMEC's solution was to use one large truss, which was as broad as the original twin truss arrangement. This had little visual effect, but made the roof easier to construct and erect, and provided more stability at intermediate stages of construction. In addition, the roof-lights were replaced by windows along the sides of the truss, which eliminated some serious problems in forming and sealing the roof-light apertures.

Broadly based company. The AMEC Group is a large engineering and construction group, whose companies include the full range of civil engineering, building construction, building services and off-shore construction companies. Of particular significance was their steelwork fabrication and erection company, whose designers, together with their advanced analytical systems, produced an improved steelwork design which made a significant impact on the economics of the roof. The structure for the seating was made from precast concrete, a speciality of another firm within the group, who produced a particularly effective design which was erected in just eight weeks.

Risk analysis. Decisions were made on several items of work that involved financial risk. For example, a design for external works was proposed in the tender which absorbed all the surplus excavated material from the project. This included an existing large mound of soil that was expected to contain industrial contamination. Some pre-tender soil analysis indicated that the contamination was limited, so only a small quantity would have to be removed from the site. This was a very economical solution, because the alternative was to remove all of the material in the mound from the site and dispose of it elsewhere. However, this competitive edge carried the risk that the landscaping scheme may not have been acceptable, or that the client may have insisted that all the material should be removed.

The tender sum was almost UK£9 million. Given the level of competition, this was a very keen price, and AMEC's management were required to be very effective in order to keep control of the project.

Notes

[1] H. Koontz and H. Weihrich: *Management.* Ninth international edition, McGraw-Hill, Singapore, 1988, p. 4.

[2] ibid. p. 15.

[3] ibid. p. 18.

[4] ibid. p. 16.

PROJECT MANAGEMENT ORGANIZATION

2

2.1 Introduction

This chapter explains how project management organizations are designed and maintained. It begins with a review of the functions of project management, on which the design of any organization structure must be based. These functions are used to define a matrix project management structure in the form of a general model which is developed for the design of organizations for construction projects. The roles of the staff in the organization are explained, especially the crucial role of the project manager. Finally, two case-studies provide practical illustrations of some of the principles.

2.2 Project management functions

The discussion of construction projects given in Chapter 1 makes it possible to derive a general list of functions necessary to manage a construction project successfully. To facilitate a comprehensive discussion, it is assumed that the contract for a project includes the design as well as the construction of the works. These functions can be considered in three groups, as illustrated by tables 2, 3 and 4.

Client performance functions

These are the functions necessary to satisfy the client's performance objectives, relating to the technical planning, design and physical construction of the project, and financial control systems. These functions are necessary to ensure that the project will produce the results that the client requires, and will be finished to the required performance and quality standards. These are called "client performance functions", and are usually performed by professionally and technically qualified people, such as architects, engineers and building economists, supported by technical and clerical staff, working within the skills and knowledge of their own discipline. Generally, construction projects are unique, so the performance functions will have to be defined specifically for each project. Nevertheless, it is possible to formulate a generalized model, as shown by the functions listed in table 2, from which readers will be able to generate their own, more detailed functional structures.

Table 2.   Client performance functions (performed by staff managers and technical staff, from both client and contractor)

Inception
Client briefing
Feasibility studies – economic and engineering
Site selection
Obtaining preliminary planning and other legal permission for the works

Design
Site and other investigations
Preparation of the scheme or outline design, and general specification
Preparation of a general specification
Preparation of the detailed design
Preparation of the detailed specification
Obtaining final planning and other legal permission for the works

Finance
Preparation of a preliminary cost plan
Value engineering, within the design process
Preparation of the full financial budget
Implementing and maintaining financial monitoring and control systems
Implementing and maintaining payment and accounting systems

Contract
Draft contract documents, and secure client approval
Supervise execution of the contract
Analyse and negotiate any variations and claims
Draft subcontract documents, and negotiate

Construction performance
Conduct a thorough constructibility analysis
Design the temporary construction works, in relation to the permanent works
Prepare the quality plan
Supervise the construction work as it proceeds

Commissioning
Prepare as-built drawings and other documentation
Draft operating and maintenance manuals

Production functions

The second group of functions are those that are based on the view of a project as a commercial production process, concerned with physical progress, completion on time and within budget. These are called "production functions", and are listed in table 3. *The performance of these functions is the duty of "managers", staff whose principal role is to achieve results through other people, rather than by doing the work themselves.* Although managers are usually professionally qualified in some relevant discipline, as managers they rarely exercise their professional, technical skills directly, and must resist the temptation to do so.

Contractor's performance functions

The third group of functions, shown in table 4, are the "contractor's performance functions". These are the functions necessary to support the contractor's management functions, providing specialized advice and services. Health and safety is an increasingly important function within this group, reflecting increasing concern worldwide with the quality of people's working conditions.

Table 3. Production functions (performed by the client's project management team and the Contractor's line managers)

Planning
The basis of control
Setting quantified project objectives
Setting quantified section and individual objectives, based on project objectives
Identify required skills and resources

Organizing
Division of work
Design of organization structures and jobs
Planning for organizational change during the project

Staffing
Recruiting and managing permanent management staff
Recruiting and managing permanent functional staff
Selecting, appointing and managing external consultants
Selecting, appointing and managing specialist and trades subcontractors
Selecting, appointing and managing general subcontractors

Leading
Motivating all project staff
Building and sustaining teams
Encouraging participation by all concerned

Coordinating
Harmonizing project and individual goals
Negotiating
Problem-solving

Controlling
Installing effective and regular progress, quality and cost review procedures
Taking corrective action, and following it through

Table 4. Contractor's performance functions (performed by the contractor's staff managers, and their professional and clerical staff)

Technical services
Making engineering analyses, designing temporary works, and testing for the permanent works
Designing and planning the temporary works
Advising managers and planners on technical aspects of design and construction

Plant and equipment
Acquisition of plant and equipment
Giving technical advice on the use of the plant and equipment
Maintaining the plant and equipment in serviceable condition
Controlling the location and use
Controlling costs and finance

Planning services
Analysing and planning methods of working
Implementing planning techniques and systems
Compiling and maintaining databases of production information

Commercial services
Estimation of costs at tender stage
Designing and managing cost control systems
Compiling and maintaining databases of cost information
Procuring all the contractor's resources
Making payments to suppliers and subcontractors

Administrative services
Making financial returns to HQ
Managing personnel
Administering the site office
Managing the stores
Implementing and maintaining administrative systems
Ensuring compliance with local legal requirements

Functions and goals

These three groups of functions relate very closely to the three goals of project management given in figure 2: performance functions satisfying the performance goals of the client and the contractor, and production functions satisfying the time and cost goals. All these functions will be discussed in the following sections.

Management terminology is commonly based on analogy with military organization structures: the production managers are concerned directly with "combat", and are called "line managers". Performance managers support the line managers, by providing resources, information, special skills (such as engineering) and are called "staff managers". Because this terminology is commonly used in management, it will be used in this book.

2.3 Client performance functions

Inception

As shown in table 2, these functions include feasibility studies, client briefing, site selection, obtaining preliminary planning and other legal approvals for the works. Generally, the time and energy spent on thorough analysis of the project at the inception stage is a sound investment. Too often, however, this stage is not given the thorough consideration of construction management, so aims and objectives are inadequately transposed into strategies in sufficient detail, and unforeseen – but foreseeable – problems arise during the construction phase of the project. Too often, there is pressure on management to "get something moving", whereas it would usually have been more prudent to wait, research, analyse and plan.

The principal output of the inception functions is the "Project Brief". An excellent reference work for the inception functions is O'Reilly's aptly named publication *Better briefing means better buildings*.[1] This booklet gives a succinct summary of this crucial project phase, and in particular lists the "functions of the brief" and "attributes of a good brief". These are reproduced in table 5.

Design

The process of design includes all the technical functions listed in table 2. All these functions will be required to conform to national and international standards, codes of practice, or standard procedures, and so there is no need to explain them further in this book. The crucial, senior management, implication is that there is an enormous wealth of technical knowledge to be acquired, and it is for this reason that firms specialize in certain countries, or form joint ventures with firms resident in certain countries. The technical requirements are usually strictly enforced, so mistakes can be costly.

Table 5. Characteristics of a good project brief

Functions	Attributes
A channel of instruction To convey decisions and information between the client and all the other parties involved	*Clarity* Purposes of the brief should be made clear and carefully distinguished from one another
To stimulate discussion To facilitate the setting of priorities, analyses, problem identification and information flow. It should provide a collective "thinking through"	*Priorities* The degree of importance or firmness of particular items should be shown; which requirements are likely to be necessities, which are no more than wishes
A record To record decisions, information, agreements, etc.	*Consistency* The brief should be consistent within itself, and with any other related projects
A tool for evaluation The brief should provide the yardstick against which the achievements of the designers and project managers can be measured	*Completeness* At any stage in the development of the brief it should be complete as far as the team's understanding and expectations have developed
A basis for estimating resources The brief should include a specific and quantified estimate of all the major resources that will be required, and an overall budget under about 20 headings	*Realism* The brief should be realistic in terms of aims, resources, context and quality to be achieved (clients tend to expect more than they can afford)
A contractual document The brief will form the technical specification for the agreement between the client and designers, project managers and possibly other parties (such as specialist suppliers)	*Relevance* The brief should contain only information and decisions directly relevant to the project
A living document The brief should be developed, in very clearly defined stages, to reflect the progress of the understanding and exploration of the project, and amended to incorporate new knowledge	*Logic* The brief should have a logical structure and presentation. It should distinguish between what the client expects from the project, and how it is intended to achieve these expectations. It should work from the genearl to the particular
	Flexibility The brief should be specific enough for decisions and actions to be taken but flexible enough to encourage exploration of problems, options and uncertainties
	Scope The scope of the project must be carefully defined.

Source: O'Reilly, 1987. See page 50, note 1 for full reference.

Finance

These functions include all the expected and well-defined functions described in table 5, including the preparation of a preliminary cost plan and eventually a full financial budget, together with use of comprehensive monitoring and control systems.

Of contemporary relevance is the use of value engineering techniques, which have been well-developed in the United States, and less so in Europe.

In essence the techniques require the designers, and often the constructors, to analyse designs to discover improved means of achieving the desired functional performance in a more cost-effective way. The objective is to provide the same result at better value, rather than cutting costs by lowering the specification. This is a process which attempts to marry creative design skills with those of the construction economist, so its successful application requires considerable experience and competence in running group-based management processes. For this reason, it is usually better to use a specialist to run some value engineering studies at strategic points during the design process.

Contract

Construction contracts are usually based on standard forms, notably FIDIC for international work. This is a specialized subject, and will not be discussed further in this general text.

Construction performance

These functions include the analysis of the constructibility of the design, which relates closely to value engineering. Constructibility, sometimes known as buildability, aims to improve construction efficiency by analysing the method by which the design will be physically realized. The subject has been developed in the United States and also in the United Kingdom.[2] Some of the principles are given in table 6.

Table 6. Principles of buildability

Investigate thoroughly—this relates also to the requirements of briefing
Consider access by people, plant and materials at the design stage
Consider storage at the design stage
Design for minimum time below ground
Design for early enclosure of buildings, to minimize the effects of bad weather
Use suitable materials
Design for the skills available
Design for simple assembly
Plan for maximum repetition/standardization
Maximize the use of plant and equipment
Allow for practical tolerances – research has shown that this is one of the most important   and often neglected aspects of buildability
Allow a practical sequence of operations
Minimize return visits by trades, so avoiding waste of the tradesman's time
Plan work to avoid damage by subsequent operations
Design for safe construction
Communicate clearly, bearing in mind the knowledge and interpretive skills of the recipients

Source: Construction Industry Research and Information Association, United Kingdom.

Taken together, constructibility and value engineering are important tools in the project manager's armoury. They offer opportunities to reduce construction costs, and to ease the construction process, through the application of professional knowledge and skills, and so supplement the use of management skills to achieve these objectives.

Commissioning

These functions include the documentation listed in the table. Considering this subject more generally, experienced managers will know that the difficulties experienced during the commissioning phase are often underrated, and the time allowed for this process is easily underestimated.

2.4 Production functions

Planning

Planning is principally concerned with setting objectives, and deciding on the ways and means of achieving them. Another vital principle is that *planning forms the basis of control. Without a plan to set the parameters, performance cannot be measured.* This principle will be discussed in more detail in the chapters on control of time and cost, but it is also a general theme throughout this book. Generally it is the case that many construction managers do not plan their projects with sufficient diligence and competence. Too often a lack of planning is blamed on the difficulty of making plans in the uncertain environment of construction work, whereas in fact this uncertainty requires more thorough analysis than in more predictable environments. In addition, one of the benefits of thorough planning is the formulation of contingency plans, which prepare managers for actions when unexpected circumstances drive the original plan off course.

In general terms, planning and its relationship with other management functions is described in figure 5. In construction project management, plans are prepared for the whole project, then in more detail for sections of the project, and so on in a hierarchy that at the highest level may have a time span of several years, down to first-line supervisors who have to plan their work each day. This concept is illustrated by figures 6 and 7. Each plan must aim to achieve objectives that contribute to the fulfilment of overall project objectives, and must be quantified in terms of time, cost and performance. Plans have to be prepared by the managers who are responsible for the work, not by specialist planners, whose job is to provide technical assistance data, systems, analyses to assist the line managers in their planning. This is because the execution of a construction plan requires considerable personal commitment, which cannot be generated unless the ideas, logic and experience embodied in the plan are those of the manager responsible for its execution. It must be "my plan" or "our plan", not "their plan".

Organizing

"A formalized intentional structure of roles and positions."[3] The characteristics of construction projects create a need to consider two distinct organizational factors:

Figure 5. Plans as the foundation of management

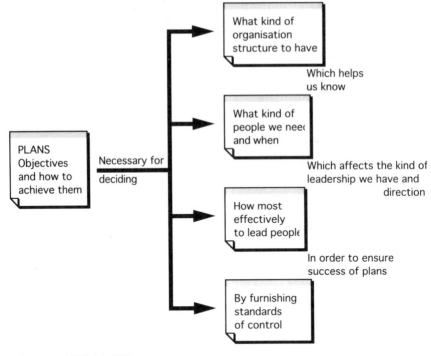

Source: Koontz and Weihrich, 1988.

1. How best to subdivide the work of the project into sections that create a managerially cohesive subject for the exercise of knowledge, skills and resources.

2. The need to plan changes in the organization structure and staffing as the project progresses, and the nature of the work develops.

    Case-study B, at the end of this chapter, illustrates the application of these factors.

    Management textbooks give a wide variety of bases for the subdivision of work, a process which is sometimes called "departmentation". Examples are:

1. By simple number – i.e. a decision to arrange people into groups of five, ten or some other number

2. By time – for example having a completely different management team for day shifts and night shifts.

Figure 6. Determining the size and shape of the inner planning frame or window

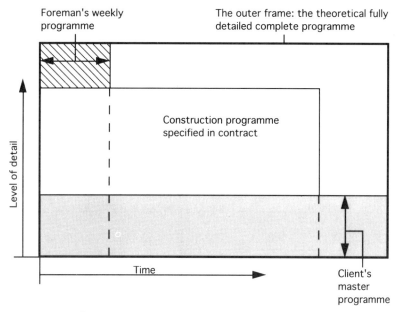

Source: Neale and Neale.[4]

3. By function – in case-study B, the division on the work in the sections was done on this basis.

4. By territory or geography – in case-study B, the structures section was subdivided on the basis of geography, each subsection being a number of bridges reasonably close together.

5. By customer or product – case-study B is an example of a substantial highway, which was constructed by the Roads Division of the civil engineering subsidiary of the contractor.

Generally, in construction project organization, the primary division of work is by process or geography, or both, and case-study B is a good example of the reasoning behind this. The characteristics of the process are one of the most fundamental and obvious bases for organization structures in most technical organizations. The secondary basis for organization is usually territory or geography. In some very large projects, the organization has been primarily on a geographical basis, with process secondary. This design works well when the purpose of the geographical split is to reduce a single large project to a number of smaller ones e.g. West site, East site, each of which is then organized as a discrete project.

Staffing

As shown in figure 5, staffing (what kind of people we need and when) is the function of bringing the right people together in the organizational

Figure 7. Relationship between duration and level of detail*

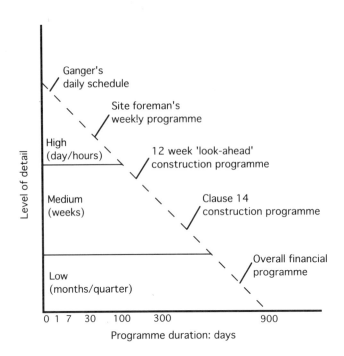

Programme duration: days

* For example, a programme for a foreman may be one day in duration but require every hour in the day to be accounted for, whereas a programme for a financier may cover three years but require assessment every three months.

Source: Neale and Neale.[4]

structure. Very few international contractors employ directly all the staff required for projects. In many cases they will employ very few staff, making use of a wide range of consultants, subcontractors, agencies and suppliers of labour. For contractors who adopt this strategy, the permanent staff may be only a small core of managers and their immediate supporting staff, whose staffing role is to identify, employ and control other organizations who undertake a wide variety of project tasks.

This staffing strategy has the great advantage of flexibility. As was explained in Chapter 1, one of the characteristics of the construction industry is that a contractor's workload at any time may comprise only a small number of large projects of long duration – say 15 projects with an average duration of 3 years. In addition, in earlier sections of this chapter it was explained that the demands made by a project for staff with specific skills and knowledge changes as the project progresses. This type of workload makes it difficult for a contractor to maintain a continuous workload, so having only a small core of permanent staff reduces the scale of this problem.

It is reasonable to assume that this will be the strategy adopted by most international contractors, so the staff required for major projects will be discussed under the following headings:

The permanent management staff of the contractor.

The permanent functional staff of the contractor.

External consultants, the suppliers of specialist services.

Specialist or trades subcontractors.

General subcontractors (sometimes called "domestic" subcontractors).

The permanent management staff of the contractor comprise the project manager's team. Many successful project managers have built up core teams with whom they move from project to project. Building these teams is one of the major aspects of leadership, and will be explained in more detail in the next section.

Generally, the core management team comprises a group of senior managers whose expertise and experience spans all the major management activities. This will include the control of a wide range of site construction work, and financial control of income and expenditure. As one of their prime leadership functions, each of the senior managers will build their own teams, and so on. So, the usual permanent management staff are a series of interlocking teams who have worked together before, and can establish good working practices quickly when moved to a new project. These people are the core staff of the contractor, who are essential to establish the company's presence in a new location. They need good conditions of service, and planned personal development programmes. The company must show their clear commitment to these managers.

The permanent functional staff of the contractor are the functional equivalent of the permanent management staff, and comprise technical and administrative staff. Most major contractors have developed special expertise in aspects of construction work, and this expertise is an important factor in gaining competitive market advantage. It is the technical staff of the project team that hold this knowledge, so again they are the core staff of the contractor's organization.

Other permanent functional staff are the construction planners, and the general and financial administrators. The principle employed here is the need to establish an approach to organization and to maintain systems that are uniform throughout the company, although allowing the necessary flexibility to accommodate the differing circumstances of individual projects. Ideally, staff should be able to move into another project, and find their way around these systems immediately.

External consultants is a general term for the services that the contractor "buys in" to supplement the permanent staff. Ideally, these can be selected to provide exactly the service required by the specific project, and should be paid for directly out of income arising from their work on the project. A good example is design consultants, who may be selected for their expertise in, for example, foundations or air-conditioning, and whose fees are paid for out of the item in the contract sum specifically allocated for this work. Other examples are agencies who supply engineers and other technical personnel on the basis of short-term contracts.

In practice, few contractors would recruit new consultants for each and every project, because this would be exposing them to the continual uncertainty of working with new firms and new people. The need for the contractor to meet the project objectives of performance, time and cost is paramount, and consequently project managers will make determined efforts to ensure that their consultants will perform also. Although it is possible to draw up a comprehensive list of criteria for the selection of consultants – which would include measures of the technical competence of the staff, the financial strength of the organization, the quality of the firm's computing and other systems, and so on – the prime criterion is the historical performance of the consultant, especially on any previous occasions that they may have worked with the contractor.

Thus, the staffing arrangement used by most major contractors is to maintain a small core staff, and to draw as necessary on a group of consultants with whom they have established good working relations over a period of time. Naturally, there will be times when even these firms fail to perform, and they will be replaced by new ones, so creating a rolling programme of external relationships. In addition, all projects will contain elements that are new to everyone, so providing another reason for new firms to join the group. In managerial terms, this is an exercise in team-building, where the members of the team are independent firms rather than directly employed staff. Building these teams is one of the prime duties of project managers.

For the modern construction project, it is the *specialist or trades subcontractors* who do most of the physical work required by the project. One of the arts of managing the work on site is the efficient organization of these contractors and the control of the interfaces between them. The term usually applied to this is "packaging". The work to be done is subdivided into packages of activities which require a body of knowledge, skills and resources that could reasonably be found in one organization. In civil engineering construction, common packages are earthworks and concrete work, and in building foundations and cladding. Of course, the extent of the package depends in part upon the firm who will be employed to do it. Many subcontractors started as simple labour contractors, taking on the labour element of some parts of construction on a contract basis, and growing in expertise and resources until they could take on substantial parts of projects to provide a complete construction service. Case-study C gives examples of such subcontractors, and illustrates some of the issues involved in packaging.

General subcontractors are those who undertake work that may also be done by large numbers of directly employed workers. Again, these subcontractors have wide-ranging expertise and resources, but most commonly in international projects they provide labour on a contract basis. In countries with abundant labour, these will be local labour contractors. In other circumstances, there will be a need to use companies who specialize in importing and employing labour.

Most countries in the world have construction industries that can provide most of the specialist, trades and general subcontractors. If the project is in a familiar locality, the principles of identifying and employing them are the same as those for the other resources described earlier. However, if the project is in an unfamiliar locality, then there is a strong argument for working in joint venture partnership with a local firm. The requirements of international clients are so demanding that it is often foolhardy to enter into contracts to deliver construction projects to performance, time and cost objectives while relying to a large extent on a group of almost unknown resources with whom the contractor has not established good working relationships. Obviously, contractors have to choose the right local partners, otherwise they simply compound the problem!

Leading

Leading is primarily a human relations function, and is almost entirely concerned with ways of getting the best out of people at work. The leadership role is dominated by the project manager, who has to assemble and maintain the project team, and to drive the project to a conclusion. One of the most perceptive analyses of the human factors in successful project management was published by Baker and Wilemon.[5] Their findings are summarized in the box on p. 34.

What emerges from Baker and Wilemon's research is the principle that human project organizations have to be designed carefully, taking into account all the relevant factors relating to the specific project. This is consistent with the approach adopted in this book, and these first two chapters have been devoted to an exposition of the principles on which construction project organizations can be designed.

There is great emphasis on teamwork, and the need to make sure that the objectives of all those who are engaged in the project are consistent. In the traditional Client-Designer-Contractor (CDC) method of client procurement, it is well-known that this is often not the case. This is one of the reasons why clients use procurement methods such as Construction Management (CM), in which there is more emphasis on teamwork and working for a common goal.

Baker and Wilemon's discussion of the project manager's role and qualities paints a picture of a person who is given free rein to manage, subject only to overall controls based on end results. Vested with

Summary of major research findings regarding the human element in project management

There is no single panacea in the field of project management. Some concepts and principles work well in some environments, while others are more suited to different environments.

It is important to vest the project manager with as much authority as the environment permits. Once vested with this authority, the project manager is well-advised to use expertise and work challenge as influence modes, rather than formal authority.

Project organizational design must be tailored to the specific task and the environment, but higher levels of authority for the project manager result in less probability of cost and time overrun.

The confrontation or problem-solving approach is generally more successful than the smoothing approach or the forcing mode of conflict resolution.

Participative decision-making styles are generally more successful than other styles. Commitment, teamwork and a sense of mission are important areas of attention in project management.

To attain high levels of perceived success, effective coordination and relations patterns are extremely important. Also, success criteria salience and consensus among the client, the contractor and the project team are important.

Source: B. N. Baker and D. L. Wilemon, 1977.

considerable power, the project manager nevertheless manages by using human managerial skills rather than the naked use of power. "Confident" and "verbally fluent" are descriptions applied by Baker and Wilemon to successful project managers, who face up to problems and discuss their solution in an entirely practical, rational way.

Readers may like to return to the sections in Chapter 1 which describe the characteristics of construction projects, and they will see the relevance of this analysis of the human relations aspects of project management. Clearly a project management team which has been carefully selected for its human qualities and teamwork potential, and vested with the authority to take such actions as are necessary to expedite the project, will be well-suited to these characteristics.

Coordinating

This function will be explained by a direct quotation from Koontz and Weihrich.[3]

> Some authorities consider coordination to be a separate function of the manager. It seems more accurate, however, to regard it as the essence of managership, for the achievement of harmony of individual efforts toward the accomplishment of group goals is the purpose of managing. Each of the managerial functions is an exercise contributing to coordination.

Even in the case of a church or a fraternal organization, individuals often interpret similar interests in different ways, and their efforts toward mutual goals do not automatically mesh with the efforts of others. It thus becomes the central task of the manager to reconcile differences in approach, timing, effort or interest, and to harmonize individual goals to contribute to organizational goals.

The best coordination occurs when individuals see how their jobs contribute to the goals of an enterprise. They are able to see this only when they know what these goals are. If, for example, managers are not sure whether the goal of their firm is sales volume, quality, advanced techniques, or customer service, they cannot coordinate their efforts to achieve any objective. Each would be guided by his or her own ideas of what is in the interest of the firm or, without any such conviction, might work for self-enrichment. To avoid such splintering of efforts, the dominant goal of an enterprise should be clearly defined and communicated to everyone concerned. And, naturally, goals of subordinate departments should be designed to contribute to the goals of the enterprise.

The relevance of this explanation to construction is illustrated by Baker and Wilemon's paper on the human element in project management, and by case-study C.

Coordination is a difficult art. Although communication is an essential part of coordination, it is not achieved by comprehensive written communication with everybody. Oral, face-to-face communication is the most effective way to coordinate with others, and this requires well-planned and objectively managed meetings, which are clearly and succinctly minuted. A senior project manager, who has just successfully managed the construction of a huge new car factory, told the author of this chapter, "When you have a problem with someone, don't write a letter, go and see them and sort it out. Confirm the agreement with a note if you feel you have to."

Coordinating the work of a construction project is more readily achieved when as many of the parties involved are actually present on the site, and so readily available for meetings as required. This is especially true for projects in which the contractor has a design responsibility. In most cases, designers are used to working from their offices, wherever they may be, and visiting the site only infrequently. For major projects, however, there is a strong case for requiring the designers to join the project office, or at least to establish a substantial satellite office, in the interests of promoting a team spirit as well as to facilitate coordination. In projects when the design and construction phases overlap – sometimes called "fast-track construction" – this is essential, and the contractor should insist on this as part of the contract with the designers.

Controlling

The managerial function of controlling is the measurement and correction of performance in order to make sure that enterprise objectives and the plans devised to attain them are accomplished. This is illustrated by figure 8.

Figure 8. The control cycle

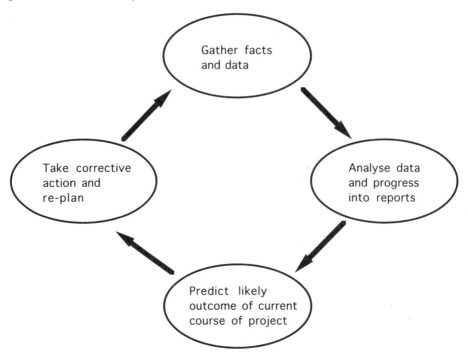

The core principles for effective control are:

1. Effective planning forms the basis for effective control. If the project work is not planned, it cannot be controlled, because there are no standards of performance against which to measure whether the work is under control or not. Therefore, one of the most important functions of planning is to set out targets for achievement.

2. Control is achieved by taking corrective action. It is a human function, not a system function. Project offices abound with paper- and computer-based "control systems". "Let me show you my control system" is a common invitation to one of the authors when he visits construction project offices, but invariably these systems simply monitor actual project performance, usually in financial terms. Few such systems compare actual progress with what was actually planned, and fewer still offer some form of prediction for the likely overall future result of current performance. Project control is actually exercised by managers, who interpret the evidence provided by systems and from their own observations, and make predictions about future performance. They then take actions to ensure so far as is possible that the project objectives will be achieved.

Figure 9 is a good example of a simple project control chart. It is derived from an actual chart used to monitor the performance of package contractors for the construction of a major international airport. It plots

Figure 9. Example of a simple control chart

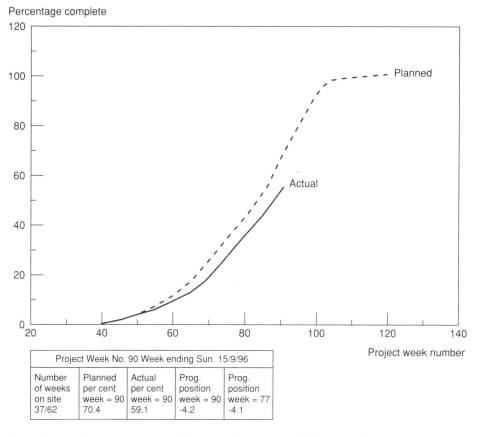

Percentage complete

Project Week No. 90 Week ending Sun. 15/9/96				
Number of weeks on site 37/62	Planned per cent week = 90 70.4	Actual per cent week = 90 59.1	Prog. position week = 90 -4.2	Prog. position week = 77 -4.1

planned performance – in this case in terms of the package contractor's earnings (which is quite a good measure of progress) – against time. Actual performance is plotted weekly, and the difference between these two lines gives an estimation of the package contractor's progress against time. The chart was produced automatically by a computer system, with a minimum of input, and was available each week in time for the weekly progress and coordination meeting between the project staff and the package contractors. It was simple, clear, cheap, timely, and accurate enough to form the basis of management decisions on the progress of the work.

Another good basis for monitoring and control is the "milestone principle". This involves the analysis of the work of a project to establish a number of points against which progress will be monitored. A good milestone is a stage of the work where completion can be easily and unequivocally recognized. A good example is "building watertight" i.e., structure, roof and cladding complete to the extent that rain will be excluded from the building, so that water-sensitive work can start. Either the building is watertight, or it isn't – in cases of dispute, it would be possible to test this by using a hosepipe! Thus, this would form a good monitoring point, a date could be set for this to be achieved, and a dispassionate assessment can be made of performance at the due date. This basis for monitoring progress is especially favoured by construction managers, because it is quick, clear and very effective.

2.5 Contractor's performance functions

The functions which are performed by the contractor's staff are listed in table 4 (see p. 23). They are described in the sections which follow.

Technical services

In many ways, this function is the core of a construction company, because it represents their expertise in the act of physical construction. Nevertheless, in management terms, this is a technical support function, and the staff involved do not have any direct control over the physical progress of the work.

In companies whose main business is the construction of work designed by others, this function is mainly concerned with the design of temporary works, and generally advising the project staff on testing, overcoming technical problems, and other technical support. However, in the case where a company undertakes a considerable volume of work which includes the design of the permanent works, it is increasingly the case that the technical services function will become a separate design company, often undertaking work for firms other than its parent contractor. Thus, in case-study A, the design of the Velodrome was done by the design and build company of the group. In reality, this company coordinated the design work done by individual specialist designers, including the structural steelwork design which was done by the group's steelwork company under a design, supply and erect contract.

Plant and equipment

This is a specialized mechanical engineering and financial function. The technical performance of modern construction machinery requires a high level of expertise to select the best items for the work in hand, and to maintain them in a serviceable condition. In addition, the costs of the machinery are such that the investment by the company in plant and equipment may comprise the major part of its capital assets. Usually, therefore, the plant function becomes another separate company, hiring its assets to the parent company, and often others. This commercial arrangement encourages the management and technical staff to concentrate on what they should be best at – providing efficient plant and equipment in such a way as to make good use of the capital invested in it by the company.

Planning services

As was explained under "Planning" in Section 2.4, the responsibility for planning rests entirely with managers. However, planning construction work is a technically demanding and complex process, so usually contractors have specialist planners who assist managers in the preparation and presentation of their plans. Typical functions include the compilation and maintenance of comprehensive databases of performance data, and the use of computer-based planning systems for analysis and presentation of plans and schedules. The sophistication and performance capability of modern information technology can be used to great effect in this function, but managers must be sure that their role as the ultimate planners of construction work is not obscured by this technology and its planning service exponents.

Commercial services

With the exception of cost estimation, the functions listed under this heading in table 4 are common to almost any commercial enterprise. Cost estimation is very different, for the reasons given in Chapter 1 which explained why construction work is unique. Generally, therefore, estimators have to be experienced construction managers or engineers, and much reliance has to be put on their experience and judgement.

Administrative services

These services provide the general administrative functions of the company.

2.6 Project organization

The relationship between production and performance management

A project organization is required to bring together all the functions listed in tables 2, 3 and 4, described in Sections 2.3 to 2.5 above, to achieve the client's and the contractor's objectives. Clearly in a major project the performance of these functions demands a very substantial body of skills and knowledge, and requires a large number of people to perform their duties in a coordinated way. Generally, project organizations are designed in such a way that production managers are wholly responsible for achieving results, and the functional, performance specialists advise and assist in achieving the technical and quality performance of the project. This type of organizational task allocation allows individual production managers to focus on the required end results of their parts of the project, and allows the performance-related personnel to maintain, develop and apply their particular skills and knowledge. In many particular cases tension and conflict will arise when performance demands do not coincide with the need to maintain progress. There is a variety of ways to design an organization to reflect these distinct roles, but in essence they can be explained in terms of line-staff relationships, and matrix relationships, although these two concepts lie at ends of a spectrum of variations. They are illustrated in figures 10, 11 and 12, and discussed in the following sections.

Line-staff project management structures

Figure 10 shows a structure for a contractor's site organization, based on line-staff relationships. The project manager is, of course, in complete charge of all the project staff, within general company personnel policies. The production manager, often called the works manager, controls all the physical construction work of the project – he is "the outside man" – responsible directly to the project manager. These two managers control the essential core of the project, on which the bulk of the client's money is being spent, so they must work very closely together. In order to facilitate this, at least one major international contractor has a management policy that they share a single office, thus easing the tasks of communication and coordination.

The production manager delegates the work to section managers, under a division of work based on the explanation given under "Organizing" in Section 2.4. When the contract includes design, it may well be the case that one of the sections is the design management section, which will have direct responsibility for liaising with the client and the client's managers and technical staff. These managers are responsible for achieving time, cost and performance objectives in their sections – it has been said that their job is to "make the project grow". They have their own support staff.

The staff managers control departments whose role is to support the line managers in functional responsibilities listed in table 4. When the contract includes design, they will also support the project manager in the management of the design process, and this will include the inception, design, construction performance and commissioning functions shown in table 2.

Staff managers in a line-staff organization structure have no direct control of the physical work of the project. They act in an advisory, supportive capacity only, and the ultimate responsibility lies with the line managers.

Matrix management structures

Matrix, grid or project organization is, essentially, the combination of functional and product departmentation in the same organization structure. Generally, each section has a manager, whose responsibilities are for the achievement of time and cost objectives. The functional managers are responsible for achieving the technical performance of their functional task allocation. This form of organization is common in construction, including design organizations. The project manager is, essentially, a customer of the

Figure 10. Line-staff organization structure (contractor's project staff)

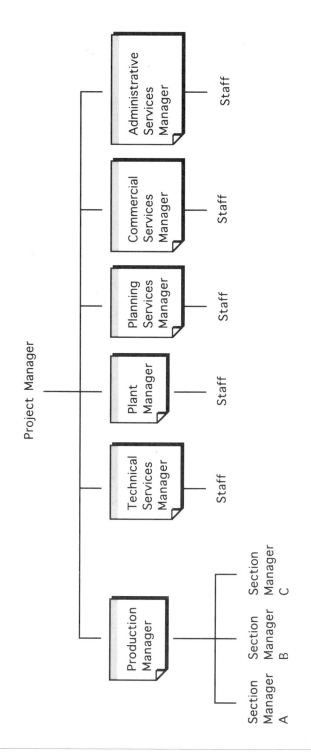

Figure 11. Matrix organization structure (contractor's project staff)

Project Manager	Inception Team	Design Team	Finance Department	Contract Department	Construction Team	Commissioning Team
Section Manager						
Section Manager B						
Section Manager						

Figure 12. Matrix organization structure (client's organization)

Project Manager	Technical Services Manager	Plant Manager	Planning Services Manager	Commercial Services Manager	Admin. Services Manager
Section Manager					
Section Manager B					
Section Manager					

functional departments, using their services to satisfy the requirements of the project client.

A matrix organization for a contractor's project site is shown in figure 11, and one for a client's project team is shown in figure 12. The case-studies at the end of this chapter give some examples from actual projects.

The essential difference between the matrix and line-staff organizations is that in the matrix the functional managers do have authority over their allocated domain, and the line managers have to come to agreement with them on the method of work – they cannot be overruled, there has to be an agreement. This requirement adds great power to the organizational design, because it reinforces the importance of achieving performance, quality objectives, which in the construction industry have so often been overridden in the interests of making progress. Quality is becoming of increasing importance throughout the world, so the matrix form of project organization is recommended in this book.

Problems that occur with matrix organization structures include:

Conflict and role ambiguity between functional and project managers. Conflicts frequently occur between the need to maintain progress and the need to maintain standards. Often the resulting solution will be influenced by the personalities involved, rather than the managerial and technical arguments. This is where the project manager has a key role to play, in selecting and managing the project staff, and creating a good team spirit.

Imbalance of authority and power of either type of manager will distort the matrix. The responsibilities of all those involved must be carefully defined, and controlled.

These conflicts may give rise to excessive written communication as managers try to protect themselves. Generally, the solution to this is to have more meetings, which encourages face-to-face contact. However, these meetings have to be carefully planned and managed, otherwise managers will simply spend all their time in meetings, which is just as unproductive as spending it writing memoranda.

2.7 Relationships between client and contractor project teams

In most major projects, both the client and the contractor will appoint project managers. The task of the client's project manager is to manage the functions listed in table 2, and to generally control the execution of the project so that the client gets the results expected. It is very important for the client's project manager to be appointed at the outset, so that he/she can be a party to the development of the project brief, and generally participate in the inception stage. Through this, he/she will have a fundamental understanding of the aims, objectives and constraints of the project, which should improve the quality of decision making.

The main focus of any project is the execution stage, and this is primarily conducted through the "construction performance" listed in table 2. It is at this stage that the client's project manager will have most staff, especially when the client chooses to supervise the construction work directly. It is, of course, essential that the supervisory staff communicate directly with the construction staff, because the whole momentum of the project can falter if all supervision is centralized. However, with many people communicating with each other, often across contractual boundaries, it is easy for communication and authority to become confused and acrimonious. There has to be discipline, and this is achieved by the two project managers formulating an agreed communication and authority structure, defining who can communicate with whom, and about what. The decision-making power of all concerned must be carefully defined. The main channel for communication should be between the two project managers. Some construction project managers insist that this is the only channel, so that they can keep complete control of all exchanges of information. This is known as single-point communication and, where this is feasible, it is a good practice.

Case-study B

PROJECT ORGANIZATION STRUCTURE

11 km of rural highway

This case is based on an actual project, on which one of the authors was the planning and systems consultant. The contractor did not wish the project to be identified.

Brief description of the project

This project was for the construction of part of a major highway through undulating countryside. This is illustrated by figure 14. There are three lengths in cutting towards the ends, and also in the centre of this section of the highway. Between the cuttings run two sections where the road is on earth embankments. Within the embankment sections there are 14 underbridges, providing for nine simple agricultural access tracks, three major roads, one substantial river and a railway. Over the cuttings are six overbridges for agricultural access, two for minor roads, and one for a major road.

Strategic planning

The strategy was easy to formulate. The embankments were formed from the material excavated in the cuttings, and this could not be moved along the line of the road until the underbridges over the river, railway and major roads had been completed. Therefore, these became top priority, and when complete the main, bulk excavation could be done, followed by the construction of the bridges over the sections in cutting. Road-building itself could start when a sufficient length of embankment had been completed. The plan for roadworks was that once started, the programme would be scheduled so that road-building could proceed continuously until completion. With such a plant-intensive activity, the cost of transport to and from the site was substantial, so this requirement obviously made good economic sense. The start of road-building was in fact delayed significantly beyond the earliest date that it could have started, so that once work began continuity could be achieved.

Organization structure

Thus the organization structure was one which required a concentration of bridge-building knowledge and skills at the beginning and end of the project, bulk earthmoving as an intensive central phase of the project, and road-building occupying the latter part of the project duration. The project was divided into four functional sections, each under the control of an experienced section manager.

The sections were:

Structures, which included items such as large drainage culverts as well as all bridges

Earthworks, which included all excavation work required to bring the road up to the formation level

Figure 13. Organization structure for project of case-study B

PROJECT MANAGER		Chief Engineer	Plant Manager	Planning Engineer	Chief QS	Office Manager
		Section Engineers	Fitters		Section QS	Clerks Timekeeper
W O R K S M A N A G E R	Structures Section Manager					
	Earthworks Section Manager					
	Roadworks Section Manager					
	Drainage Section Manager					

Roadworks, including all work from sub-base to surfacing, including kerbs where necessary, and all diversions of existing roads

Drainage and miscellaneous works, which included all other items of work not included in the other three sections as well as all the drainage works.

The project organization structure is shown in figure 13.

An alternative form of organization structure was considered and rejected. This was a geographical division, based on the principle that – until the bridges were completed – the river and the railway were such serious obstacles to transport and communication that the site was effectively divided into three distinct parts. This organization structure was rejected on the grounds that it would be difficult to coordinate all the earthmoving and roadbuilding equipment across three sections. Nevertheless, the structures section was effectively subdivided on this basis, with each subdivision comprising a number of bridges which were quite close together.

Each section had a section foreman (a line manager), and a section engineer (who was in control of technical performance). In practice, they worked as a section management team, and in many cases the boundaries

Figure 14. Section through rural highway (case-study B)

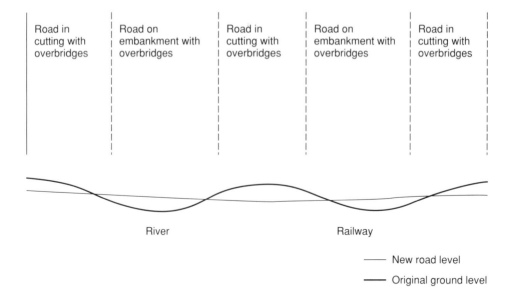

| Road in cutting with overbridges | Road on embankment with overbridges | Road in cutting with overbridges | Road on embankment with overbridges | Road in cutting with overbridges |

River   Railway

—— New road level

—— Original ground level

of the line and staff management functions were less distinct, because individuals brought their own experience and skills to bear on both technical and managerial problems.

Each section manager was directly responsible to the works manager, who was solely responsible for the "outside work" on the project. The works manager was directly responsible to the project manager, to whom the performance managers, such as the chief engineer, chief quantity surveyor and the office manager, were also responsible.

Each section was subdivided further into individual responsibilities. In the case of structures, a team of one foremen and one engineer would look after all the work on a number of bridges, which was a geographical split. On the other hand, management of roadworks was organized more on the basis of the process – the stone road base being under the control of one team, the bitumen surfacing under another.

Organizationally, the changing demand for the services for each section team throughout the project was difficult to manage. The skills required for each of these major operations was quite different, and thus different personnel were needed throughout the project for the work to be done efficiently. However, the level of demand on the different sections varied greatly throughout the project. Having foreseen this problem the project manager solved it by negotiating with other project managers in the same company for an interchange of staff at critical times, and several of the company's projects were scheduled together to make the best use of these shared resources.

Case-study C

WORK PACKAGING

Groundworks for a large dining and recreation facility on a military base

For reasons that will become obvious to the reader, the parties involved in this case-study did not wish to be identified.

Brief description of the project

The contract was for the design and construction of a large dining and recreation facility for a military base. The requirements were for a dining room that could also be used as a function and entertainment room, several smaller rooms for games and meetings, catering facilities, and other miscellaneous rooms (staff, lavatories, etc). Planning permission was granted on the condition that it would be of single-storey construction. The client invited tenders on the basis of a client's functional brief and the standard, comprehensive specification used by the military organization.

Tendering procedure

For the tender, the contractor engaged an architectural practice to prepare an outline scheme design that satisfied the client's brief, and a structural engineer to make preliminary designs for the structure. These were selected from a dozen or so firms with whom the contractor had established good working relationships on other projects. The selection process was based on discussions with those firms who were considered by the contractor to have the required expertise, and who had the capacity to take on this work. The final selection was commercial, and was largely based on how much of the tendering risk the consultants were prepared to take. In the very poor market conditions which prevailed at this time, both the architectural and the structural consultants were prepared to work on a "no-win, no-pay" basis. Their work was specified in detail in work packages, which included the preliminary designs that they had done for the tender, and prices for these packages were negotiated. These consultants also assisted in the preparation of packages for other design and supervision packages, and in the estimation of prices for these. All the consultants' packages were organized to cover the work to be done according to traditional professional disciplines: architect, structural engineer, building services engineer, cost engineer, and so on. Written into their package specifications was the requirement that they would coordinate their work, and define the limits of their packages, to the satisfaction of the project manager.

This information, prepared by the consultants, gave the contractor sufficient information upon which to prepare package specifications, on which to invite bids for the detailed design and the construction of the building. These bids were then analysed, and formed the basis of the contractor's tender.

When the contractor won the contract, the entire project and packages were reviewed in detail in order to produce the building required by the client and the best commercial result for the contractor. This review involved a more detailed analysis of ways in which the project work had been divided into packages, and the content of each package, and was conducted with the participation of the potential package contractors.

Design development

Most of the detailed design work required to develop the design from the outline to working drawings stage was to be done by the package contractors, and included in their "design-supply-and-fix" packages. The design element of these packages was to be supervised and coordinated by the architectural and structural consultants. To formalize this process, the organization of their work packages was made more comprehensive, incorporating a rigorous "design development procedure". This laid out in detail each element that had to be designed, and by whom, together with a series of checks and approvals through which each package design had to pass, with time scales and deadlines.

Organization: Construction packages

Some examples of the construction packages are described below.

The original intention was to group all the work up to and including the floor into a single groundworks package. This included all the excavation, drainage, access road, car parks, foundations and the floor itself. The advantage to the contractor was that all the complex coordination required in these operations would be delegated to a single package contractor. In the event, no subcontractor could be found who was prepared to take this package, largely because of the diversity of expertise and resources required, but also because they too were apprehensive about the coordination of such a diversity of activities.

The final decision was to divide this work into three packages: roadworks and drainage; foundations; and the floor. The first two of these represented clear distinctions between the expertise and customary divisions of traditional trades contracting. However, the concrete floor would usually have been included in the foundations package, but for this building the ground conditions had influenced a design decision to use long-span precast concrete flooring units. The foundation contractor was unwilling to undertake the work of installing these units, so a design-supply-and-erect package contract was arranged with a precast concrete company.

The frame of the building and the external cladding formed two other design-supply-and-erect packages. Thus the construction of the building to the stage of being watertight was divided into five packages. The contractor's job was to coordinate these.

Coordination: Managing the interfaces between packages

This approach to the management of construction projects gives the project manager a fundamentally different job from that of a traditional approach in which the contractor undertakes all the work by directly employed operatives. Instead of being a labour master, the project manager's job centres around technical coordination and control, and negotiating on problems as they occur. It is actually very difficult to coordinate four packages such as those described. Each designer tends to work concurrently, but independently, in geographic locations remote from each other. Unless the project management staff are competent and diligent, there is every chance of design developments not being passed on to the other designers

In this project, the tight price influenced the contractor to staff the project at an inadequate level. The project manager and his assistants were, therefore, very much overworked, with the consequence that there were two major coordination problems. Firstly, although from the drawings the top of the foundation wall appeared to be of adequate size to support the base of the steel columns, in practice the holding-down bolts were too near the edge, and coincided exactly with some of the the main reinforcement. Consequently, the side of the foundation would break away when the bolt hit the reinforcing steel as it was drilled in. This was not discovered until steelwork erection started, and work then had to stop for three weeks until the bases were redesigned and new ones made.

The second problem was for the installation of the floor slabs. The original package specification required the foundations, slabs and steel frame to be constructed in stages, so that cladding could begin at one end and follow the other activities across the building. In the event, the flooring contractors' quotation ignored this, and their tender was based on installing all the units in a single, intensive continuous four-day activity. Consequently, all the foundations had to be complete before any of the slabs could be installed, and in turn this meant that no steelwork could be erected until all the floor was finished. All the package contractors used the disruption caused by this problem to negotiate to their commercial advantage, with the result that the project was delayed and the contractor lost a considerable amount of money – far more than it would have cost to provide a full project management team.

Perhaps the most astonishing lesson to be learned is that really basic problems like this can occur in substantial projects, run by an experienced international contractor, in 1993. It emphasizes the truth of the old aphorism that management is largely a question of making sure that simple things are done well, always.

Another lesson is the crucial importance of the management of the interfaces between trades and packages. Interfaces must be defined competently and in great detail, based on proper method statements describing how the work will be done in each package. Managers must then monitor and control the work so that these interface agreements are actually put into effect.

Notes

[1] J. J. N. O'Reilly. *Better briefing means better buildings.* Building Research Establishment, Garston, Watford, United Kingdom, 1987.

[2] CIRIA (Construction Industry Research and Information Association): *Buildability: An assessment.* Special publication No. 26, CIRIA, London, 1983.

[3] H. Koontz and H. Weihrich: *Management.* Ninth international edition. McGraw-Hill, Singapore, 1988, p. 18.

[4] R. H. Neale and D. E. Neale: *Construction planning.* Thomas Telford, London, 1989.

[5] B. N. Baker and D. Wilemon: "The human element in project management," in *Project Management Quarterly*, Vol. VIII, No. 1, Mar. 1977.

SYSTEM SUPPORT FOR PROJECTS

3

3.1 Data flow in contractors' organizations

Those involved in the day-to-day management of activities on construction sites are usually assisted by head office staff. The extent and nature of this help varies from organization to organization and from construction project to construction project. Superficially most companies' information systems appear to have little in common in terms of how the companies do business or how they manage construction. However, research has found more similarity where these systems are considered in terms of data, rather than in terms of what a managerial function is called or who does it.[1]

An overview of the typical flow of data in a contractor's organization is given in figure 15. This identifies three different sets of procedures of a construction project: pre-tender procedures (which include those undertaken prior to and during the preparation of a bid for a project), preconstruction procedures (those initiated following a successful bid and prior to work starting on site) and construction procedures (procedures involved in the construction process). Several data flow maps providing an increasing level of detail are provided in the research referred to above and give a useful benchmark with which contractors can compare their own data flows.

Several support systems usually exist to service the data flows shown in figure 15. Table 7 identifies the main systems normally found in construction organizations as well as where they are usually located.

Table 7. Support systems required in a contractor's organization

Support system	Location
Design (including architectural, structural and services design)	Head office
Measurement (during design)	Head office
Estimating and tendering	Head office
Tender planning	Head office
Contract planning	Head office/site
Site measurement	Site
Site accounting	Site
Head office accounting	Head office
Personnel	Head office
Site management	Site
Plant management	Head office
Head office management	Head office
Marketing	Head office

Figure 15.   Overview of data flow in a contractor's organization[1]

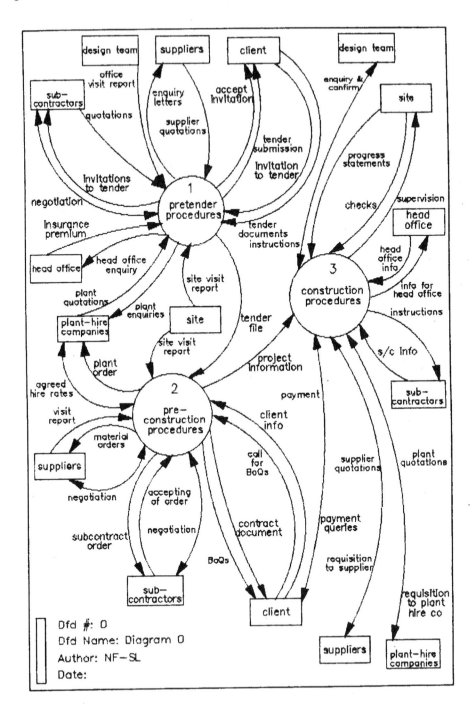

Figure 16.   Flowchart of technical and accounting systems

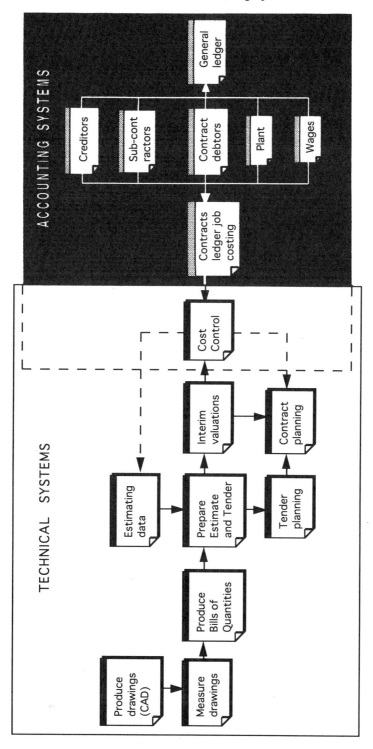

Computer systems that assist head office staff in managing the data shown in figure 15 fall into two categories – *Technical systems* and *Accounting systems*. These are illustrated in figure 16. Accounting systems have been in existence for a longer time and have gained more widespread acceptance than technical systems. This chapter concentrates on technical systems and stresses aspects of these systems to be considered for successful implementation.

The software available to the construction industry generally does not distinguish between head-office and site-based operations. Few proven "off-the-shelf" systems exist which exploit the many technical innovations (such as bar-code readers, remote television, hand-held computers) that are currently available. For the purposes of this chapter, no distinction has been made between computer systems based at head office and those located on a construction site.

3.2 Technical systems

This section gives a brief overview of software that is currently available in each of the technical areas shown in figure 16. The advantages and disadvantages of different proprietary computer packages are not within the scope of this book. Rather, the emphasis is to *highlight strategies for the successful implementation of these systems*. Each application is dealt with in terms of:

o   the functions the software performs

o   the operations involved in using the software including:

 —   a schematic flowchart (showing the relationship between various operations)

 —   the data required to operate the systems and their sources

o   key advantages and disadvantages of using a computer system

o   potential problems associated with using the software

Producing drawings using CAD systems

The functions of CAD software
CAD systems (Computer Aided Drawing, Draughting or Design) may be used by designers and draughtsmen to prepare:

o   fully detailed two- and three-dimensional drawings (including plans, elevations, services details, dimensions, notes, specifications and other similar "attributes")

o   three-dimensional visualizations of designs

o   measurements based on CAD drawings

Figure 17.   Flowchart of CAD

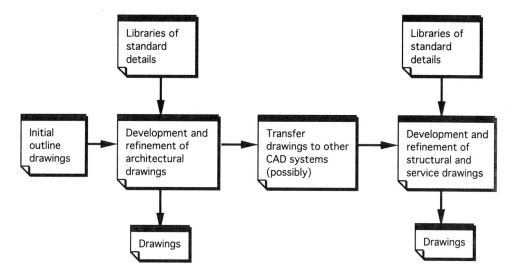

The operations involved

Figure 17 provides a simplified flowchart of the operations involved in using CAD systems.

Sources of CAD data

o   Unique nature of structures
Each structure is unique. It is therefore not usually possible to re-use designs or to use "off-the-shelf" designs.

o   Similar nature of materials/components
Many construction materials and components are widely used in buildings and other structures. Recognizing this, several suppliers provide CAD drawings of their products for use by designers. For example, CAD files of standard special bricks are readily available as are drawings of sanitaryware and windows. These details (possibly supplemented by other frequently used "in-house" drawings) can then be incorporated in the production of CAD drawings and provide a valuable productivity aid to designers.

o   Interdisciplinary use
Several different professions contribute to the design of a structure. It is clearly advantageous to avoid repeating work already completed by others (for example, where architectural drawings are re-used by structural engineers to facilitate the design of a structure). If those concerned use compatible CAD systems it is possible for drawings to be exchanged. However, when incompatible systems are used, the transfer procedure is more complicated and necessitates CAD data from one system being "translated" into a format which the receiving system can interpret.

Key advantages and disadvantages

o   The drawing process

　　—   Once the skills of using a CAD system have been acquired, these systems allow drawings to be produced more quickly and in greater detail than is possible with traditional manual methods.

　　—   Certain CAD facilities make it easier to produce drawings than by hand. One such facility is "layering" (a "layer" may be thought of as a sheet of tracing paper which can be switched on or off electronically). The advantages of this become apparent when the detail required on various drawings is considered. Some may include a basic outline of a structure as well as dimensions, notes, positions of services and so on. These can become so overcrowded that they are unintelligible. Layering makes it possible to store specific information on a particular layer and switch it on or off as required. Details, such as electrical light and plug points, may thus be stored on a "layer" and either included or excluded when shown on screen or produced on paper.

　　—   A further advantage of "layering" (and CAD systems) is that potential conflicts between services can be identified when complementary layers are "switched on". These may then be rectified before construction work starts.

o   Provision of standard details
As already identified, the repetitive nature of many building components can be accommodated by CAD facilities which allow such details to be stored and re-used at a later date.

o   Visualization
Some CAD systems provide powerful three-dimensional facilities which simulate the views available whilst walking through a structure. Such aids are being used increasingly to "sell" designs and to identify clashes between services.

Potential problems

o   CAD systems can be time-consuming and complex to learn.

o   The facilities provided by some systems are more suited to a manufacturing environment than to architecture and construction.

o   As already stated, the exchange of drawings between different CAD systems requires a translation process. This transforms drawings created on one system into a "transfer format" which can then be interpreted by other systems. The "transfer format" that is currently widely accepted is the Data Exchange Format (DXF).

However, DXF does not have the status of a British, European or international standard. Work is under way within the International

Organization for Standards to produce a formal international standard for two-dimensional drawing transfers as well as the futuristic "product model" exchange TP(STEP) which will eventually replace DXF.[2] Until a proven and widely used alternative to DXF is available, users who wish to transfer drawings between different CAD systems are advised to use systems that support the DXF format.

Measurement of construction work

The functions of the software

Measurement of work from drawings is an essential part of construction. In the United Kingdom, and in those countries who use it as a model for their construction industries, the term "quantity surveyor" is applied to those involved in this task and "bills of quantities" to the documents which record the work measured. Readers not familiar with these terms should substitute others (for example, "cost engineer" and "work schedules") where these are felt to be more appropriate.

Measurement software:

o   allows dimensions to be measured (or "taken off") from drawings

o   calculates quantities from these measurements (frequently called "comping up")

Bill production software:

o   collects together quantities of similar items ("abstracting")

o   prints out bills of quantities

The operations involved

o   Dimensions are entered into a system using either a keyboard or a digitizer.

o   These may be referenced to geographic (or other) areas/locations.

o   The dimensions are then associated with suitable bill item descriptions (selected from a library of descriptions or from previously completed projects where no appropriate descriptions exist, these will need to be composed at this stage). The data stored for each bill item typically consists of:

— a code by which items are classified (in the United Kingdom commonly used classifications are the SMM7[3] or CESSM3);[4]

— an item description;

— the units that the item is measured in;

— the estimated price per unit.

Figure 18.   Flowchart of measurement and bill production

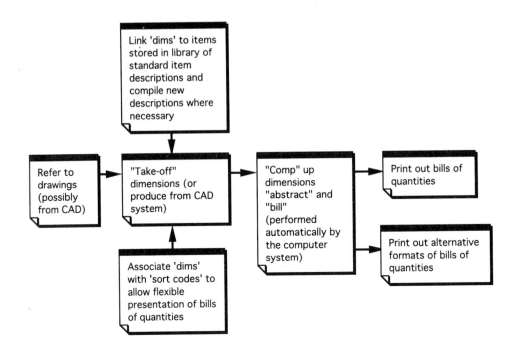

o   Bills of quantities are then produced (these systems complete all the tasks required i.e. "comping" up dimensions, "abstracting" similar bill items and finally producing a bill).

Sources of data
o   CAD systems
    CAD makes use of coordinate geometry to identify the positions of drawn data. It is therefore possible for these systems to calculate distances as well as areas and volumes bounded by specified points. To conform with the measurement practices in common use, the measurements produced by these systems need to be arranged in accordance with a standard system of measurement (e.g. SMM7 for the building industry and CESSM3 for the civil engineering industry in the United Kingdom). This requirement has proved to be a stumbling-block – the automatic generation of bills of quantities from CAD systems is still to be realized. It is worth noting that some use is made of "CAD measurements" where these do not need to conform to a method of measurement (for example, where those involved are able to define their own measurement standards. Examples of this are to be found in the house-building industry in the United States and

South Africa, where CAD measurements have been used to prime estimating software since the mid 1980s).

o   Libraries of bill item descriptions
     It is time-consuming and costly to compose clear, concise, legally binding bill item descriptions. To be used effectively, bill production systems need to be primed with bill item descriptions that have already been prepared at some earlier stage. Libraries of such descriptions and/or previous jobs are frequently used to provide this data.

o   Libraries of bill item rates
     Bill production systems are frequently used to provide approximate estimates. The item library facilities described above are extended in many systems to include monetary rates. Appropriate software is also provided to complete the arithmetic required to produce priced bills of quantities and these systems may be used to prepare approximate estimates of construction cost during the design process.

o   Specifications
     Software is also available which allows specifications of materials and workmanship to be stored, recalled and modified according to the requirements of individual projects.

Key advantages and disadvantages
o   Calculations and sorting
     Computer-aided bill production systems perform the calculations and sorting required to produce bills of quantities (i.e. "comping up" of dimensions, "abstracting" and "billing"). The fact that these tasks are done as a by-product of the measurement process means that much tedious manual and error-prone work is avoided.

o   Alternative methods of presentation
     Many of these systems have facilities which allow bills of quantities to be presented in different formats (e.g. trade, locational or elemental order). This is usually accomplished by linking dimensions to suitable "sort codes". No extra work is involved in producing these alternative bills as the same set of dimensions is used to generate all bills. These facilities are particularly relevant to those involved in design and build operations as different formats will prove useful to those involved (e.g. "trade" order bills for estimators, "locational" bills for planners).

o   Consistent bill item descriptions
     Using a library of bill item descriptions leads to more consistent presentation of bills of quantities than is feasible with manual systems. This leads to a more precise understanding of the work involved and a more professional image of those responsible for measurement.

o   Digitizers
     Digitizers are electronically sensitized drawing boards and styluses.

When used as measurement devices, drawings are placed on the digitizer and measurement software calibrated to the scale of the drawing. Lengths and areas are marked off (or, in the cases of curved elements, traced) using the stylus and the system then automatically calculates appropriate lengths and areas. These devices have proved particularly useful in practice. Although they involve scaling drawings (and the inaccuracies that this entails) they are frequently used to quantify alternative designs throughout the design process.

Potential problems
The problems likely to be experienced with these systems are those normally associated with using computer systems. These are discussed in Section 3.4.

Estimating based on bills of quantities

The functions of estimating software
o   Computer-aided estimating (CAE) systems produce estimates of construction work based on bills of quantities.

o   They also allow estimates to be converted into tenders by the addition of amounts of money to allow for mark-up, risk, overheads and so on.

The operations involved
o   Bills of quantities should first be entered into a CAE system

o   These items then need to be linked to performance data (preferably already stored in the CAE system being used)

o   Performance data can then be changed if necessary

o   Up-to-date quotations need to be obtained and entered into the system

o   Rates for "one-off" items need to be built up

o   "Preliminary and general" costs need to be calculated

o   Mark-up needs to be added

o   Bills of quantities may be produced at any stage

o   Other reports can also be printed out as and when required

Sources of data
o   Bills of quantities
    Before CAE systems can be used to price bills of quantities they need to be "primed" with the data for a project (such as bill item descriptions and quantities). If this task is done manually it is time consuming to complete and susceptible to error. Alternatives include Electronic Bills of Quantities (EBQs), and Optical Scanning (OS). Problems associated with these methods are described below.

Figure 19. Flowchart of computer-aided estimating

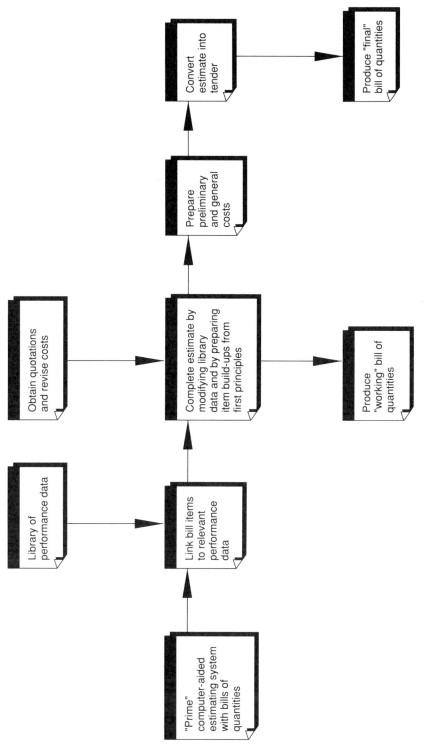

o   Libraries of performance data
     Records of past performance on previous contracts are essential if
     contractors are to estimate for new work at realistic rates. CAE
     systems allow performance data to be stored in a structured way and
     retrieved as required. Estimators can then base estimates on production
     rates achieved in the past and/or modify outputs according to the new
     conditions anticipated. A library of performance data is thus an
     essential element of a CAE system and needs to be exploited if the
     full benefits of computers are to be reaped in this area.

Key advantages and disadvantages
o   Calculations
     Estimating involves many different calculations; item rates need to be
     worked out, multiplied by item quantities and totalled to produce
     trade and overall totals. Computer systems are ideally suited to
     operations such as these.

o   Simulation of different construction methods
     CAE systems allow several different methods of construction to be
     simulated for each tender. It is possible, for example, to prepare an
     estimate based on subcontract rates and then compare the cost arrived
     at to that of similar work performed by an in-house labour force. The
     manual effort associated with doing comparisons such as these is
     usually considered to be prohibitive.

o   Application of mark-up
     Most CAE systems provide facilities which allow mark-up to be
     distributed over the estimated costs of bill items in a variety of ways.
     The manual effort required to do these calculations is prohibitive.

o   Post-tender use of estimating data
     Most CAE systems provide reports which split the costs of bill items
     into categories of labour, plant materials, subcontract, overheads and
     mark-up. This information is extremely valuable to site managers who
     need cost budgets to work to. It is possible to obtain this information
     from manual systems but the ease and speed with which CAE systems
     produce it is sufficient to convince some contractors to computerize
     their estimating departments.

o   Speed and quality
     Few users of CAE systems are willing to cite speed of producing
     tenders as a major benefit of their systems. However, most agree that
     the quality and detail of data produced enables better decisions to be
     made.

Potential problems
o   Entering bills into a CAE system
     As already stated, bills of quantities need to be entered into a CAE
     system before it can be used. The problems of manually entering these

documents have already been described. Two alternative approaches are available:

○ Electronic Bills of Quantities (EBQs) which are an electronic form of the paper documents. These are currently not widely used, though isolated instances of successful application have been reported. This lack of use must, in part, be due to the fact that no standard for exchanging data between different parties exists. Those that have successfully employed EBQs have made use of ASCII documents as a transfer vehicle. Work is currently under way by EDICON to prepare a standard for interchange, but at the time of writing this had not been completed.

○ As an alternative to EBQs some use has been made of *optical scanners* which, in effect, create "electronic bills". However, the accuracy of scanned images is dependant upon the quality of source documents being excellent and it is also necessary for bill data to be presented consistently. As some bills do not satisfy these requirements, the use of scanners has not been widespread in this area.

○ Collecting performance data
CAE systems need to provide libraries of past performance so that relevant data can be used in the preparation of new tenders. However, considerable effort is required to classify and assemble sufficient data to make a worthwhile contribution to the preparation of a tender. Some vendors of these systems provide general performance data but these are generally used as a supplement rather than a primary source of performance data.

○ Package contract element
Where extensive use is made of package contractors there is less of a requirement for CAE systems to incorporate comprehensive libraries of "performance data". In these circumstances estimating revolves more around a knowledge of the capabilities and pedigree of package contractors than of production rates. However, major contractors still need a knowledge of production rates if they are to estimate how long individual work packages are likely to take. Library facilities are thus a valuable element of CAE systems.

○ Estimator's "gut feel"
Some estimators are hesitant to use computer systems because they feel such an approach will inhibit them applying their "gut feel" to a job. Apprehensions such as these are generally voiced by older, more conservative estimators. Most CAE packages provide facilities which are flexible and it can be argued that they enhance estimators' ability to exercise "gut feel" once experience in such a system has been gained.

Planning construction activities

The functions of planning software

o   In their basic form, these systems aid the planning of construction projects by producing bar charts based on critical path analysis.

o   Most of the planning systems currently available also provide presentation aids and flexible reporting facilities.

o   Frequently costs of construction can also be entered into these systems thus providing information on financial aspects as well as timing and sequence of construction operations.

The operations involved

Planning is required for the preparation of a tender and during construction.

o   Tender stage
     Most Computer-Aided Planning (CAP) systems require the following data to be entered for each activity:

     o   an activity description

     o   an activity duration

     o   the relationship between an activity and other activities

     o   the resources used to complete each activity

     o   various sort codes (to allow similar activities to be collected together at a later stage)

     The following general data are also required:

     o   calendar(s)

     o   holiday periods

     o   the working hours per day (or week)

     o   the availability of resources

o   Contract stage
     Where tender programmes have been prepared using a CAP system, the following additional activities are necessary:

     o   monitoring of progress

     o   updating and modification of logic

     o   production of revised programmes

Where tender programmes have been prepared manually, or where the level of detail required at contract stage is greater than that available from the tender plan, it is necessary to complete the activities for both the *tender* and the *contract* stages.

Figure 20. Flowchart of construction planning

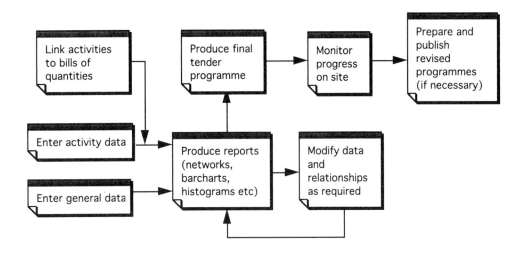

Sources of data

○ Performance data
Construction projects are seldom the same but the individual activities of which they are constituted frequently involve similar operations. Usually construction planners have libraries of performance data (not unlike those used by estimators) which they use to calculate the durations of construction activities. However, few (if any) CAP packages provide such "library" facilities. Planners requiring a computer system to store this data use general purpose programmes such as databases or spreadsheets.

○ Activity data
Although construction projects involve the same type of activities as those of previous jobs they are rarely arranged in the same sequence or subject to the same constraints. There is therefore minimal opportunity for critical path programmes prepared for one project to be re-used on another.

Key advantages and disadvantages

○ Speed and accuracy of calculation
CAP involves many tedious calculations which may need to be repeated many times to achieve an optimum solution. CAP systems provide measurable benefits over manual systems because they perform the necessary arithmetic quickly, accurately and do not suffer from fatigue.

○ High quality presentation
CAP systems provide reports that could not be provided, within the constraints of time and quality, by manual systems. In addition, the nature of CAP software means that extra reporting facilities (over and above manual systems) are available. For example, it is generally possible to display screen reports before printed documents are called for. CAP systems also allow bar charts to be presented in a variety of different ways (e.g. sorted by critical activities, or into different areas of a construction site and so on). This is important because the people who refer to these documents do not all have the same requirements (e.g. a plumbing package contractor does not require the same information as a major contractor's site manager).

○ Simulation of "what-if" scenarios

   ○ CAP systems are valuable pre-tender planning tools because they make it possible to alter methods of construction easily and quickly. For example, the implications of different methods of construction, different sequences of construction operations and so on can readily be assessed. The effort required to achieve this using manual planning methods is prohibitive.

   ○ These systems are also valuable *construction planning* aids. Using the facilities outlined above these systems make it possible to evaluate the effects of different courses of remedial action (e.g. different methods of construction, additional resources and so on) when progress has "fallen" behind programme.

Potential problems

○ Links to bills of quantities
CAP programmes reflect the timescale that construction is to be completed in. Although a link between the data stored in computer-aided estimating systems and this time-scale would seem obvious, few computer systems provide it. There are several reasons for this:

   ○ the way bills of quantities are presented does little to encourage this link

   ○ historically planners and estimators have worked separately and have an understandable "resistance" to change

   ○ some managers advocate that estimators and planners and planners work independently so that they, in effect, check each others work.

Notwithstanding these considerations, it is likely that computer systems which provide for a marriage of estimating data with planning data will become available. The benefits of this approach are illustrated in the next section on cash flow forecasting.

o   Size of construction project
    The size and level of complexity of a construction project generally
    determines the sophistication of the planning system (manual or
    computer) to be used. Similarly there are simple and sophisticated
    CAP systems. Not only do construction projects need to be matched
    to planning software but also to the CAP literacy of planning staff.

o   Revised programmes
    It is usual to revise programmes from time to time during the
    construction period. CAP systems may be used to advantage here as
    the "what-if" facilities described above considerably ease this task.
    However, care needs to be taken to avoid the confusion that may
    result if revisions are published too frequently.

Cash flow forecasting

The functions of cash flow forecasting software
    In the context of this chapter a Cash Flow Forecast (CFF) refers to a
prediction of the financial feasibility of a construction project viewed either
by a client or by a construction contractor. It involves calculations which
take into account the timing and amount of funds that flow in and out of
an organization. Cash flow is of prime importance to the profitability of a
project and to an organization. CFF systems:

o   prepare a cash flow forecast for a construction project

o   and for a company.

The operations involved

o   To calculate a CFF for a project the value of construction work needs
    to be apportioned to the duration of the project. This is a laborious
    task which entails allocating the items found in a bill of quantities to
    specific activities found in a critical path (Because of the number and
    complexity of the calculations involved, some contractors prefer to
    make use of statistical methods (such as standard graphs e.g.
    Californian envelope) of predicting approximate cash flows or to only
    calculate cash flows for large tenders.)

o   Once this allocation has been completed, CFF parameters need to be
    defined. These typically include:

    o   when payment is to be requested from the client;

    o   the delay between requesting payment and obtaining it from the
        client;

    o   the frequency of paying labour directly employed by the main
        contractor;

Figure 21. Flowchart of cash flow forecast

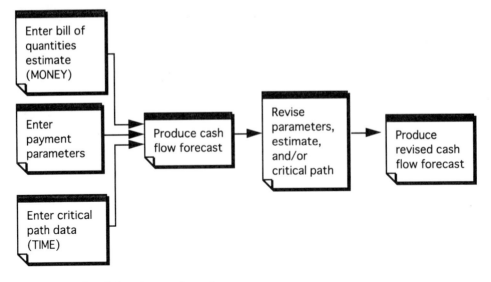

- o   the delay in paying plant;

- o   the delay in paying materials;

- o   the delay in paying subcontractors;

- o   the interest available on credit balances;

- o   the interest payable on debit balances.

Sources of data
- o   Estimate
    An estimate provides the monetary basis of a cash flow. Where these are prepared using CAE software, estimating data can be transferred to CFF systems. However, where manual estimating methods are used, CFF software will need to be manually primed with estimate data.

- o   Critical path programme
    CAP programmes provide a time-scale against which the costs included in an estimate can be allocated. As with the estimate, if a CAP system has been used to prepare a construction programme, these data do not have to be recaptured.

Key advantages and disadvantages
- o   Calculations
    As with other operations involved in producing tenders CFF involves many calculations. Forecasts may need to be done many times to achieve an optimum solution. Computer systems are ideal for this type of problem.

Potential problems
o   Allocating bill items to a time-scale
    The main problem is that of allocating each bill item to an activity in a CAP system. Part of this problem is that the manner in which most bills are produced bears no resemblance to the way buildings are constructed. For example, it is usual to have the external brick wall of a building as a single item in a bill of quantities. This clearly causes problems when trying to work out how much work is contained on each floor of a tall building (floors may not be typical and a certain amount of brickwork may also occur in basement(s)).

o   Compatibility of data
    This is also a problem as it may be found that the way data is stored in a CAE system is not compatible with the CAP programme being used.

Claims for interim payments (valuations)

The functions of valuations software
o   To monitor and document the value of work completed during a given period.

o   To prime site control systems (see Section 3.2 under "Cost control")

The operations involved
o   Bills of quantities need to be entered into a Computer-Aided Valuation (CAV) system.

o   Progress on site needs to be monitored.

o   The amount of work completed during each valuation period (usually one month) needs to be entered into a CAV system.

o   Reports are printed out.

o   Valuation claim is then submitted to client's financial representative for checking and authorization.

o   The actual payment made by the client needs to be entered into the CAV system.

o   Actual payments (to suppliers, subcontractors, workmen etc.) are entered into the system.

Sources of data

o   CAE systems
    Where a CAE system has been used a valuation system is relatively easy to introduce. Some work may need to be done to the manner in which the tender data are stored but this is minor compared to the effort required in setting up a CAV system on a stand-alone basis.

Figure 22. Flowchart of valuations

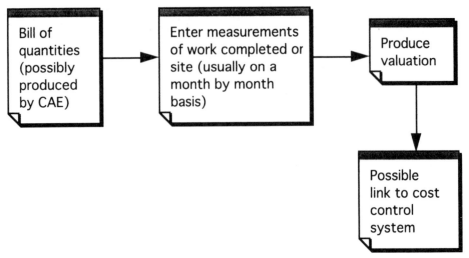

Key advantages and disadvantages

o   Calculations
     Doing monthly valuations involves many repetitive calculations.
     Computer systems are ideal for this type of application, as already
     discussed.

Potential problems

o   Reworking of some items
     Where valuations systems are primed with data from CAE systems,
     some editing of this data may be required. This is because short cuts
     taken at tender stage (especially with package-contract items where
     lump sum amounts are frequently entered for many bill items instead
     of splitting the sum into its constituent amounts) are not acceptable
     to client's financial controllers at contract stage.

Cost control

The functions of cost control software
     Cost control (CC) involves comparing the budgeted costs of
construction with those actually incurred. As such this area is of paramount
importance to senior managers.

The operations involved

o   Budgets need to be established.
o   Actual expenditure needs to be monitored. Two specific operations
     are involved:

     o   measuring the quantity of work completed over a specific time
          period, and

     o   measuring the resources expended achieving it.

Figure 23. Flowchart of cost control

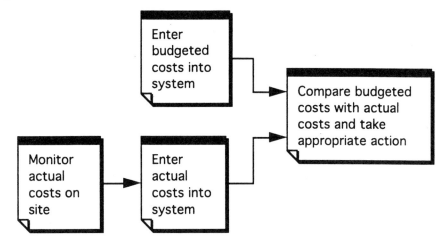

o   Actual costs need to be entered into the system.

o   The CC system then compares budgeted and actual expenditure.

Sources of data

o   Budgets

    o   Calculations and documentation completed as part of the preparation of an estimate and tender usually provide these budgets.

    o   Where computer-aided estimating (CAE) systems have been used to prepare estimates and tenders, the task of "priming" computer-aided CC systems with budgets is considerably eased. (This requires considerable effort when estimating is done manually and a computer system is used for cost control.)

o   Actual expenditure

    o   This is generally done by clerical staff entering data measured by others at a computer terminal.

    o   Potential exists to exploit more sophisticated computer techniques (such as card readers – which may be used to monitor staff starting and finishing work).

Key advantages and disadvantages

o   Computer-aided CC systems offer advantages of speed and accuracy over manual systems.

Potential problems

o   To be in a position to take remedial action, budgeted and actual costs need to be compared in a timely manner by site management personnel. Cost control systems that rely on traditional practices of month-end accounting have limited merit on a construction site because comparisons are generally produced too late to allow corrective action to be taken.

o   It is for this reason that "site costing" procedures (where delivery notes are entered into a system separate from the accounting system) have gained favour amongst many construction contractors.

o   Budgets need to be arranged in categories that match the way in which costs are to be monitored on site. When implementing estimating and cost control systems, careful attention needs to be paid to the coding system used to identify labour, plant materials and subcontract resources. If this is not done, it is likely that estimate data will need considerable manipulation before being used to prime cost control systems.

o   Cost control systems should permit a comparison between actual and budgeted costs as well as quantities of materials (and other resource categories). Some general accounting packages do not permit this.

o   Monitoring construction activity involves considerable work. The financial benefits that may accrue as a result need to be weighed up against the costs of collecting this information.

3.3   Accounting systems

Computer-aided accounting systems have been around for, what is in the time-scale of computer applications, a very long time. These systems abound but many are suited more to manufacturing than to construction. To be effective in a construction environment they should, as a minimum, provide normal accounting facilities such as creditors and a general ledger. In addition it is essential that they provide "construction related" facilities. These are not found in other industries and cater, for example, for the methods by which payments are made to subcontractors (especially in the area of retention where amounts are held back from such payments).

General purpose wages systems are also readily available but purchasers should be sure that the systems they use also cater for the vagaries of the construction industry.

3.4   Spreadsheet applications

No discussion on "Construction computing" would be complete without reference to spreadsheet applications. They may be used as a vehicle to create "home-grown" computer systems for some of the areas described above. Spreadsheet programmes are not, however, without drawbacks. The following factors should be considered before time and money are invested in them:

○ *Programmes need to be developed*
Spreadsheets are general purpose systems that need to be "programmed" to perform specific functions. Construction personnel generally master the skills necessary to accomplish this task fairly quickly, but if spreadsheets are to be used to solve construction computing problems, time needs to be spent developing programmes.

○ *Solutions may be cumbersome*
Spreadsheets can be programmed to accept complex formulae and store large amounts of data. However, the manner in which these systems cater for complicated requirements may become cumbersome and other more efficient computer programming tools may be more beneficially used.

○ *Not easy for third parties to use*
Generally spreadsheet systems are developed by enthusiastic members of staff and work well whilst they are operated by the author. The approach adopted in developing most spreadsheet-based systems is, however, not to provide menus of commands specific to the application in question. These systems are therefore generally more difficult to operate by third parties (e.g. clerical and/or trainee staff) than dedicated systems where programmes have been written for a particular purpose.

3.5 Problems of implementing computer applications

Many computer systems are not fully exploited. Some are never used and simply gather dust. What makes one installation successful whilst another one meets with resistance from the time it is installed? The following suggestions stem from observations of successful computer systems over the years:

○ Implementing a computer system is a major task and needs to be carefully planned. This involves the appropriate sequencing of installation tasks including the timely training of staff.

○ In most cases much thought needs to be put into structuring data long before work on the computer system starts.

○ Training of staff is of paramount importance and is expensive. Managers need to be aware of and committed to these costs if installations are to be successful.

○ Staff need to be motivated to use systems. Identical installations may be found to operate well in one environment and be labelled as a failure in another. Staff who are not committed to an application are likely to make it fail. Conversely, staff who are committed will make a system work and possibly overcome problems and shortcomings along the way.

o Members of staff sometimes balk at changing from existing manual methods to computer-aided ones because of a natural "resistance to change" (and, possibly, a lack of familiarity with computer systems). Older staff are probably more prone to show this reluctance and even when convinced of the merits of a particular system may be tempted to delay implementation until after their retirement.

o If possible, cultivate a "local expert" within the department a system is implemented in. This will reduce expensive calls to software vendors.

o Manual systems have evolved checking procedures which are tried and tested. This has not yet happened with computer applications. Clearly checking the arithmetical accuracy of "comping" is a waste of time but other checks related to different methods of working need to be instituted. Perhaps a reason for this is that manual measurement systems have evolved to such a degree (and incorporate checks) that those involved feel that the advantages outlined above are not sufficient to warrant the move. New systems are certainly not as widely accepted and provide what some see as only marginal benefits.

3.6 Hardware

The current use of computer technology has evolved to a stage where computer systems are controlled by localized groups of end users. The reasons for this trend from earlier more centralized control of computer installations by computer departments extend beyond the availability of cheaper and more powerful personal computers. Thorpe[5] identified dissatisfaction with the service provided by these departments as one such reason. Central Information Technology (IT) departments have not been removed but greatly reduced in size with modified objectives concerned with the guidance of IT strategy rather than the control of all IT objectives.

Notes

[1] N. Fisher and S. L. Tin: *Information management in a contractor*. Thomas Telford, London, 1992.

[2] *A simple guide on how to do "IT"*, CAD Data Exchange in the Construction Industry. National Economic Development Office, London, 1992.

[3] *SMM7, standard method of measurement of building works* (authorized by agreement between the Royal Institution of Chartered Surveyors and the Building Employers Confederation). Seventh edition. Royal Institution of Chartered Surveyors, 1988.

[4] Institution of Civil Engineers. *CESMM3, civil engineering standard method of measurement*. Third edition. Thomas Telford, 1991.

[5] A. Thorpe: "Construction integration: The role of data transfer". Paper presented at the SERC workshop entitled "Integration of Construction Information", at Armathwaite Hotel, Cumbria (United Kingdom), May 1993.

CONTROL OF QUALITY AND QUALITY ASSURANCE

4

4.1 Quality and assurance control, and certification

This chapter covers quality control, quality assurance and quality assurance certification. The subject will be understood better if the terms are defined at the outset and then explored in more detail in the rest of the chapter.

Quality in general
Something of superior value, something good, better or best, providing value for money.

Quality in terms of the production of an end product
The achievement of agreed requirements – Client satisfaction.

Quality control (QC)
Procedures to control the processes involved in producing the end product, in order to achieve the required quality.

Quality assurance (QA)
The demonstration that the agreed requirements will be, or have been met. This is usually achieved by means of a Quality Management System (QMS).

Quality assurance certification
Formal, public recognition that an organization has a satisfactory QMS and has demonstrated that the procedures and systems are employed correctly. Quality assurance certification is rapidly becoming a requirement for pre-qualifying in the world's construction market.

4.2 Quality and its achievement

Commonly quality is thought of as something of superior value, something good, better or best, providing value for money. However, these are abstract qualities – they have no substance, and cannot be measured or controlled. Before quality can be managed it must be related to something specific and quantifiable. The requirements must be identified and agreement between the parties involved in the contract must be obtained. Quality is achieved when agreed requirements are achieved.

Quality is concerned with people and their attitudes rather than bureaucracy and paperwork. To be a quality-minded organization is to be a customer-oriented organization. A major contractor's customers are its clients, its consultants, its package-contractors; in fact, everyone with whom it deals in its daily business. To ensure quality at the workplace the senior manager must lead by example, by efficient management of the whole construction process and by communicating a genuine commitment to excellence throughout the organization.

4.3 Obtaining client satisfaction

We have stated that to be quality-minded is to be customer-oriented and that quality is achieved when agreed requirements are achieved. In a construction project one particularly important customer is the client. In terms of this relationship, quality is achieved when the client is satisfied, better still when the client is delighted. Properly managed QA/QC will assist in this goal; however, client satisfaction is a much broader issue. It should permeate all levels of the organization and all stages of the construction project and extend beyond the formal "quality" department. It should not only be considered when approaching project completion as is so often the case with contractors seeking final account settlements. There are some key actions which will assist in bringing the client to an awareness of satisfaction.

Bringing the client to an awareness of satisfaction:

o   understand the client's expectations;

o   identify who will approve the works;

o   obtain approval as the work proceeds;

o   plan for practical completion;

o   give full and complete client briefings;

o   identify and monitor key milestones, referring to them in client reports;

o   plan ceremonies at key stages of the project;

o   complete a fully finished section early in the project and obtain approval;

o   do not hide your difficulties – keep the client aware;

o   ensure all your site activities reflect your attitude to quality;

o   remember; all contacts with the client will affect client satisfaction.

Section 1.4 defines what clients require from a construction company: a project completed on time, within budget, and to the required standard of quality. The drive for increased quality in construction has come, in the main, from construction clients. Contractors must respond to this initiative if they wish to compete in the world's construction market. In the contemporary construction environment, and even more so in the future, failure to recognize the importance of quality will result in an organization being unable to tender for the prestige projects. This must lead to a reduction in market share and even to the failure of the company.

4.4 The quality management system (QMS)

Scope of the QMS

Quality assurance (QA) is the demonstration that the agreed requirements will be, or have been, met. To achieve this a quality management system (QMS) must be established. This is a carefully structured and documented assembly of information and systematic working methods that describes how an organization will consistently achieve its customers' requirements. The system must include all aspects of the organization's business, providing control, reducing inconsistency and producing a platform for implementation. An effective QMS will assist a quality-minded organization in demonstrating that a good quality product can be produced with regularity. However, poorly devised QA and QC procedures can result in excessive "paper mountains" and will probably have little effect on the quality of the end product.

For an organization managing major construction projects the QMS will consist of two or three distinct parts:

Scope of the quality management system:

○ Head office/Corporate QMS;

○ Project office/Site QMS;

○ Production facility/Factory QMS (if applicable).

Corporate QMS

The corporate QMS covers activities that are the responsibility of the head office. It is wise to restrict detailed procedures to activities that are unique to the head office. Items such as company policy for projects should define the guidelines for project management but not prescribe, in detail, how such policies are to be implemented. Section 1.2 describes construction as a highly mobile business, building wherever required. There should be flexibility at project level to develop specific detailed procedures to suit individual situations. This is particularly important for international projects where the requirements of a country, remote from the organization corporate office, may be significantly different.

Scope of the corporate QMS:

○ Policy-making;

○ Company organization;

○ Communication;

○ Personnel (including training);

○ Safety;

○ Company policy for projects.

Project QMS

There are several different methods of establishing a project-based QMS. It will certainly reflect and expand the corporate QMS but must not contradict it. A typical QMS for a major construction project will include the following: (titles of documents may vary but principles will remain)

○   Project quality plan;

○   Project procedures manual.

Project quality plan: This is a succinct project policy statement, developing the principles of the corporate QMS. The plan states the procedures and techniques to be used to meet the contractual requirements and the corporate QMS requirements, and to provide appropriate verification that they have been achieved.

Project procedures manual: This details procedures and techniques and amplifies the quality plan. It must clearly state the person responsible for each activity and what that person is required to do.

Scope of project procedures manual:

○   Project management;

○   Procurement/purchasing;

○   Planning/resources management;

○   Financial management;

○   Quality.

It is advisable to ensure that the quality plan and procedures manual are kept as simple as possible as these will be the basis for assessment for QA certification. (This is covered later in the chapter.) It is not the purpose of QA to produce bureaucratic burdens, however, strategic planning and single-mindedness are required to prevent the procedures becoming so unwieldy that they detract from the primary objective to produce a quality project.

Case-study D
PROJECT PROCEDURES MANUAL
Vintners Place, London, United Kingdom

The following case-study[1] provides an example of the items included in a project procedures manual. The project is a 25,000 m^2 prestige office block in central London with six storeys above ground and two basements. This was a speculative development by a British/Japanese consortium, completed at the end of 1992 under a management form of contract.

The project procedures manual provided detailed procedures for the following items:

o   Project management:

  — Project policy;

  — Project organization;

  — Safety;

  — Communication;

  — Reporting;

  — Client/customer relationship;

  — Design management;

  — Off-site management;

  — On-site management;

  — Control of package contractors and suppliers;

  — Site establishment/common site services.

o   Procurement/purchasing:

  — Package contractor selection;

  — Tender preparation, evaluation and reporting;

  — Package contractor documentation;

  — Suppliers/materials ordering.

o   Planning/resources management:

  — Programming principles;

  — Works package content;

  — Package contractor's tender and contract programmes;

  — Progress monitoring and reporting;

  — Control of information.

o   Financial management:

  — Financial control, monitoring and reporting;

- — Contract administration;
- — Legal and Insurance.
○ Quality:
- — Control of QA documents;
- — Quality audits – internal, package contractors and suppliers;
- — Quality rating of works packages;
- — Package contractor requirements:
    ○ Quality plans;
    ○ Inspection and test plans;
    ○ Non-conformance and corrective action.

See Case-study E, p. 98 below for further information on this project.

Factory QMS

Organizations that have production facilities must produce a factory QMS. This is similar to the project QMS but deals with production aspects. Some elements of the package contractor's quality system, which is described later, will also be included.

4.5   The QMS and major contractors

How much disruption will be caused by establishing a QMS?

Provided the QMS has been established with adequate planning and forethought the disruption to an already efficient organization will be kept to a minimum. A good company will have quality procedures already in place, and a well-planned QMS will build on these procedures and formalize and rationalize the process throughout the organization. The QMS should be seen as facilitating efficiency rather than restricting innovation and flexibility.

Once the QMS has been set up can it be amended?

The quality plan and procedures manual can be amended to reflect changes in requirements or to refine the systems. This is particularly true during the early stages of QMS development, but it is also possible even after certification of the system. However, document changes can be costly and should be kept to a minimum. The manual must include a procedure for amendments, to ensure that changes are correctly communicated and actioned throughout the organization.

Is a quality consultant necessary?

Many organizations employ a quality consultant to advise on certification. Whilst there are many good, effective consultants there has also been an increase in consultants seeking to benefit from the recent rush towards QA registration. The following questions should be asked before choosing a consultant:

o   Does the consultant understand the construction industry?

o   Does the consultant have experience in the construction industry?

o   Is the consultant registered with the appropriate certification body?

o   What is the consultant's success rate for achieving certification?

o   Does the consultant only offer a standard solution and if so, does that solution meet the organization's needs?

Does a QMS guarantee a quality product?

Quality standards apply to management systems and not products, therefore neither a QMS, nor quality certification will necessarily guarantee a quality product. However, following registration, the certification body will periodically audit the QMS. Findings from such audits will be given to the organization for immediate action. Depending upon the seriousness of the default findings a follow-up audit may be arranged. Failure to action such findings will result in certification being withdrawn.

The stated aims of quality assurance are to improve the quality of the output of an organization. However, the assessment can only audit against the QMS. As such, it is unwise to assume that a company operating a QMS is necessarily producing a high-quality product. Neither can it be said that companies require a quality certified management system in order to produce products to the highest quality. It is also possible to register part of an organization, rather than the whole. For example, a head office may be certified without its production facility. Therefore, it is advisable to investigate claims of certification by suppliers and subcontractors.

4.6   The QMS and package contractors

What are the implications of the QMS on works packages?

Commonly, the work content of major projects is split into discrete works packages. Thus the role of the major contractor is now more of "project coordinator" than "labour master". The resultant fragmentation of the construction process has particular implications for quality control and assurance. To obtain customer satisfaction the major contractor must ensure that each supplier and package contractor provides a quality product. In addition, as the various components are assembled on site the interfaces between them must have the same quality checks as the individual elements.

To ensure that quality control measures are suited to the needs and requirements of different works packages, the major contractor grades each package for quality, based on value, complexity and design content. The precise requirements for quality documentation depend on the quality grading of the package. However, in general, each package contractor or supplier must produce documentation, and ensure that the relevant procedures are followed. This will apply even if the individual package contractor is not registered as quality assured. (Registration is covered later in the chapter.)

Documents required for a package QMS:

o   Project quality plan;

o   Inspection and test plan.

The problem of employing package contractors who are not "quality assured":

There is a very real difficulty here for the major contractor. Typically, the main contract document will require QMS procedures along with appropriate certification. However, market forces may lead the major contractor to employ a package contractor who has no QMS, and may also have little understanding of formal quality procedures. If such package contractors are used the major contractor must invest considerable time, and effort, in setting up the necessary procedures in order to comply with the main contract.

Project quality plan

This is similar to the major contractor's plan but refers only to the works within the package. The plan must be project-specific, reflecting the requirements of the project specification. A standard company quality plan will not suffice.

Inspection and test plan

This breaks down the work package into sequential stages and details the essential control procedures, inspection requirements and related documentation as follows:

Scope of the inspection and test plan:

o   Controlling specification – refers to contract document clauses;

o   Verifying activities – states inspection or test required;

o   Verification record – states format and location of results;

o   Inspection authority – defines the level of inspection;

o   Hold stage – identifies approval required before proceeding;

o   Acceptance criteria – states who accepts and what is acceptable.

4.7 Quality assurance certification

What is quality assurance certification?

QA certification gives public recognition that an organization meets the requirements of the appropriate QA standard and is registered as quality assured. The international series of standards are known as ISO 9000. In some countries quality standards may be given different names, for example BS 5750 in Britain and EN 29000 in Europe. Nevertheless, the standards are similar in format and content and are interchangeable throughout the world. Organizations trading in construction worldwide are advised to become registered to one of these standards.

Definition of the ISO 9000 series of standards[2]

The ISO 9000 series of international standards for quality systems tell suppliers and manufacturers what is required of a quality-oriented system. They do not set out extra special requirements which only a very few firms can – or need – comply with, but are practical standards for quality systems which can be used by all industry. However, the standards were originally designed for use in the manufacturing industry and require careful interpretation when applied to construction.

The principles of ISO 9000 are applicable whether you employ 10 people or 10,000. They identify the basic disciplines and specify the procedures and criteria to ensure that products or services meet the customer's requirements.

Is certification essential?

To date, certification is not mandatory, but organizations may be required to comply with certain of the procedures under the terms of contract for a particular project. In fact, due mainly to client pressure, quality assurance certification is rapidly becoming a requirement for pre-qualifying in the world's construction market. This is also likely to apply to suppliers and package contractors that are engaged by the major contractor. For example from April 1993 the Hong Kong Housing Authority, with a large-scale development plan of 70,000 dwellings per year, requires all prospective contractors to be certified prior to tendering for work.

How is certification obtained?

Figure 24 describes the several stages required to obtain quality assurance certification, and identifies the parties involved at each stage.

The QMS must operate for a satisfactory period of time prior to assessment. This period is agreed with the certification body – this is typically from 6 to 18 months from having no system to being registered, but will obviously depend on the existing systems in place within an

---

Figure 24. The route to quality assurance certification

Action   Participants

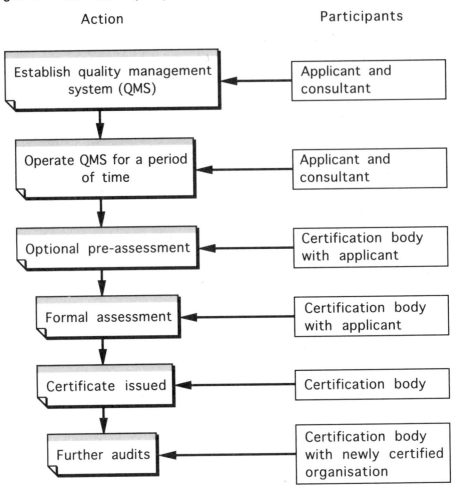

Action	Participants
Establish quality management system (QMS)	Applicant and consultant
Operate QMS for a period of time	Applicant and consultant
Optional pre-assessment	Certification body with applicant
Formal assessment	Certification body with applicant
Certificate issued	Certification body
Further audits	Certification body with newly certified organisation

organization. Following this period the certification body assesses the organization, by auditing the quality system. This is, basically, a check to see that the organization is doing what its system says it should.

If the results of the assessment are satisfactory the organization's name is registered with the appropriate government body and a certificate is issued.

Details of how to obtain a list of approved consultants and contact certification bodies are given at the end of the chapter.[3]

How much does certification cost?

The costs will vary considerably depending on the size and type of organization as well as the standard of its existing quality systems. In Section 4.5 we stated that a good company will have quality procedures

Figure 25. Costs of quality assurance registration

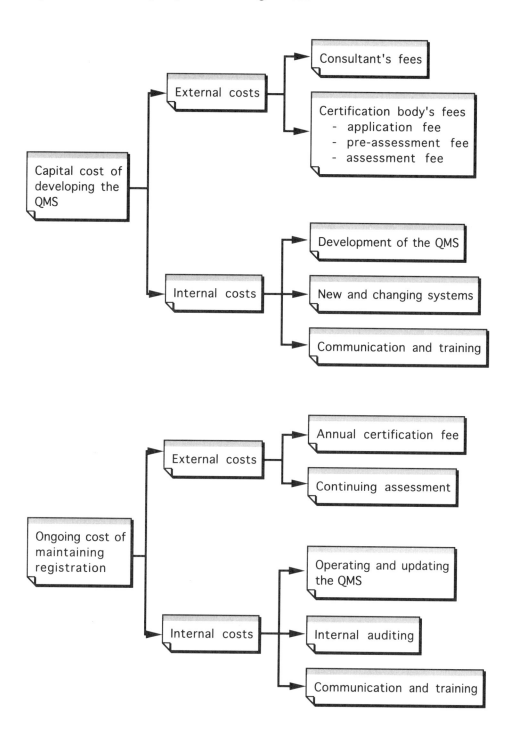

already in place and a well-planned QMS will build on these procedures and formalize and rationalize the process throughout the organization. In this case costs will be much lower than if no formal quality systems exist at all.

Evidence from the major construction companies in the United Kingdom suggests that, compared to turnover, costs are insignificant. Furthermore, the benefits of QA, although hard to quantify precisely, will increase efficiency and productivity.

The cost of QA registration can be divided into two parts:

o   The capital cost of developing the QMS;

o   The ongoing costs to maintain registration.

In turn, these can be split into external costs and internal costs, as shown in figure 25.

4.8   Summary of main conclusions

> Quality is achieved when agreed requirements are achieved.
>
> Quality is achieved when the client is satisfied.
>
> The quality management system (QMS) describes how an organization will consistently achieve its customer's requirements.
>
> The establishment of a QMS in an already efficient and quality minded company will cause very little disruption and costs will be insignificant compared to turnover.
>
> Package contractors must be brought up to the quality standards required in the main contract – a process which can be costly and time consuming for the major contractor.
>
> Quality assurance certification is rapidly becoming a requirement for pre-qualifying in the world's construction market.

Notes

[1] Vintners Place, London. Client: Wates City of London Properties plc. and the Sumitomo Corporation (Japan). Major Contractor (Management Contractor): Laing Management Ltd., London, United Kingdom. Vintners Place was one of three projects used as test cases to enable Laing Management to achieve QA certification.

[2] Adapted from BSI Quality Assurance: *BS 5750/ISO 9000/EN 29000:1987 – A positive contribution to better business.* Part of the "Managing in the '90s" series, Department of Trade and Industry, London, 1993.

[3] Details of approved quality consultants can be obtained from BSI Building and Construction Business Development, Linford Wood, Milton Keynes, MK14 6LE, United Kingdom. Details of certification bodies can be obtained from the National Accreditation Council for Certification Bodies, Audley House, 13 Palace Street, London SW1E 5HS, United Kingdom.

PART 1: SITE LAYOUT AND FACILITIES

5

5.1 Why is the planning of site layout and facilities necessary?

The construction site is one of the primary resources available to the contractor. In fact the site becomes the "factory" for the production of the building project. The aim in planning site layout and facilities is to produce a working environment that will maximize efficiency and reflect the organization's attitude to the project, its commitment to the safety and well-being of the workforce and its determination to satisfy the needs of its customers. The planning and management of construction site layout and facilities should be given priority throughout the construction period. Concentrating on the efficient organization of the "construction factory" maximizes the benefits of innovative techniques such as prefabrication and automation in construction.

Decisions made in the planning and management of construction site layout and facilities are critical to the successful completion of the project. Incorrect or ill-advised decisions prove costly, and lead to inefficient working, a demoralized workforce and a site that is unlikely to be safe or conducive to producing a high quality product. For example, the wrong choice of type or location for a tower crane may mean that, at worst, certain sections of the project cannot be built, or at least, may result in the necessity of hiring additional mobile craneage, double-handling of materials and so on.

5.2 Labour-related and materials-related facilities

The site layout and facilities planning process is complicated, time-consuming and intellectually demanding. It is a skill acquired from experience over a long period of time. In most companies the planning method is not written down but remains locked in the minds of experienced personnel – they consider it almost "second nature". Each facility in the "construction factory" will affect, or be affected by, one or all of the key resources, namely:

— labour;

— plant and equipment;

— materials and components.

Figure 26 itemizes the major construction site facilities and aspects of site layout and shows how they relate to these three primary resources. These facilities are usually provided by the major contractor and are often called "common-user" facilities.

> **Example from figure 26**
> The sizing of a storage area is primarily dependent upon the amount of materials required at different stages of construction. Its location depends upon the position and lifting capacity of cranes or lifting plant. Storage location will have a secondary effect on the workforce for smaller items that are carried to the workface. However, the size of the canteen is dependent upon the size of the workforce, and its location will affect the travelling time between the workface and the facility, and thus affect both worker morale and productivity. These principles are developed later in this chapter.

5.3   The sizing and location of labour-related facilities

An assumption of requirements for both labour-related and materials-related facilities is made at tender stage, in order to produce correct costing for the tender. Following the award of the contract the site management team develop the tender proposals and produce a site plan showing the relationship between the permanent works, the site boundary and the temporary facilities. Figure 27 shows the main factors affecting the sizing and location of the key labour-related facilities. These factors are developed in the appendices.

> Fundamental principle: Allocate the best space to the most important facility

Most managers plan site facilities using a combination of knowledge from previous experience, company policy and statutory legislation. The fundamental principle is to allocate the best space to the most important facility. The site plan will change as construction progresses and this must be considered and planned before work commences. The decision processes for labour-related facilities are complex and iterative and require both labour and materials-related facilities to be planned at the same time. However, as an illustration, they have been simplified and summarized in figure 29 which should be read in conjunction with figure 30 to understand the interrelationship between labour and materials-related facilities. A common fault is to concentrate on the initial activities and requirements forgetting that the needs towards the end of the project are different to those at the start. Failure to plan properly will significantly reduce worker morale and efficiency, and ultimately increase time and cost, and reduce quality.

Figure 26. Relationship between construction site facilities and labour, plant and materials

Aspects of site layout and facilities		Primary resources affected		
Main aspect	Related items	Labour	Plant	Material
Safety	Signage	■		
	First aid	■		
	Access ways	■	■	
	Site cleanliness	■		■
	Lighting	■		
	Existing services	■		
	Fire prevention	■		■
Welfare	Canteen/mess rooms	■		
	Drying/changing rooms	■		
	Toilets/washrooms	■		
	Car parking/transport	■		
	Worker accommodation	■		
	Time office	■		
Offices	Major contractor	■		
	Package contractor	■		
	Client/design team	■		
Access	Delivery access		■	■
	Site access roads		■	■
	Pedestrian access	■		
Storage, etc.	Off-loading areas		■	■
	Long-term storage	■	■	■
	Workface storage	■	■	■
	Tool storage	■		
	Secure stores	■		■
	Hazardous material store	■	■	■
	Prefabrication areas	■	■	■
	Batching plants	■	■	■
Transportation	Hoists	■	■	■
	Craneage		■	■
	Horizontal transportation	■	■	■
Rubbish removal	Site cleanliness	■	■	■
Temporary services	Electricity/gas/water	■	■	
	Drainage/surface water	■		
	Existing services	■	■	
Testing	On-site laboratories	■		■
Security	Hoarding/fencing	■		
	Site access	■	■	
	Secure stores	■		
	Identification passes	■		
Image	Signage	■		
	Hoarding/fencing	■	■	
	Site cleanliness	■		
	Public relations	■		

Figure 27. Sizing and location of labour-related facilities: Key factors

Facility	Factors affecting sizing of facility						Factors affecting location of facility							
	Statutory requirements	Company policy	Past experience	Size of workforce	No. of package contractors	Site location/Expected usage	Phase of project	Company policy	Past experience	Size of site	Congested/Uncongested site	Location of related facilities	Minimum travel time	Phase of project
Canteen/Mess room	□	□	□	□		□	■	■	■	■	■	■	■	■
Drying/Changing Room	□	□	□	□		□	■	■	■	■	■	■	■	■
Toilets/Washroom	□	□	□	□		□	■	■	■	■	■	■	■	■
Residential accom.		□	□	□		□	■	■	■	■	■			■
Car parking areas		□	□	□		□	■	■	■	■	■	■		■
Time office		□	□	□			■	■	■	■	■			■
Site offices		□	□		□		■	■	■	■	■			■
First aid room	□	□	□	□			■	■	■	■	■			■
Personnel hoists		□	□	□		□	■			■	■			■

Figure 28. Sizing and location of materials-related facilities: Key factors

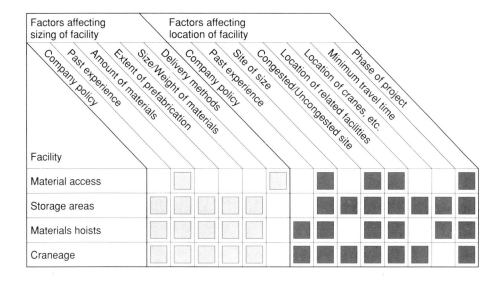

Figure 29. Simplified representation of the decision process for planning labour-related site facilities

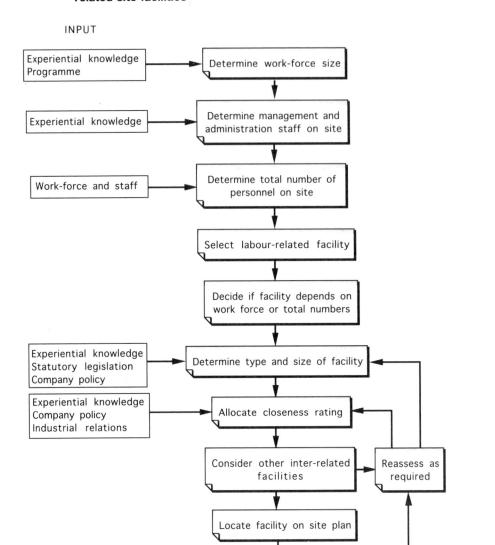

Example from figure 29: Sizing and locating the site canteen

Determine workforce size:
Assume that peak workforce size is 500 and average is 350.

Determine management and administration staff numbers:
Assume a peak of 100 and average of 75.

Determine total number of personnel on site:
600 maximum, 425 average.

Select facility:
Site canteen. At this stage the manager must decide if the facility will cater for peak numbers or average numbers with alternative measures taken for the overflow at peak. Decide if facility size depends on workforce or total numbers: this will depend on whether staff and workforce will use the same canteen; custom varies in different countries.

Determine size of facility:
Plan area determined by seating requirements and allowance for catering, etc. Most countries have statutory legislation which refers to welfare accommodation. Most temporary units can be stacked and so reduce the area of site taken up, however circulation within the canteen area will be a priority and affect decisions to plan a split-level facility. It is also likely that the facility size can be reduced at the start and end of the project.

Allocate closeness rating:
At this stage the manager must decide the importance of this facility being close to the workface. This will obviously have an effect on other facilities and the closeness rating is a method of prioritizing the facilities with regard to location. For instance, the use of dispersed canteens located next to the workface may be considered to minimize workforce travel time at rest breaks. Local practice and industrial relations considerations will be influential here.

Consider other interrelated facilities:
At this stage the manager must relate the canteen to other facilities such as toilets, washrooms and site offices. Decisions on the canteen cannot be made in isolation. The size and closeness rating may need to be reconsidered due to the influence of the other facilities.

Locate facility on site plan:
Allocate the best space to the most important facility. The manager must decide the relative importance of the canteen. The size and closeness rating may need to be reconsidered once more. Avoid moving the canteen during the project unless absolutely essential.

5.4   The sizing and location of materials-related facilities

Figure 28 on page 91 shows the main factors affecting the sizing and location of key materials-related facilities. These factors are developed in Part 2. Figure 30 is a simplified representation of the decision process for the planning of materials-related facilities.

Figure 30.   Simplified representation of the decision process for planning materials-related site facilities

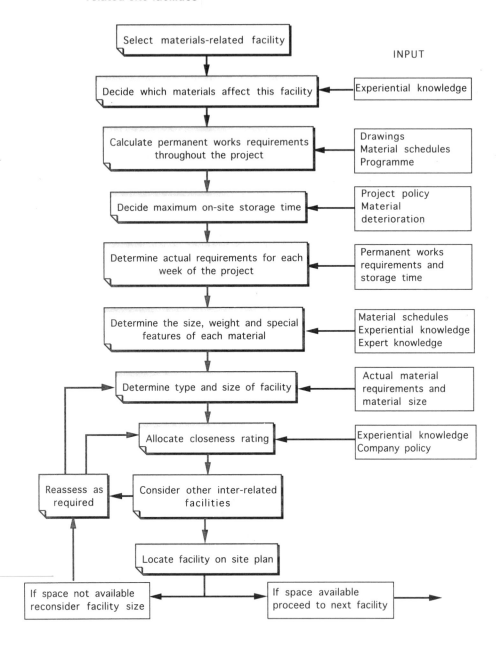

MANAGING INTERNATIONAL CONSTRUCTION PROJECTS: AN OVERVIEW

Example from figure 30: Sizing and locating site craneage

Select facility:
Craneage

Decide which materials affect, or are affected by, this facility:
Likely to be the major items of plant, structural frame, cladding, prefabricated elements, etc. But craneage can also be used for other, non-essential activities such as the loading out of materials, rubbish removal, etc.

Calculate permanent works requirements throughout the project:
From the drawings and schedules the manager must establish what materials and components are required and relate these to the construction programme.

Decide maximum on-site storage time:
The manager must decide how much in advance of the fixing dates the various items are to be delivered. This will obviously differ depending on the type of material or component and also upon the extent of on-site storage space available. There is a compromise between holding minimum stocks on site to prevent damage, and ensuring sufficient materials are available for efficient working.

Decide actual requirements for each week of the project:
Some items will be delivered and installed straight away, with others delivered and stored for future use. The first priority will be the items which must be installed using craneage, with a second list of other items which could use craneage if it was available but could be transported in other ways if necessary.

Determine size, weight and special features of each material:
These parameters will influence the decision on type of facility, and its location.

Determine type and size of facility:
This will depend upon the items to be lifted, available site space, possible locations, etc., and also upon the relative merits of mobile cranes and tower cranes. Local practice will be influential here.

Allocate closeness rating:
For craneage, weight and position for pick-up and final installation or lay-down are the overriding considerations.

Consider other interrelated facilities:
At this stage the manager must relate the craneage to other facilities such as unloading areas, lay-down and storage areas. In addition the proximity of adjacent buildings, highways, etc., will affect type and location. The size and closeness rating will need to be reconsidered due to the influence of the other facilities.

Locate facility on site plan:
In the case of craneage the weight and position of the items to be lifted are the key criteria, but other factors such as the pros and cons of cranes sited inside or outside buildings, and the practicality of removing the crane at project completion must also be considered. The size and closeness rating may need to be reconsidered once more, along with the possibility of reducing the size of prefabricated components in certain areas to optimize the craneage provision. In practice, the cranes will be sized and located based on items that must be crane-handled, with any additional capacity used on non-critical activities.

5.5 The use of computers to assist in the sizing, location and management of site facilities

Knowledge-based systems

Research in the United States has begun to explore the use of knowledge-based computer systems to assist in the sizing and location of site facilities.[1] Using similar algorithms to those shown in figures 28 and 30, these systems aim to combine the information storage and computational capabilities of the computer with the human ability to discriminate between alternatives. The systems are linked with graphics software to allow for interaction during the planning process and the production of a site layout plan as the output. To date, such systems are not available commercially, but as knowledge-based systems develop, their application to site layout planning is also likely to develop.

Computer-generated construction sequence and drawings

Computer-aided design packages have been used to produce site plans that can be updated on a regular basis to reflect the changing site environment.[2] This practice relies on adequate computer-generated information being available from the design team to use as a basis for the layouts. To date the practice has only been employed on projects with a complex interface with the general public or where there has been the requirement to generate sequence plans for briefing outside bodies.

Coordinated design information

Where computer compatibility between design team, client and contractors can be achieved, materials schedules, construction programmes and site layouts may be linked to produce coordinated information for site facilities and site layout. This practice is currently in its infancy with few successful applications, but is likely to develop along with the increased use of computers in construction.

The use of information technology in construction is developed further in Chapter 8.

5.6 Characteristics of construction projects and implications for site layout and facilities

Section 1.2 describes the characteristics of construction projects. One of the challenges of construction is that each project is unique, even where the design is similar. There are differences in the location, ground conditions, workforce and site management that necessitate a flexible management style in order to complete the project on time, within cost-plan and to the required quality. The requirements of a major project located in the heart of a major city are significantly different to one in a largely rural area, and this characteristic has a considerable effect on the sizing and location of site facilities. To reflect this aspect it is helpful to distinguish between these two types of site:

— Congested sites:

  — building plan area greater than 90 per cent of the overall site area;

  — often city centre projects.

— Uncongested sites:

  — building plan less than 90 per cent of the overall site area;

  — often rural area projects.

The 90 per cent figure is an approximation and a number of projects have some features of both congested and uncongested sites. The term uncongested does not mean that layout planning is unnecessary, in fact, uncontrolled site activities tend to expand to fill the available space, so planning is always required.

5.7 Summary of main conclusions

The construction site is one of the primary resources available to the contractor.

Efficient planning of site facilities and layout is essential for a well-run site.

Most site facilities can be described as principally labour-related or materials-related.

The methods of planning site facilities are complex and iterative and require both labour and materials-related facilities to be planned at the same time.

Fundamental principle: Allocate the best space to the most important facility.

Congested and uncongested sites produce different problems for the site planning team.

Case-study E

SITE LAYOUT AND FACILITIES

Vintners Place, London, and Glaxo Medicines Research Centre, Stevenage, United Kingdom

Introduction to cases

The planning and management of site facilities and layout on two major projects in the United Kingdom is considered below. Vintners Place is a speculative office development in the historic centre of London. The Glaxo development is a research complex on a "green field" site on the edge of Stevenage, a medium-sized town in the south-east of England. To keep this section brief the case histories only cover craneage and canteen facilities.

Project descriptions

VINTNERS PLACE, LONDON, United Kingdom. (Vintners)

A 25,000 m² speculative "landmark" office development in the heart of the City of London, less than 500 metres from the Bank of England. Internal and external finishes are of a very high standard, designed to attract high profile, corporate tenants. The construction project included newbuild, some refurbishment and internal fit-out to developer's standard. The building footprint almost completely fills the available site, being bounded to the south by the River Thames, the north by a dual carriageway road and the remainder by existing historic buildings. The five-storey steel and concrete structure, clad with pre-cast concrete panels and granite and limestone facing, reduces to four storeys at the south end to maintain site lines from the river to St. Paul's Cathedral. Figure 31 shows the construction site layout.

Client: Wates City and Sumitomo Corporation. (United Kingdom/Japan)

Major contractor (management contractor): Laing Management Ltd. (United Kingdom)

GLAXO MEDICINES RESEARCH CENTRE, STEVENAGE, United Kingdom. (Glaxo)

A 166,000 m² research facility on a 73-acre "green field" site, for 10 low-rise concrete-framed structures clad with pre-cast concrete panels. There is a very significant building services element in the project. Figure 32 shows the construction site layout.

Client: Glaxo Research & Development Ltd.

Major contractor (principal contractor): Laing Morrison Knudson (LMK) Joint Venture (United Kingdom/United States)

Craneage – Deliveries and materials handling

Vintners Place

The significant factors affecting craneage were the proportion of the site covered by the permanent works and the location of the site in the middle of a city centre. Three tower cranes were used as shown in figure 31. Materials and components were off-loaded from the road to the east of the site (times restricted to 11.00–16.00 due to traffic congestion), and from barges moored to a temporary jetty on the River Thames (affected by tidal flow). Some special deliveries were made from the major highway to the north where times were restricted to 19.00–7.00. Package contractors booked time periods for deliveries and craneage giving 7-days notice. Traffic control, craneage and deliveries were managed by a central materials coordinator. Smaller materials were off-loaded from the small side road to the west of the site and distributed through the building via the goods hoist as shown in figure 31.

Figure 31. Vintners Place, London — Site plan

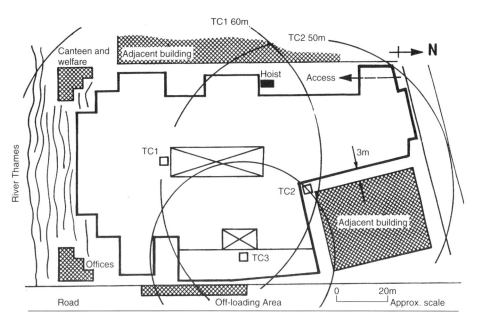

Key TC = Tower crane

Glaxo Research

The main criteria affecting materials handling on the Glaxo project was the need for efficient movement around site. One of the first operations was to construct the ring road around the edge of the site, as shown in figure 32. All vehicles were checked in and out of security at the entrance and traffic flow was restricted to one-way. In this case craneage was provided by the individual package contractors for each of the buildings (positions shown in figure 32). It could be argued that this resulted in more cranes than if they had been provided by the major contractor. However, each package contractor was able to provide craneage appropriate to their needs.

Figure 32.   Glaxo Medicines Research Centre, Stevenage, United Kingdom – Site plan

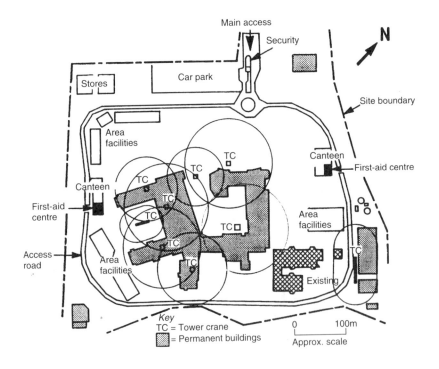

Canteen – workforce welfare facilities

Vintners Place

Workforce peak: 500. Canteen provision: 150-seat canteen, temporary units, triple-stacked on a temporary steel gantry over the River Thames. Other welfare facilities such as toilets and drying-rooms were located in the same triple-stacked block. Towards the end of the project when the gantry was dismantled the welfare facilities and offices were moved to a nearby vacant building. Had this building not been available then they would have to have been moved into an area in the completed building. Use of the canteen was not high due to the proximity of various sandwich shops and fast-food outlets.

Glaxo Research

Workforce peak: 2,000. Canteen provision: 2 × 250-seat canteens, one situated at each end of the project near to the other welfare blocks. Both canteens were located close to the circulatory site road to ease worker access. The canteens coped with the maximum numbers by serving meals in shifts. At peak, canteen usage was 1,600, i.e.: 80 per cent, mainly due to the location of the project, which had few alternative eating venues, and the high standard of catering. The canteens were temporary units located in landscaped areas such that they could remain until very near completion. Prior to the units being installed the preliminary landscaping works were completed with the resultant ground level left 400 mm below the required finished level. Once the units were removed the topsoil and grass were placed with no need for further earth-moving or excavation.

Notes

[1] D. Tommelein, R. E. Levitt, B. Hayes-Roth and T. Confrey: "Site plan experiments: Alternative strategies for site layout design" in *Journal of Computing in Civil Engineering*, ASCE, Vol. 5, No. 1, Jan. 1991, pp. 42–63.

[2] One Ludgate Place, London (Part of the Ludgate Development). Client: Rosehaugh Stanhope Developments. Major contractor (Construction manager): Bovis Construction Ltd.

PART 2: KEY CONSIDERATIONS FOR SITE LAYOUT AND FACILITY PLANNING

The aspects of site layout and facilities listed in figure 26 are explained below. Many of the items relate to more than one key aspect, but for clarity are only described once. Methods of sizing and locating the facilities are covered in Chapter 5, Part 1.

5.8 Safety

Safety is covered in detail in Chapter 6. However, there are a number of safety aspects that directly affect site layout and facilities.

Signage:	Key considerations:
Appropriate use of signs has a significant effect on site safety, labour morale, work efficiency and the image of an organization portrayed to employees and the general public	Signs enable the workforce to move efficiently to the workface, and they communicate key information: Safety statistics, emergency evacuation procedures, etc.
In many countries certain signs are mandatory (for example health and safety regulations, certificates of insurance, etc.) However, these should be seen as a minimum requirement	Poorly written, inappropriate, incorrect or damaged signs should be changed immediately. For example, a "Danger! Work at High Level" sign, left in place when the hazard no longer exists, can lead to workers ignoring signs on other occasions.

First aid:	Key considerations:
Many countries have statutory regulations regarding the provision of first-aid facilities	Consider additional facilities at the workface
Organize emergency action teams — training, practice, communication, etc.	Produce an emergency response procedure — for evacuation, fire or other major incident. This should be practised regularly.
Plan for getting an injured person from a remote area of the site to the emergency services — use of cranes, hoists, etc.	Decide extent of first-aid provision by package contactors

Access ways:	Key considerations:
Clear, well-marked access ways for labour and plant are essential, not only for safety but also for efficient working	Provide additional lighting to cover for cut in mains power supply — can personnel find their way out in an emergency?

Keep clear of materials at all times	Ensure construction sequence allows for safe access ways throughout the project — particularly true for stair cores in multi-storey construction
Ensure plant and labour are kept separate	

Site cleanliness:	**Key considerations**
Relates to issues such as labour morale and project image as well as safety	In many countries specific environmental legislation requires close control on the disposal of waste materials
Ensure that all rubbish, but especially flammable material is cleared as it arises	This is a politically sensitive topic that requires careful consideration and may lead to different approaches in different countries
Decide package contractor's responsibility for rubbish removal	Maximize re-use of excavation spoil on site if possible
Ensure adjacent roads are kept clean at all times — wheel spinner, road brush, etc.	

Lighting:	**Key considerations:**
General safety or access lighting — to enable personnel to enter, leave and move about site safely.	☐ in some countries sunrise and sunset times vary dramatically with the different seasons;
	☐ lighting levels will dramatically reduce when partitions are erected;
	☐ regular maintenance of safety lighting is essential;
	☐ battery back-up lights should be provided for emergency use
Task lighting — additional local lighting of the workface to enable work to be done to the required quality:	☐ often provided by the package contractor;
	☐ power requirements must be considered for temporary power supplies
Security lighting — usually 2 hours, to assist in maintaining a secure site:	☐ beware causing a nuisance to local residents by excessive night-time security lighting

Existing services:	Key considerations:
Must be located prior to commencement and marked to prevent accidents and damage	Specific action will depend on whether clearly they are to be disconnected, to be used as temporary supplies, or to form part of the permanent works

Fire prevention Key considerations:		Fire prevention Action to minimize the fire risk:	
Construction sites are high fire-risk areas	The project must have a fire prevention policy, that clearly identifies individuals responsible for fire prevention, and describes action to be taken	Site cleanliness and the regular removal of rubbish are essential	Offices, canteens or other welfare facilities should not be located inside a building under construction unless absolutely necessary
An evacuation procedure should be produced and regular practices held		The burning of rubbish on site should be completely banned	Certain areas should be designated "no smoking" areas
		Restrictions on "hot water" (burning, welding, cutting, etc.) should include permits to work and the provision of fire extinguishers at the workface	

5.9 Welfare facilities

The quality of welfare provision will directly affect site labour morale and worker efficiency. Industrial unrest is often caused by poor welfare provision.

Canteen and mess rooms:	Key considerations:
Provide good quality food at a reasonable price, a fast and efficient service and a clean, tidy environment	National statutory legislation may apply regarding size and nature of provision

Decide project policy on staff/labour integration

Provisions for a city-centre project will differ significantly from a rural project

Produce a clear policy on where food can be consumed

Ensure facilities do not cause a fire or hygiene risk

Consider additional workface facilities for short breaks to reduce travel time, but beware additional fire and hygiene risks

Consider providing pay-phones, cash-dispensing facilities and other services for the workforce

---

Drying and changing rooms:

National statutory legislation may apply regarding size and nature of provision

Ensure facilities do not cause a fire or hygiene risk

Consider showers for some trades

Key considerations:

Requirements will alter throughout a fire or hygiene risk

Decide if package contractors are to be segregated — consider local work practice

Some activities, such as asbestos removal or work in contaminated ground, require special, completely separate, facilities

---

Toilet and wash rooms:

National statutory legislation may apply regarding size and nature of provision

Ensure facilities for female staff and labour are provided

Key considerations:

Decide project policy on staff/labour integration

Consider additional workforce facilities to reduce travel time, but beware additional hygiene risk

---

Car parking and personnel transport:

This has a significant effect on labour motivation, timekeeping and impact on local residents

Ensure good quality surfacing and efficient access/egress

Consider security aspects — of car theft and also material theft using cars

Key considerations:

Provision for a city centre, congested site will differ from a more rural site

If car park cannot be located close to the workforce, additional personnel transportation should be provided

Consider impact on local roads, particularly at peak travel times

---

Workforce accommodation:	Key considerations:
Necessary for large projects remote from other accommodation	Consider security and hygiene implications

Time office:	Key considerations:
To enable the workforce to register time of arrival for work, and time of departure	Provision will depend on local practice regarding the control of labour

5.10   Office facilities

Generally there are three main groups of offices as listed below. As a fire precaution, offices should not be located within a building under construction unless absolutely necessary. Office requirements will change during construction, and also the major contractor must complete and hand over the project to the client. As a result their sizing and location must be carefully planned to minimize costs and loss of productive working time.

Major contractor's office:	Key considerations:
Consider proximity to workforce for site based personnel Consider facilities for visitors	Consider conference facilties and administration areas

Package contractor's offices:	Key considerations:
Size based on number of packages, but also on extent of on-site design work required — for example, services contractors Decide if package contractor supply or free-supply	Decide if offices can also be used as messrooms for smaller contractors — beware additional fire and hygiene risks

Client and design team's offices:	Key considerations:
Will be specified by the client	Consider advantage of the design team being project-site based, in terms of detailed design development, early approval of package contrator's drawings, etc.

5.11 Access

Access and egress of a major construction site must be restricted for safety and security reasons. However, it must also be managed efficiently to ensure good worker morale, minimum time to deliver goods and a positive impression on the general public.

Delivery access:	Key considerations:
Plan for largest delivery vehicle — height, width, chassis clearance, etc.	Include for turning circles or alternative reversing arrangements if space is not available
Ensure facility is also suitable for small deliveries	Needs will change significantly over the construction period

Site access roads:	Key considerations:
Ensure pedestrian-safety — crossing places, barriers, etc.	Ensure roads are kept clear and well marked
Consider use of permanent roads completed except for final finishes	Ensure efficient traffic flow — one way traffic is best
Include turning areas	Prevent unauthorized stopping or parking

Pedestrian access:	Key considerations:
Must be separated from vehicular access	Security considerations are essential
Ensure safe passage from access point to offices and welfare facilities	Provide clear signage giving directions, warnings, etc.

5.12 Storage

The main types of storage areas are considered in this section. The sizing and location of these areas, to maximize usable space and ensure efficient handling of materials, is dealt with earlier in Chapter 5.

It is essential that a materials delivery and storage plan is produced as soon as the contractor is appointed. Once the works have commenced an effective and flexible system must be applied to ensure efficient management of materials handling. This system will ensure that deliveries are planned in advance, correctly notified, and that all necessary plant and storage space is available when required. However it must also allow for unplanned circumstances such as plant breakdown or adverse weather.

Offloading areas:	Key considerations:
Consider local practice for delivery methods — self-unloading lorries, etc.	Ensure access for fork-lift truck or coverage by site craneage
Ensure deliveries are planned and notice given	Move materials to other storage areas, or the workface as soon as possible
Needs will change throughout the construction period as different materials require different unloading methods	

Long-term storage:	Key considerations:
Depends on space available — unlikely for city centre site	Recording of deliveries and storage locations is essential
Minimize double handling	Ensure correct storage conditions are maintained
Ensure responsibility for materials is clearly defined — are they the client's, the contractor's or the package contractor's?	
Who provides insurance?	

Workforce storage:	Key considerations:
Ensure enough materials are available for efficient working	Ensure materials do not hinder the work of other trades
Consider health, safety and fire risks	Decide how materials will be protected
Decide who will move materials to the work face	Decide how much space is available and for how long

Tool storage:	Key considerations:
Consider security and safety aspects	Decide who provides the facilities — contractor or package contractor?
Small tools are better stored near the work face to minimize transportation	

Secure stores:

Items of high value require secure storage — for example ironmongery, electrical fittings, etc.

Ensure correct storage conditions

Key considerations:

Decide who provides the facilities — contractor or package contractor?

Ensure responsibility for materials is clearly defined — who pays insurance?

Hazardous material stores:

Many countries have legislation regarding the control of hazardous materials

Key considerations:

Consider health, safety, environment and fire risks

Prefabrication areas:

Provide if space is available — unlikely in city centres

Ensure coverage by site craneage

Key considerations:

Possible uses include:

☐ pre-cast concrete

☐ pre-assembly of structural steel sections

☐ prefabrication of steel reinforcement cages for concrete works

☐ prefabrication of pipework

Batching plants and workshop areas:

Provide if space is available — unlikely on city centre sites

Consider smallscale workshops close to the workface

Key considerations:

Consider transportation from batcher to workface

Possible uses include:

☐ concrete:

☐ mortar for brick and blockwork;

☐ cutting and dressing of stonework or brickwork;

☐ timber and joinery workshops;

☐ mechanical and electrical workshops

5.13 Transportation

Transportation methods, for both labour and materials, must be considered along with storage aspects. The main transportation methods are explained briefly in this section. The sizing and location of these facilities is covered earlier in Chapter 5.

These aspects require very careful planning – decisions are made early in the project period which will be very influential in the success or failure of the project. In all cases provision should be made for unforeseen occurrences such as, plant breakdown or adverse weather conditions. The tender plan must be developed by the site team and an effective booking control system adopted for day-to-day management. It is advisable that expert advice is sought to ensure that national variations in practice and procedure are correctly considered.

Hoists:	Key considerations:
Most countries have legislation covering testing and regular inspection	Decide if personnel hoists are to be provided — consider local practice
Consider peak times for personnel hoists — meal times, shift changes, etc.	Most hoists require sections of the building envelope to be left out and are tied into the building structure
Ensure loads applied to the permanent works have been included by the designers	Plan for installation and dismantling of hoists — most hoists can be erected by hand except for the base sections
Plan for completion of adjacent works after hoist removal	Provide, and maintain, adequate protection to works adjacent to hoist locations
Provide appropriate access at all levels — fork-lift trucks, pallet trucks, etc.	Provide protection from the weather at all access locations into the building
Consider beneficial use of permanent goods lift, but ensure precautions are taken to re-commission the lift prior to hand-over to the client. Also ensure that warranty maintenance periods for the permanent works are not reduced.	

Craneage:	Key considerations:
Most countries have legislation covering testing and regular inspection	Generally two types of crane are available:
	☐ fixed crane — usually some form of tower crane;
	☐ mobile crane — telescopic or fixed jib, lorry mounted or caterpillar tracked
Obtain approval to use cranes for each change in location — for example, adjacent properties, public highways, railways, etc.	Cranes are better located outside the building to minimize works to be completed after removal
Ensure loads applied to the permanent works have been included by the designers	Decide what will be provided and what will be package contractor's supply — for example, special lifting beams, labour to hook up the materials and provide signals to the crane driver, etc.
Some operations require specially trained crane drivers — for example, cladding, pre-fabricated modular units, etc.	Allow for additional drivers and signallers to cover meal breaks and shift changes
Plan for 80 to 90 per cent usage to cover periods when crane is inoperable — for example, wind or periodical maintenance	Consider use of crane-handled cantilever access platforms for pre-loading materials into the building prior to cladding installation

Horizontal transportation:	Key considerations:
Fork-lift and pallet trucks	
Generally used for horizontal transportation of materials to and from a hoist or crane	Consider use of fork-lift type loader for loading into the side of medium-rise buildings
Decide who will supply — often free, common-user supply by major contractor	Provide suitable running surface and access into hoists or building
Ensure materials are packaged, prior to delivery, to suit plant used for on-site distribution	Ensure drivers are trained

5.14 Rubbish removal

This aspect is covered under the safety section.

5.15   Temporary services

Water, drainage, electrical power and telephone services are all required for the use of contractors during the construction period. These services are also usually provided as part of the permanent works. It may be possible to utilize some of the permanent supplies for construction purposes provided that adequate precautions are taken to prevent damage.

Temporary services:	Key considerations:
Consider employing one package contractor to provide and maintain all temporary services	Ensure all needs for temporary services are considered at the preliminary planning stage

5.16   Testing

Most major construction projects require performance testing of certain materials or elements. Some testing must be done on the installed works and therefore, this testing does not require specific additional facilities. However, some prototype testing is usually required. Where space is available provision for on-site prototype testing may be provided. Likely on-site testing includes:

Testing:	Typical on-site requirements:
Concrete quality control	Certification testing for welding operatives

The same area may be used to keep the quality control samples which have been approved by the client or his representatives. These can then be referred to throughout the project. Some of these may require considerable space and require careful planning. Typical samples will include:

Samples:	Typical on-site requirements:
Quality samples for brickwork or other finishes	Range of samples for natural materials such as stonework or wood veneers
Mock-ups of complex assemblies such as window/cladding interfaces	

5.17 Security

This aspect has been covered in the safety and access sections.

5.18 Image

Most of the preceding aspects of site layout and facilities will, in some way, affect the image portrayed by an organization to its client, its workforce and the general public. A well-planned, well-organized and well-managed site will:

Increase labour morale and aid in the maintenance of a stable, well-experienced workforce	Improve industrial relations, helping to reduce time lost to industrial action
Improve relations with the general public and adjacent building owners	Reduce complaints by the public about the works

CONSTRUCTION SITE SAFETY

6

6.1 How serious is the safety problem?

Worldwide accident statistics are not available, therefore, in order to explore the background to the safety problem, statistics from one nation must be considered. In this chapter the statistics refer mainly to the United Kingdom (UK), but studies show that similar trends are apparent throughout the world – although, in many cases, the accident figures are considerably higher outside the UK. In the UK the Health and Safety Commission (HSC) produces annual reports on accident statistics throughout industry. The surveys show that construction is one of the most dangerous industries with 581 fatal accidents between 1986 and 1992.

Each year, between 1986 and 1992, the UK construction industry has averaged 10 fatalities per 100,000 employees compared with an average of 2 per 100,000 for all other industries. Non-fatal injuries follow a similar pattern with 1,900 per year in construction, compared with an average of 700 for all other industries.

There is no doubt that maximum effort is required to significantly reduce these statistics.

6.2 The major causes of death and injury in construction

Table 8 gives the major causes of death and injury in industry along with typical examples from the construction industry.

Figure 33[1] shows the distribution of causes of fatal and major injuries in the UK's main employment sectors in 1990/1991. Falls from height caused over 50 per cent of injuries in construction compared to around 25 per cent in the other three sectors.

Figure 34[2] represents a study of the causes of the 739 fatalities in construction between 1981 and 1985. More than 70 per cent relate to falls or falling objects, and almost 20 per cent to transport and plant.

Table 8. Major causes of death or injury in construction

Major cause of death or injury	Examples from construction
Falls from heights	Falls from scaffolding, maintenance cradles, mobile access towers, ladders, roofs, etc.
Slips	Slips from roofs, into trenches, over handrails, on oil. Include trips over materials, badly fitting scaffold boards, etc.
Being struck by moving objects	Materials falling from a height (e.g.: off scaffolds) Materials being handled by cranes, etc.
Electrical hazards	Excavating live cables, misuse of electrical power tools, demolition, etc.
Confined spaces – Asphyxiation	Drainage works especially maintenance, basement excavations, large diameter piles (inspection), underground storage tanks, etc.
Machinery	Excavation plant, cranes, hoists, etc.

6.3 The cost of accidents

The most important cost of accidents, in any environment, is the human suffering of those killed or injured, and of their families. However, there are a number of other costs due to accidents which may help to influence corporate attitude and improve the industry's poor record. These costs are summarized in Figure 35.

Insured costs

Some of these costs are insured and as a result the industry may feel protected from the risk. However, insurance premiums for employers' liability, public liability, contractor's all risks and professional indemnity are linked to past performance. In many countries the link is hidden beneath the surface, but it is still there and has a definite effect on insurance costs. In the United States, where information is often made more available to the general public, there is no attempt to deny this link; premiums for employer's liability insurance are based on a classification code for the type of work and then multiplied by a factor known as the experience modification rating (EMR). The EMR is calculated from each employer's record of losses caused by worker injury over three of the previous four years. Typically, EMRs vary from 0.3 to 2.0 which therefore has a considerable impact on the insurance costs. Improving safety performance is an important way of reducing insurance premiums.

Uninsured costs

The direct uninsured costs, such as sick pay, can be readily quantified. However, the indirect uninsured costs may be overlooked in any superficial survey of accident data. Delay to projects and investigation costs may be considerable but have a relatively short-term effect. Loss of goodwill or loss of corporate image may have a very significant, long-term influence on ability to obtain prestige contracts. It should be no surprise that some of

Figure 33.   Causes of fatal injuries in industry (United Kingdom), 1990-91

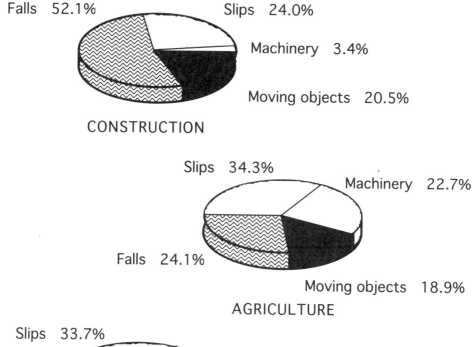

Falls   52.1%   Slips   24.0%

Machinery   3.4%

Moving objects   20.5%

CONSTRUCTION

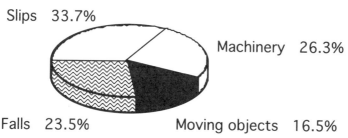

Slips   34.3%

Machinery   22.7%

Falls   24.1%

Moving objects   18.9%

AGRICULTURE

Slips   33.7%

Machinery   26.3%

Falls   23.5%   Moving objects   16.5%

MANUFACTURING

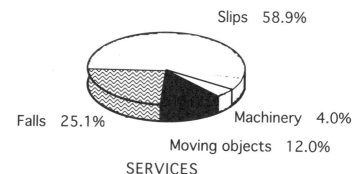

Slips   58.9%

Falls   25.1%   Machinery   4.0%

Moving objects   12.0%

SERVICES

Figure 34. Causes of fatalities in the construction industry (United Kingdom), 1981-85

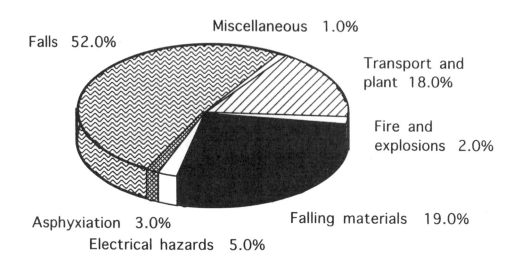

Miscellaneous 1.0%

Falls 52.0%

Transport and plant 18.0%

Fire and explosions 2.0%

Asphyxiation 3.0%

Electrical hazards 5.0%

Falling materials 19.0%

the most profitable companies in the world are those with the most impressive safety performances.[3]

6.4 Why is the construction industry unable to learn from the past?

One particularly worrying observation is that almost identical repeat situations continue to cause death and injury. The construction industry seems unable to learn from its past mistakes. There is a tendency to blame external factors for the poor safety record. Factors such as:

— the transient nature of the industry;

— the complete disregard for safety of many of its employees;

— the need to use a partially completed permanent structure, or a regularly changing temporary platform, to access works at a higher level;

— the constantly changing hazards as the project is constructed.

Figure 35.   The cost of accidents

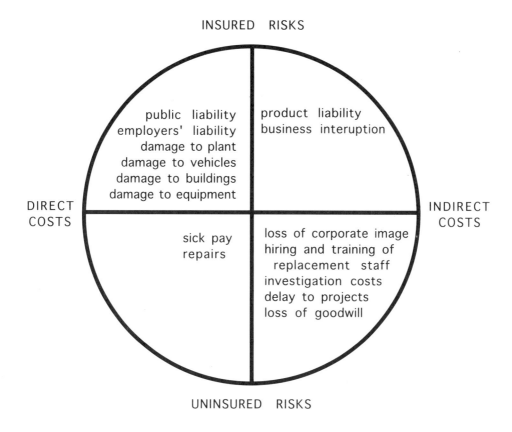

However the HSC's survey of fatalities between 1981 and 1985[2] concluded that positive action by management could have prevented 70 per cent of the deaths. Senior managers cannot escape their responsibility.

6.5   How senior managers can improve safety records

An American study on how senior managers (policy-makers) can affect the safety performance of their companies identified four distinctives of the companies with better safety records.[4]

Senior managers of organizations with better than average safety records:

— know about the accidents on their projects;
— evaluate construction managers on their safety records;
— ensure that they discuss safety with their managers on a regular basis;
— distribute accident records from individual projects throughout the organization.

6.6 Who is responsible for safety?

Every individual has a direct responsibility for safety. However, within a typical construction organization there are specific responsibilities which are described in Figure 36.[5]

In recent years lawyers have refused to accept senior management claims that they are too far removed from the workface to have a direct

Figure 36. Safety responsibilities in a typical construction organization

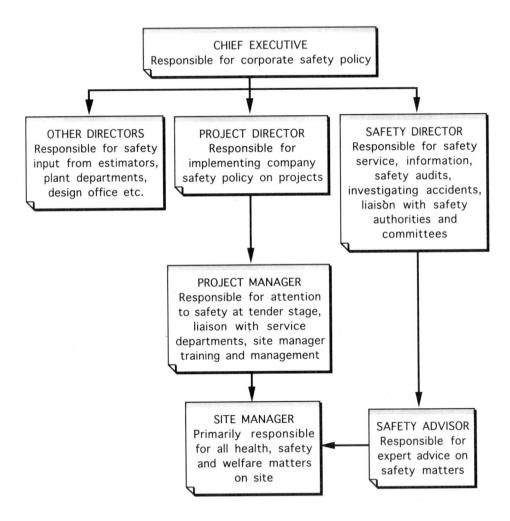

MANAGING INTERNATIONAL CONSTRUCTION PROJECTS: AN OVERVIEW

influence on safety. There has also been an increase in the prosecution of individuals as well as the organizations that they represent. In Europe a 1992 European Community directive on the management of health and safety at work has lead to member countries producing specific legislation covering managers' responsibility for safety.[6]

6.7 What is a safety policy?

Corporate safety policy

This is a statement by the corporate management regarding safety.

A corporate safety policy will include:

— Policy statement:

states what the organization will do.

— Operation of the policy:

explains how the organization will ensure that the policy is adhered to.

— Organization:

states who is responsible for safety at different levels of the organization;

explains how the policy affects departments, sections or projects within the organization.

— Communication:

explains how the policy will be communicated throughout the organization, and how senior management will be briefed on its implementation.

Divisional safety policy

A large organization with several operating divisions or companies is required to produce a safety policy for each division. This will state the division's arrangements for carrying out the corporate safety policy and will be arranged in a similar manner.

Project safety policy

The pre-eminence of safety must continue to project level. A project-specific safety policy is required.

The purpose of a project safety policy is to:

— state who is responsible for safety;

— explain how the corporate safety policy will be implemented;

— state specific arrangements for maintaining safe working conditions;

— provide a management tool to enable project safety to be monitored.

There is a danger that, once compiled, the safety policy is filed out of sight. The safety policy must be a working document, used regularly to monitor site practice. If practice begins to deviate from the policy, the major contractor must act immediately.

6.8 Safety in project planning, design and construction

Clients, designers and contractors are beginning to recognize that it is essential to consider safety throughout the project period from inception, through design and construction, to maintenance and beyond.[7] For example, the early decision to prefabricate large elements of the project will enhance safety on-site providing the operations are well planned to reflect the changed safety environment. Prefabrication enables elements to be built in an environment that is easier to control. However, installation of large prefabricated units is significantly different to *in situ* construction and safe erection methods must be included in the design process.

Irrespective of specific legal obligations for safety, all members of the project team: client, design team, major contractor and package contractor, are involved in safety management. Close coordination is required to ensure that assumptions made in the planning and design phase do not become invalid due to the construction methods chosen.

An example of lack of coordination between design team, major contractor and package contractor:

A key element of the design of a steel-framed building is its stability. This is true both during construction as well as in the final "permanent works" condition. It is common practice to pass the responsibility of temporary stability to the steelwork package contractor. The steelwork specialist should have the expertise to make due allowance in the detailed design, and the erection of the steel frame is under the control of the same specialist contractor. However, once the frame is complete and the steelwork contractor has left the site, the frame is still not in its final condition. The client's design team may have assumed that the cladding to the frame would be installed on a floor-by-floor basis, right around the building. The cladding contractor may wish to install the cladding to one side of the building before commencing the other sides. In this case both the dead load due to the cladding weight and the wind load on the partly completed building are different from the initial design assumptions. The major contractor may be coordinating the works without adequate knowledge of the assumptions made by the design team or package contractors. The result could be the collapse of the frame with resultant risk to the safety of the workforce and damage to the building.

6.9 Safety training

Lack of formal safety training is commonly considered the weakest part of accident prevention in construction.

Minimum requirements for safety training:
— Formal safety training for all personnel;
— Regular refresher courses;
— Regular "job-specific" safety instruction;
— Site safety induction prior to starting work.

All personnel must receive formal safety training. This training should relate specifically to their responsibilities and should be repeated whenever their responsibilities or environment changes. In any case, the training should be repeated at regular intervals – ideally annually – to act as a refresher and to include changes in legislation or methods of construction.

At the workface, operatives and tradesmen should receive short and specific safety instruction at regular intervals – ideally weekly. These are often called "tool-box talks" and cover aspects of safety that will be encountered on a day-to-day basis. However, these short refresher talks should not take the place of more formal "off the job" training.

The majority of accidents occur to people within their first few days on site. Therefore, prior to commencing work on a new site, or even visiting a site, each employee should receive a safety induction that will cover specific risks and location of hazards on that site, at that time. It is considered good practice to issue all personnel a safety handbook during their induction. This will enable them to take away a readily available guide to the safety aspects of the site.

Example of a site health and safety handbook

LMK, the major contractor on the Glaxo Research Facility, described in Chapter 5, issued a pocket-sized booklet to every person who entered the site.[8] This was issued as part of a comprehensive safety awareness programme which was promoted by both the client and contractor. The project's corporate image was reflected in the cover and styling of the booklet, and linked to safety posters and notices displayed throughout the site. The following aspects were included:

— Introduction and welcome from Glaxo's Chief Executive.

— Site rules.

— Annotated sketches showing: what to do in an emergency;

how to respond to an accident;

correct safety equipment;

what not to do.

— A site plan showing medical facilities and muster points.

— Examples of typical warning signs.

— Details of the safety award schemes.

6.10 Country-specific legislation

The principles of safety management are universal; however, construction practice varies from country to country – furthermore each country has its own safety legislation. Before considering trading in another country it is essential that the full requirements of that country's safety legislation are understood. Because of the complex nature of much of the legislation and the significance of correct interpretation of the law it is advisable to obtain specific advice from a national safety consultant.

6.11 The major contractor's role in making projects safer

In 1988, the UK's HSC published a guide to managing health and safety.[9] The guide described the roles and responsibilities of the various parties under the following types of construction contract: management contracting; design and manage; construction management.

The major contractor's responsibilities for managing health and safety include:

— to help the design team identify information on major health and safety matters which will be passed on to the package contractors;

— to contribute construction and health and safety expertise to the design team. This should lead to design features which are easier and safer to construct;

— to identify high-risk activities during the pre-contract planning stage and to formulate site-wide method statements for dealing with them. These will be included in the contract documents for the package contractors. High-risk activities will differ from contract to contract, but are likely to include:

  — confined spaces and excavation;

  — demolition including asbestos removal;

  — cranes and hoists;

  — scaffolding and temporary works;

  — multi-storey frames;

  — cladding and roofing;

  — hot-works (welding/burning/cutting, etc.);

  — substances hazardous to health;

— to identify essential, separately priceable health and safety items (for example, access scaffolding, edge protection and welfare facilities) which could be included in contracts with package contractors;

— to shortlist package contractors who will be invited to tender, taking account of their skills in managing health and safety;

— to produce a site safety policy that includes rules and conditions, procedures, guidance notes and codes of practice. The policy should incorporate client requirements, where appropriate, and be included in the contract documents for the package contractors;

— to set up the site organization for the management of health and safety taking into account the following factors:

   (i) overall programme for the project;

   (ii) planned procedures;

   (iii) arrangements for coordination, liaison and communication;

   (iv) safety representatives' functions and arrangements for joint consultation;

   (v) arrangements for monitoring site health and safety;

   (vi) arrangements for training, instruction and information;

   (vii) policy on the use of common facilities, plant and equipment;

   (viii) arrangements for record-keeping and statutory examinations;

   (ix) external liaison;

   (x) responsibilities of package contractors;

   (xi) responsibilities of individuals.

— to ensure that package contractors are briefed about anticipated construction methods, site/design factors, relevant hazards, precautions, general site safety rules and conditions, and are clear about divisions of responsibility. Similarly the package contractors should inform the major contractor, and interfacing package contractors, about possible hazards arising from their own activities;

— to ensure that package contractors have made plans to work safely, have priced their bids accordingly and have the necessary resources. Each package contractor should produce a contract-specific safety policy;

— to ensure that package contractors produce detailed method statements for high risk activities, to monitor the package contractor's performance against the method statements and take action where necessary. It is good practice to consider safety as the first item on the agenda of the regular package progress meetings;

— to manage health and safety on site by coordinating activities, ensuring that planned procedures are implemented and monitoring performance so that revised arrangements can be made as necessary. The major contractor should ensure that he does not become remote from day-to-day problems on site;

— to consider the creation of a joint safety committee operating on a site-wide basis and involving representatives of management and operatives from all package contractors;

— to convene regular, site-wide coordination meetings, attended by both the major contractor's staff and each package contractor's site management. Safety is one of the key aspects of coordination;

— to make site-wide arrangements for emergencies, fire prevention, safe access, lighting, etc.

However, the advice given is applicable to all major construction projects, especially those where the major contractor has some influence over detailed design and employs package contractors to construct some, or all, of the project.

Notes

[1] *Health and Safety Commission Annual Report* (UK), 1991/1992, HMSO, London, 1992.

[2] *Blackspot construction*, Health and Safety Executive (UK), HMSO, London, 1988.

[3] Cullen, Sir J.: Foreword to *Health and Safety Commission Annual Report*, op. cit.

[4] A. M. Levitt and H. W. Parker: "Reducing construction accidents — Top management's role", in *Journal of the Construction Division*, ASCE, Vol. 102, No. 3, Sep. 1976, pp. 465-478.

[5] Adapted from *Site safety handbook*, Construction Industry Research and Information Association, Special Publication 90, London, 1992.

[6] *Management of Health and Safety at Work Regulations* (UK), HMSO, London, 1992.

[7] *Total project management of construction safety, health and environment*, Thomas Telford Services Ltd., London, ISBN 0-7277-1923-8, 1993.

[8] Glaxo Medicines Research Centre, Stevenage, United Kingdom. Client: Glaxo Research & Development Ltd., Major Contractor (Principal Contractor): Laing Morrison Knudson (LMK) Joint Venture (United Kingdom/United States).

[9] Adapted from *Managing health and safety in construction: Management contracting*, Construction Industry Advisory Committee, HMSO, London, 1988.

PLANNING CASE-STUDIES

7

7.1 Introduction

Control of time is one of the prime functions of management, and delivery of construction projects on time is one of their prime objectives. This chapter illustrates the practical application of some of the planning techniques used. There is a strong emphasis on the use of information technology. This is clearly becoming a major and continually expanding suite of construction management facilities, but it is also the case that many construction managers have not yet embraced their use. Therefore, the use of computing and other aspects of information technology (such as the generation of management reports) are described comprehensively. For these reasons, whereas the first three chapters of this book were concerned with the management of construction projects at a strategic level, this chapter and the next examine specific practices. This approach is consistent with the skills required of construction managers – being able to see the broader picture, but also able, when necessary, to grasp the detail. Therefore, after studying this chapter, the reader should have a very clear understanding of the contemporary project planning process, and should be able to direct subordinates effectively.

It has been assumed that the managers of construction companies, who are the intended readership of this book, will be thoroughly conversant with the basic planning techniques used by contractors. However, it was recognized that some managers will have been appointed to senior positions without having progressed through line management positions with direct responsibility for the construction work, and so may not be familiar with these techniques. A practical book for readers who require a more comprehensive explanation of the whole process of construction planning, including a review of the management of planning and control, as well as an explanation of the techniques, is *Construction planning* by R. H. Neale and D. E. Neale (for reference see Chapter 1).

The main content of this and the following chapter comprises three case-studies (F, G, H). The first (F) applies network analysis to the construction of a concrete service reservoir. It is based on an actual project. The case-study also illustrates the application of a popular project management computer system to the planning and control of construction work, and contains numerous examples of computer-generated management reports.

The second case-study is based on a major tunnelling project in India (G), and illustrates the use of the time-chainage planning technique, which is useful for planning and controlling linear projects.

The third case-study (H) is not based on an actual project, but explains how a computer spreadsheet may be used to apply the line-of-balance technique to a project which has repetitive elements. After studying this case, the reader will see that the application of spreadsheet calculations to the time-chainage technique used in the previous case-study is fairly similar, and equally straightforward. An example, taken from an actual project, is also included in this case-study.

7.2 Objectives of planning

The managerial importance of planning and control was explained in Chapter 2. In their standard work on construction planning, Neale and Neale summarize the objectives of planning as shown in Table 9.

Table 9.   The objectives of planning

Analysis: envisaging how the work will be done, in what order and with what resources

Anticipation of potential difficulties and risks, and planning to overcome them

Scheduling resources to make the best use of them

Coordination and control of all those involved in the project, so that each party knows what is expected of them, and when

Production of data through the monitoring and control process, which will be used to make future plans more realistic

7.3 The construction planning process

The process by which effective plans are formulated is shown in table 10, which is derived from Neale and Neale. One of the authors of this book is the managing director of a substantial construction company, and this process is based on actual practice within his company.

7.4 The need for realism and simplicity

Experience has revealed two distinct approaches to planning. The first is based on the view that construction is too complicated to be planned, so managers just work it out from day to day. Alternatively, in people who hold the view that planning is important and must be done thoroughly, there is a tendency for them to attempt to plan in great detail, and to time-scales which are too long to be realistic. The managerial problem is to find a practical compromise, which yields results without overburdening managers with voluminous reports. Case-study F is an illustration of a

Table 10. The construction planning process

Initial appraisal: a preliminary review of the information provided, in which senior managers will be centrally involved

Early decisions: early decisions lay the strategic foundations for the formulation of the entire plan for executing the project, so senior management involvement is crucial

Detailed appraisal: usually delegated to planning staff, who liaise with all staff who may have relevant expertise or information, and report frequently to senior management. This detailed analysis may cause the early decisions to be questioned

Project team conferences: these provide a forum for two-way communication, in which problems are resolved and staff become committed to decisions and construction strategies

Resource analysis and scheduling: again this is usually delegated to planners and other specialists, who examine sequences, methods and resource levels which result from the decisions and strategies developed earlier

Shaping the plan: in which the results of the resource analysis and scheduling are reflected in the development of the plan, especially in regard to balancing direct, site-based costs and indirect, overhead costs. Case-study F illustrates this process in some depth

Monitoring: comparing what actually happens with what was planned, which requires an efficient system for capturing and analysing site performance data

Replanning: taking appropriate action to reflect the information provided by the monitoring process this is where control is exercised

practical level of planning for a project of this type. The case-study includes illustrations of a hierarchy of planning, in which planning is done at various levels of detail to suit the level of managerial decision-making, which is crucial if sensible reports are to be generated.

Case-study F, part 1

LUFBRA RESERVOIR

A case-study of planning and resource analysis for a construction project, using a project management computer system

Part 1. Planning

This case-study was compiled by Richard Neale and Simon Barber

Introduction to the case-study

This case-study demonstrates the use of network analysis and a standard, commercially available computer system for the planning and scheduling of a realistic construction project. The information was derived from a project for the construction of a concrete service reservoir, and was provided by the contractor who constructed it. This is not a major project, but it is nevertheless quite substantial and is compatible with the space available in this book. In addition, readers will be able to use the data given to explore the use of other systems, and so develop their own skills and knowledge of information technology applications to construction project management.

The case-study has formed the basis of training courses for site and office staff of major British contractors, run by the authors. The principal purpose of the courses was to train the staff of customers of Claremont Controls in the use of their HORNET project management system in construction management. The case-study has, therefore, been exposed to practical construction managers, and given quite a severe testing. The course assessments reinforce the authors' view that this case-study is a good demonstration of how construction projects may be planned effectively using modern computer systems. In addition, it provides a good illustration of the analytical and presentation capability of contemporary computing.

The case-study begins with a description of the project and an analysis of the construction methods, and continues by converting this into computer input. The reports include bar charts and network analysis diagrams, resource histograms and control curves. A substantial section is devoted to resource analysis, exploring strategies to improve resource usage. Part 1 of case-study F is concerned with planning, and is presented here, in the chapter on time control. Part 2 is concerned with resource analysis and costs, so is included in the next chapter, which is about control of costs, where it is called Case-study F, part 2.

The information used is reproduced by kind permission of Claremont Controls Ltd, Rothbury, Northumberland, United Kingdom, who developed and market the HORNET computer system used in this case-study.

Introduction to the project

The reservoir to be constructed is shown in Drawings R/01/36/1 to R/01/36/4 reproduced on pages 133–136. It is a rectangular reinforced concrete box, with a central dividing wall to facilitate cleaning and repairs while in use. It will be constructed on Beacon Hill, near the market and university town of Lufbra. The estimator's report of his site visit is reproduced below, and an extract from the instructions to tenderers on the following page.

WINDMILL CONSTRUCTION

INTERNAL MEMORANDUM

ESTIMATOR'S REPORT ON LUFBRA RESERVOIR

Lufbra Reservoir is described in Drawings R/01/36/1 (Location Plan); R/01=36/2 (Site Plan); and R/01/36/3 (General Arrangement). The client is the Burleigh Brook Water Authority, whose engineer is well-known for his strict enforcement of the contract documents, and the R.E. is expected to be Mr. E.R. Stephenson, who is known to us as a hard but fair man.

The site is at Beacon Hill, in attractive countryside. The existing access track is adequate for most forms of transport, but large or heavy vehicles may have some difficulties. Water and electricity supplies may be easily obtained. The first two metres of excavation (below top soil) will be in boulder clay, the remainder in weathered and heavily fissured granite. The contractors who built a neighbouring reservoir found that "the rock could be loosened by powerful ripping equipment - just", according to the engineer. All excavated material may be incorporated into the site landscaping. The underfloor drain is a simple 150 mm dia. drainage pipe surrounded by no-fines concrete.

The walls are of constant height, both floor and roof having a similar plan shape. Details of the valve chamber are given in Drawing R/01/36/4. There are no restrictions on the dimensions or volumes of concrete pours, although the engineer has indicated possible pours, as a guide only.

Construction methods are shown on our drawings WC/90/16/1 - and useful production information has been obtained from the records of Woodhouse and Thorpe Acre Reservoirs.

Site investigation shows that there are no water problems on this site.

The power line across the site can be isolated for a period not exceeding 6 months.

There is a reasonable supply of labour in Lufbra, five miles away.

The contract duration is 12 months, starting on 1st April 1990; I think we can complete this project in 9 months, so saving 3 months' overheads.

F.M. Phillipson

F.M. Phillipson
Chief Estimator   2nd February 1990

Author's note:

RE: "In the form of contract used for this project, an 'Engineer' was appointed by the client to have overall responsibility for the investigation and design of the project, and to supervise its construction. The Resident Engineer represents the Engineer on the site of the works."

No fines concrete: "This is a form of lightweight concrete obtained when fine aggregate is omitted, i.e. consisting of cement, water and coarse aggregate only" (A. M. Neville: *Properties of concrete*, p. 544. Pitman, London, 1977).

Instructions to tenderers

1. Specification is the National Water Council "Civil Engineering Specification for the Water Industry 1978" and "Advisory Note", 2nd October 1981.

2. *Additional clauses and engineer requirements*

2.1 Working area to be temporarily fenced with post and 4-wire fence.

2.2 Mechanical plant will not be allowed to operate on the roof of the reservoir during or after construction.

2.3 Batter to the sides of excavation will be allowed within the confines of the working area at the Contractor's responsibility.

2.4 Topsoil is to be stripped from the whole of the working area, except that required for the topsoil tip.

2.5 The employer will provide water for testing the reservoir any time from 6 months after the commencement of the contract.

2.6 The roof of the reservoir shall be watertight on completion and shall be tested by covering to a minimum depth of 25 mm for a period of 3 days.

2.7 Concrete may be cast in one of the following methods throughout:

	(a)	alternate bays with at least seven days between adjacent pours;
or	(b)	with shrinkage gaps;
or	(c)	successive pours away in both directions simultaneously from the first panel;
or	(d)	any other method subject to the engineer's prior approval.

Drawing R/01/36/1. Location and site plan

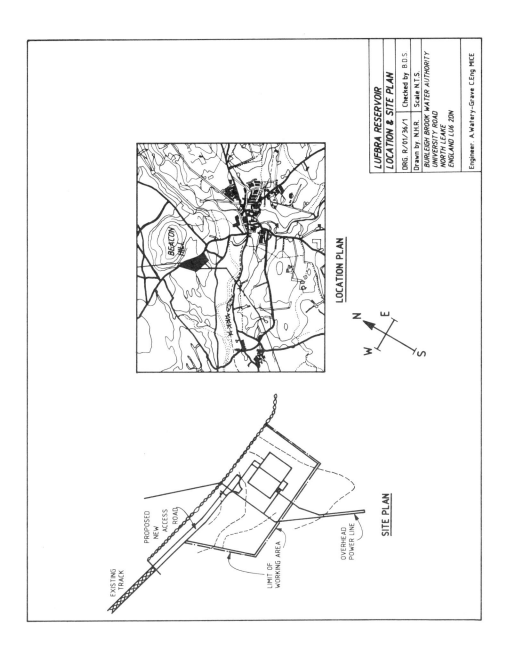

Drawing R/01/36/2. Detailed site plan

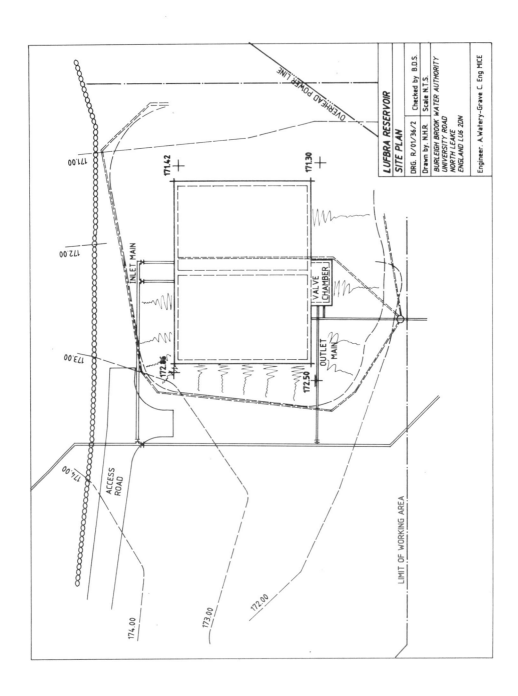

Drawing R/01/36/3. General arrangement

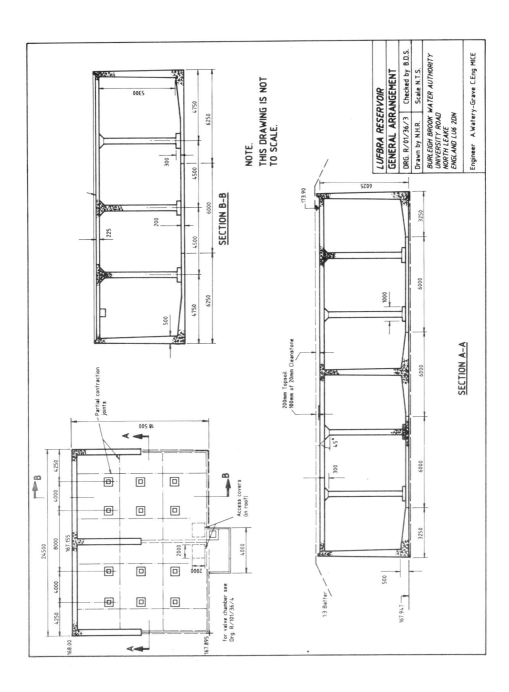

Drawing R/01/36/4. Valve chamber

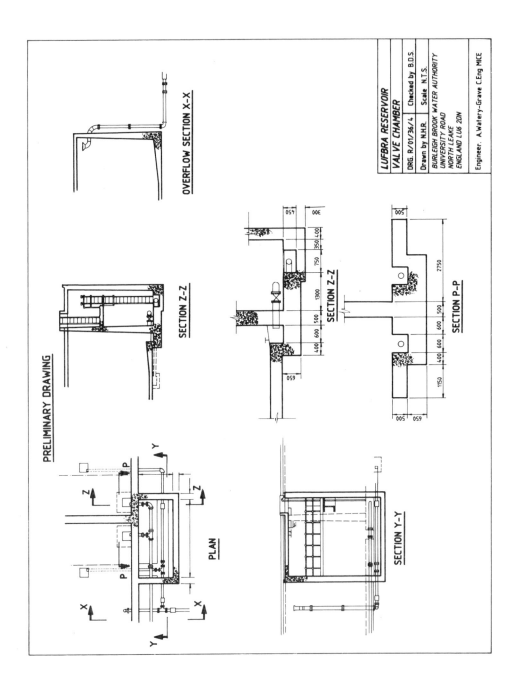

Construction strategy

The joint layout and pour design for the floor, walls and roof are shown by sketches on the following pages, figures 37 to 39. The contractor chose to use crawler-mounted mobile cranes, figure 40, and to leave out some floor and wall panels to allow the crane to be used within the reservoir, figures 40 and 41. Wall formwork is illustrated in figure 42. Using this information, strategies can be developed for the sequence of construction of the floor, walls and roof, figures 43 to 48.

The strategy is summarized tersely in boxes below.

Access to excavation

Must have a ramp for access of people, small equipment, etc., also for removal of spoil from rock-ripping.

Can make ramp

through valve chamber, which goes to base of reservoir

or

through drains, which is nearer to access road but not as deep as valve chamber.

Spoil from rock excavation can be used to make a good roadway around excavation, so that whole reservoir can be easily served by a crane from top of bank.

Floor

Column base reinforcement details enable the floor to be kept clear until columns have to be erected.

May start floor before bringing any cranes to site. Direct discharge from ready-mixed concrete trucks recommended.

Floor reinforcement details do not impose a sequence of pours. The detailing is very good for "constructability".

Figure 37. Joint layout and concrete pours for reservoir floor

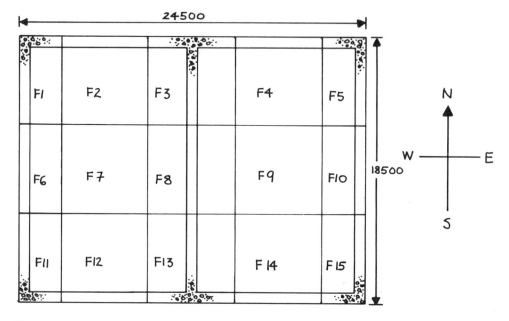

FLOOR POURS

Figure 38. Joint layout and concrete pours for reservoir walls

WALL POURS

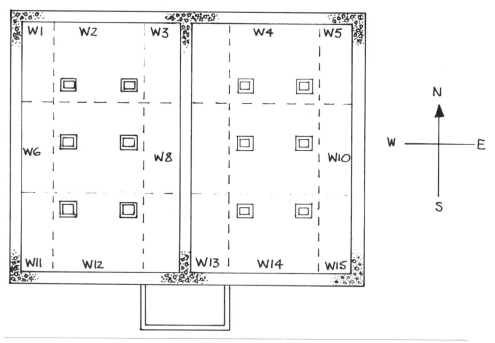

Figure 39. Joint layout and concrete pours for roof, and column numbers

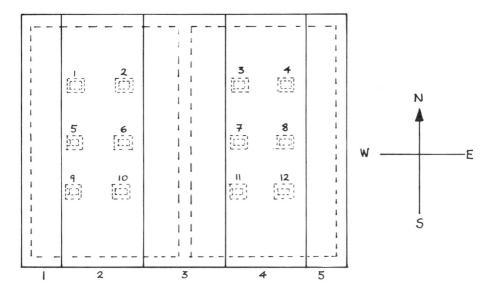

ROOF POURS

Figure 40. Access for mobile crawler crane around the reservoir

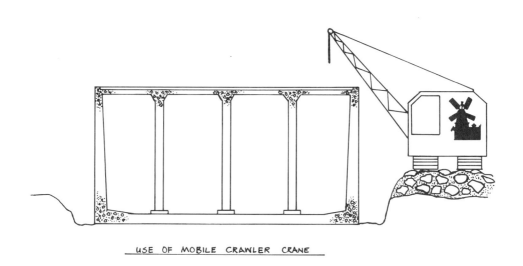

USE OF MOBILE CRAWLER CRANE

Figure 41. Access to centre of reservoir

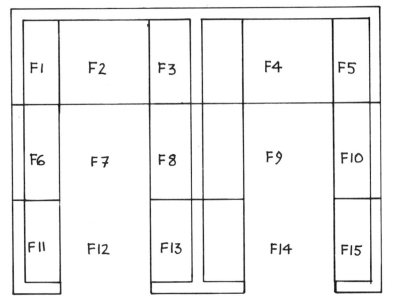

Pours F7, F9, F12 and F14 concreted last, to enable concrete trucks to drive into the reservoir

Figure 42. Wall formwork

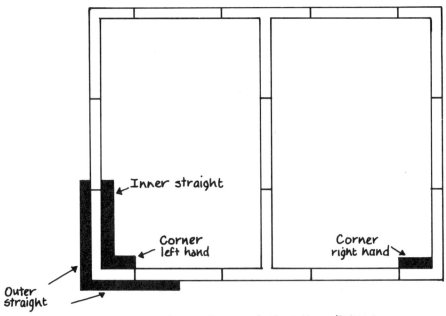

WALL POURS AND WALL FORMS
2 "Inner straights" required for tees

Walls

There are three types of pour:

straight walls;

corners, which are handed because of the internal wall taper;

tee-shaped-junctions between the cross wall and the side walls.

The easiest way is to make corner forms – right- and left-hand – which also form the inside of the wall on the shortest sides of the corners and tees. Each such form could be used for two tees and two corners, according to the handling. To form a tee requires a pair of such sections, plus three straight panels for the remaining, longer faces. This is the minimum number of panels required. (Note that these longer straight sections will also be used on the straight sections of wall.)

Valve chamber

Forming the section of reservoir adjacent to the valve chamber will damage the forms, because of the provision of starter bars for the valve chamber walls. Therefore, this should be in the last reservoir wall pour.

A special form should be made for the base of this section of wall, enabling the pipes to be built in easily. The main wall form then sits on this in the same way as for the previous wall bases.

Columns and roof

Columns may be most easily erected before the main soffit falsework and formwork is erected, using small and independent scaffolds. This gives more flexibility when planning.

A variety of pours and sequences is possible. Note that all support material has to be removed through the access hatch.

One of the key factors is the striking time of the falsework, as required by the specification; this is dependant on the air temperature during the curing period, but we have assumed two weeks.

Strategy rules for concrete pours

Plant

Ready-mixed concrete would be used on a small reservoir like this, because the amount of concrete required does not justify the cost of setting up a mixing plant.

The concrete from ready-mixed trucks may be discharged directly into the blinding, floor and wall bases. Floor sections F7, F9, F12 and F14 will be concreted last, to enable these trucks to drive into the reservoir to pour F8 and the inner points of all other wall-base pours.

A crane will be required to cover F7, F9, F12 and F14, because the discharge chute of a truck cannot reach across to the far side of the pour. This problem does not occur on the other pours because the trucks can discharge from the haul road that runs round the reservoir and the extra height will enable them to reach across.

The walls may be poured using a crane and skip or a concrete pump. A crane would also move the formwork, so if the concrete is pumped, mobile cranes must be hired when the forms have to be moved.

The most common strategy is to use a crawler crane for everything except the roof. It is difficult for a crane to reach the centre of the reservoir roof, so a mobile concrete pump will be more effective.

Floors – strategy rules

The "Instructions to tenderers", gives a number of alternative methods for pouring the concrete for the reservoir. It is proposed to adopt the method outlined under section 2.7 (a) – that the concrete be cast in alternative bays, with at least seven days between adjacent pours.

The following rules are adopted:

Work from the outside towards pours 7, 12, 9 and 14.

Tee and corner walls (panels 1, 3, 5, 11, 13 and 15) take more time than straight walls, so start floors for these as quickly as possible.

Steel-fixing and formwork can proceed concurrently, provided the operatives are sensible.

Floors – reinforcement and construction sequence

Starter-bars for the walls prevent any heavy vehicles driving onto the concrete floor slab once it has been laid, hence it is important to leave panels 12 and 14 until as late as possible.

The general sequence of activities is as follows:

Before the steel reinforcement or the floor formwork panel can be fixed, the floor blinding must be complete.

A panel can only be concreted after the steel and formwork have been completed.

Figure 43.   Activities that represent the construction of one floor panel

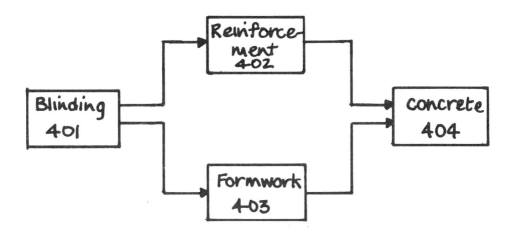

Figure 44.   Sequence for the construction of floor panels F1 to F15, leaving panels omitted for access until last (note that these are dependent upon other activities also)

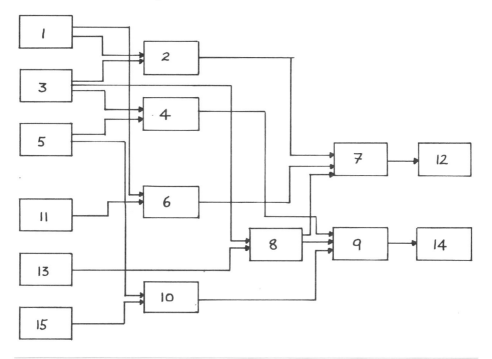

Walls

The walls will follow a similar pattern to the floor. The rules are:

The floor panel under the wall must be completed.

Tees and corners must be completed before infilling with straight walls.

Walls 12 and 14 are used for access, so are done last.

Formwork must be manufactured before the wall formwork may be started.

The starter bars for the valve chamber walls will damage the forms when panels 13 and 12 are cast. Therefore these panels should be done last.

The sequence of events for each of the panels is quite straightforward:

Once the floor panel has been concreted, the reinforcement can be fixed.

The formwork can then be erected.

The panel can finally be concreted.

(With the walls it is not possible to fix the steel and erect the formwork at the same time.)

Columns

To simplify the plan, the columns are paired to give six activities, according to the floor panels they occupy. The construction rules are:

the floor under the column must be complete before the column can be started;

columns must be completed before the scaffold for the roof is started.

Figure 45. Activities that represent the construction of one wall panel

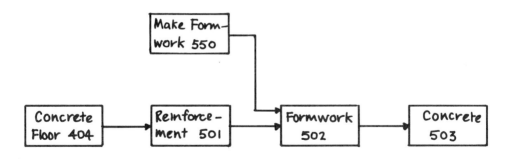

Figure 46. Sequence of wall pours W1 – W6, W8, W10 – W15

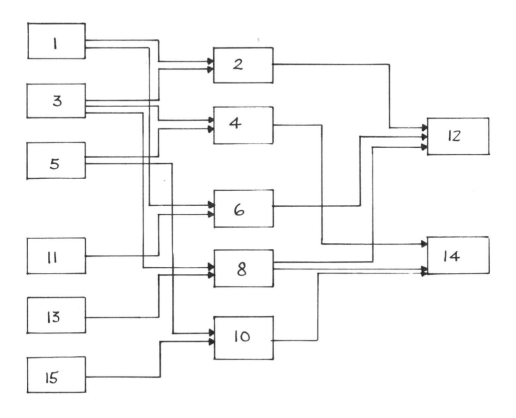

Roof

The roof will be poured in five strips, moving from east to west; the first and last pours being half width. The following rules will be adopted:

Supporting walls and columns must be completed before any scaffolding is erected.

Scaffold must be completed before soffit erection starts.

Reinforcement can follow closely behind the soffit formwork.

The sequence of panels will be 1, 2, 3, 4 and 5.

The sequence of activities is, therefore, as follows:

when the walls and columns are complete, the scaffolding can be erected;

the roof soffit and reinforcement are worked on simultaneously, with a lead of one day to ensure the reinforcement will have a form to lay on;

the panel is concreted;

curing and striking follows on.

Notes:

Curing and striking have been combined in one activity. A more accurate representation would be to use separate activities, where the curing activity is given a seven-day-week calendar.

The scaffolding cannot be erected for the next panel until it has been struck from the previous panel.

Figure 47. Activities that represent the construction of one roof panel

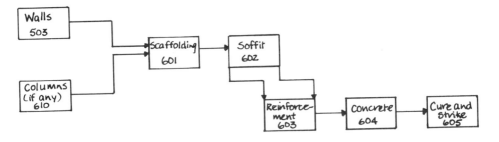

Figure 48. Sequence for the construction of roof pours P1 – P5

Bills of quantities

Simplified bills of quantities are given on the following pages.

Number	Item description		Unit	Quantity	Rate	Amount
	Summary sheet					
Part 1	General items	Page 2				89 840.00
Part 2	Reservoir					
	Earthworks	Page 3				31 360.00
	Concrete	Page 4				57 728.92
	Ancillaries	Page 5				
		Page 6				125 988.60
Part 3	Pipework	Page 7				10 780.84
Part 4	Access	Page 8				6 615.76
				Tender sum		322 314.12
					Page total	

Number	Item description	Unit	Quantity	Rate	Amount
A 1.1	Insurances	Sum			4 120.00
A 2.1	Resident engineer office & equipment	Sum			2 800.00
A 2.6	Testing of works	Sum			200.00
A 2.7	Temporary works fencing & access	Sum			3 000.00
A 3.1	Contractor's office	Sum			6 300.00
A 3.2	Provisions of services	Sum			1 900.00
A 3.7	Contractor's supervision	Sum			41 720.00
A 4.1	Provisional sum for daywork	Sum			18 000.00
A 4.2	% adjustment on daywork	10%			1 800.00
A 4.3	Provisional sum for supply of all ladders & covers	Sum			10 000.00
				Page total	89 840.00

Number	Item description	Unit	Quantity	Rate	Amount
	E 4 General excavation				
E 4.1.1	Topsoil for re-use	m³	250	3.48	870.00
E 4.3.4	Subsoil for re-use	m³	200	3.48	696.00
E 4.5.5	Fragmentary rock for re-use	m³	700	4.24	2 968.00
E 4.6.5/1	Fragmentary rock for disposal	m³	100	8.70	870.00
E 4.6.5/2	Solid rock for disposal	m³	1 000	11.74	11 740.00
	E 5 Excavation ancillaries				
E 5.2.2	Preparation of surface rock	m²	500	0.70	350.00
	E 6 Filling and compaction				
E 6.1.4	Filling to structure excavated material	m³	200	2.34	468.00
E 6.1.6	Filling to structure fragmentary rock	m³	700	2.34	1 638.00
E 6.2.5	Filling to structure imported material	m³	200	11.88	2 376.00
E 6.3.1	100 mm thickness topsoil from site	m²	2 500	1.30	3 250.00
E 6.3.2	200 mm thickness topsoil imported	m²	450	4.24	1 908.00
E 6.3.5	100 mm thick gravel imported	m²	450	3.36	1 512.00
	E 7 Filling ancillaries				
E 7.1.1	Trim slopes	m²	850	0.34	289.00
E 7.2.4	Lay Terran PR 140 on roof	m²	450	1.78	801.00
	E 8 Landscaping				
E 8.3.1	Grass seed to general areas and roof	m²	2 050	0.56	1 148.00
E 8.3.2	Grass seed to slopes	m²	850	0.56	476.00
			Page total		31 360.00

Number	Item description	Unit	Quantity	Rate	Amount
	F 1-5 Provision of concrete				
F 1.2.3	Design mix grade 15	m³	36	51.43	1 848.24
F 4.4.3	Design mix special structural design	m³	530	71.94	38 128.20
	F 6-8 Placing of concrete				
F 6.1.1	Blinding concrete	m³	36	64.22	2 311.92
F 7.2.3	Wall and floor base	m³	163	34.16	5 568.08
F 7.3.2	Suspended slab	m³	105	29.84	3 133.20
F 7.4.3	Walls	m³	247	23.00	5 681.00
F 7.5.3	Columns	m³	12	70.62	847.44
F 7.8.0	Upstands	m³	3	70.28	210.84
				Page total	57 728.92

Number	Item description	Unit	Quantity	Rate	Amount
	G 1 Formwork rough finish				
G 1.4.3	Vertical floor and floor joints	m²	60	33.58	2 014.80
G 1.4.4	Vertical base slab	m²	54	38.30	2 068.20
G 1.4.5	Vertical reservoir walls	m²	440	31.54	13 877.60
G 1.4.6	Vertical valve chamber	m²	75	31.54	2 365.50
	G 2 Formwork fair finish				
G 2.1.5	Horizontal to roof and chamber	m²	428	36.14	15 467.92
G 2.3.5	Battered to walls and chamber	m²	654	31.54	20 627.16
G 2.4.3	Vertical to columns	m²	95	48.40	4 598.00
G 2.4.5	Vertical to chamber access	m²	72	31.54	2 270.88
G 2.6.6	Curved to column heads	m²	7	50.06	350.42
	G 5 Reinforcement				
G 5.2.3	High yield bars 10 mm	t	1	1 109.94	1 109.94
G 5.2.4	High yield bars 12 mm	t	15	982.10	14 731.50
G 5.2.5	High yield bars 16 mm	t	30	67.92	26 037.60
G 5.2.6	High yield bars 20 mm	t	15	35.28	12 529.20
	G 6 Joints				
G 6.3.1	Floor roof and wall joints	m²	88	28.86	2 539.68
G 6.7.1	Seal horizontal rebate including formwork and expandite	m	240	1.42	340.80
G 6.7.2	Seal vertical rebate including formwork and expandite	m	65	1.36	88.40
				Page total	121 017.60

Number	Item description	Unit	Quantity	Rate	Amount
			Brought forward		121 017.60
	G 8 Concrete ancillaries				
G 8.1.2	Steel trowel finish	m²	850	0.84	714.00
G 8.3.2	Cast in pipes	nr	9	48.00	432.00
	W 3 Waterproofing					
W 3.3.1	Waterproof membrane to roof expandite proofex 12	m²	450	8.50	3 825.00
			Page total		125 988.60

Number	Item description	Unit	Quantity	Rate	Amount
	I 1 clay pipes				
I 1.1.2	Under floor and perimeter drain 1 m deep	m	165	14.58	2 405.70
I 1.1.7	Perimeter drain up to 6 m deep	m	13	73.78	959.14
	I 4 SI pipes				
I 4.1.1	In chamber and overflow (pipe supplied)	m	20	15.60	312.00
I 4.1.2	Washout pipes	m	10	6.50	65.00
	J 4 fittings (all supplied)				
J 4.1.1	Bends	nr	2	36.00	72.00
J 4.1.2	Junctions	nr	2	34.00	68.00
J 4.5.1	Adaptors	nr	9	54.00	486.00
J 4.9.1	Steel special	nr	4	28.00	112.00
J 8.1.1	Gate valves	nr	4	62.00	248.00
	K 1 manholes				
K 1.5.1	Precast chamber to sluice valve 1.5 m	nr	2	284.00	568.00
K 1.5.5	Precast chamber to sluice valve 4 m	nr	3	672.00	2 016.00
	L 1 to 7 pipework supports and protection				
L 1.1.0	Excavation in rock	m³	100	20.00	2 000.00
L 5.1.1	No fines concrete surround to pipe	m	178	6.50	1 157.00
L 6.0.1	Wrap flange with serviwrap	nr	8	8.00	64.00
L 7.3.0	Concrete thrust blocks	nr	4	62.00	248.00
				Page total	10 780.84

Number	Item description	Unit	Quantity	Rate	Amount
	Access track				
E 4.1.1	Topsoil for re-use	m³	52	5.64	293.28
E 6.4.1	Replace topsoil to rear of kerbs	m³	52	5.04	262.28
E 7.2.2	Prepare formation level	m²	320	0.70	224.00
R 6.4.1	*In situ* concrete kerb to access	m	140	23.74	3 323.60
R 7.2.5	Hardcore base depth 150 mm	m²	320	3.26	1 043.00
R 7.9.2	Type A 14 material depth 50 mm	m²	320	1.78	569.60
X 1.2.3	Permanent timber post and wire fence	m	200	3.30	660.00
X 2.3.5	Metal field gate	nr	1	240.00	240.00
				Page total	6 615.76

Approximate estimates of durations

In order to plan the construction of the reservoir, it is necessary to estimate the output of the resources to be used, and the duration of the construction activities. So as to plan in a realistic and practical way, the planner has to decide on an appropriate and realistic level of detail. Thus, the estimates of duration calculated below are quite detailed but nevertheless based on simplifications of what will actually happen. This plan would be more than adequately detailed for the purpose of planning and controlling the work, at the level of the construction manager, for the whole project at its outset. As the work proceeds, each section manager will expand the plan in greater detail, to a shorter time-scale, when specific groups of operatives and equipment would be identified individually.

Concrete

Volumes are taken from bill of quantities items F6-8
Estimated outputs are in person-hours per cubic metre

	Quantity m^3	Output mh/m^3
Blinding	36	0.55
Wall and floor bases	163	2.20
Suspended slab and upstands	108	3.00
Walls	247	1.75
Columns	12	5.50
Total	570	

Assuming:

4-person crew

blinding done as formation available, to no set pattern

other pours (except roof) as layout drawing

roof pour is done in strips, basically as pour drawing

Bases to wall and floors:

15 bases gives 163/15 x 2.20/4 = 6 crew-hours per pour
(OK for a day's work)

Walls:

13 pours + valve chamber, say 14 pours

This gives 247/14 x 1.75/4 = 7.72 crew-hours per pour
(OK for a day's work)

Suspended slab:

4 strips (actually 5 but two end strips are 1/2 size)

This gives 108/4 x 3/4 = 20.25 crew-hours per day
(This is too long, so pour in original pattern shown, or in half strips)

Reinforcement

Quantity of steel from the bill of quantities, items G 5.2.3 – G 5.2.6

Total tonnage = 61 tonnes

Output average is 22 person-hours per tonne

	Weight (tonnes)	Person-hours (@ 22 ph/t)	Duration (days) 2 persons	Duration (days) 4 persons
Bases	18.76	413	26	13
Walls	28.43	626	39	20
Slab	12.43	274	17	9
Columns	1.38	42	3	2
Total tonnes	61.00			

Formwork

Values from the bill of quantities, items G 1.3.5 to G 2.6.6

	Total area m²	Output ph/m²	Total ph	Duration with 4 persons (days)	Duration per hour (days)
Bases	109	2.30	251	8	0.53
Walls	1 216	0.90	1 094	34	2.43
Soffit	428	1.70	728	23	5.75
Roof joists	30	1.85	56	2	—
Columns	79	1.45	115	4	—

There may be a case for having just three persons.

Make formwork

Outer panels	6 025 mm high, vertical
Inner panels	5 700 mm high, for tapered wall
Straight sections (4 No)	6 250 mm long
Corner sections (2 No)	4 250 mm long, to suit inner tapered wall

Therefore minimum area required is

2 inner str 6 250 long = 2 x 6 250 x 5 700		71.25 m²
2 outer str 6 250 long = 2 x 6 250 x 6 025		75.31 m²
2 inner corners 4 250 = 2 x 4 250 x 5 700		48.45 m²
		195.01 m²

At 1.8 ph per m², this gives 351 person-hours.

Crew of 4 persons would take 10.96 days (11 days).

Scaffolding

Mean depth reservoir	= 5 500 mm
Area = 2 x 11 500 x 17 500	= 402.5 m²
Volume	= 2 214 m³
At 0.13 ph per m³	= 288 ph or 144 ph per tank
	= 18 person-days

Use of the HORNET project management system

This section of the case-study explains how the information developed so far is now used within a computer system. The detail of data input has been given in appendix 1 to this case-study, which shows a limited number of actual screen displays, principally to illustrate the relative ease of use of contemporary computing for those unfamiliar with it. (There are systems now available which use "windows technology" which are even easier to use.)

A broad description of the use of the system is given below, showing the essential steps required to input the Lufbra reservoir data, and examples of reports available from the system.

Project calendar and planning data

All projects must have a project calendar explicitly defined. This sets up the whole planning process, relating dates to project week numbers, noting holiday periods, and so on. This information is summarized below.

Design and tender documents complete	Wed., 4 Jan. 1990
Tender documents available	Wed., 18 Jan. 1990
Tender date	Thur., 16 Febr. 1990
Contract date	Mon., 2 Apr. 1990
Contract start	Mon., 30 Apr. 1990

When using a computer system, it is possible to use more than one calendar. This will enable activities performed during normal working hours to be distinguished from activities that continue through rest days. An example of the latter is concrete curing.

Having entered this data, the next step will be to enter the resource requirements for the activities in the project, which facilitate an assessment of requirements for the projects.

Examples of activities

Some examples of activity data are given below, a brief description illustrated by extracts from the data listing of the system. The full data listing for activities is given in appendix 2 to this case-study.

101 Set up site

This is the start activity. It represents the erection of the resident engineer's and contractor's accommodation, covered by bill items A 2.1 and A 3.1. Note that these items must also include for dismantling, activity 1 000.

102 Construct access track

This activity requires some supervision so it cannot begin until some site accommodation is available. Therefore, the contractor planned to erect the essential site facilities in the first week so that the access track could begin in the second week. Thus activity 102 had start-to-start relationship with activity 101, with a delay of one week. This was entered as shown on the screen, "SSG" meaning start-to-start link with the specified delay measured on the "global" calendar (i.e. no holidays).

The access track is covered by the items on page 8 of the bill of quantities; except for the permanent fencing, item X 1.2.3, and the gate, item X 2.3.5. The work of constructing the site access is to be subcontracted to Lufbra Roadworks Ltd. (LRL).

103 Temporary fencing

As required by point 2 of the "instructions to tenderers", this activity requires some supervision, so it has a start-to-start relationship to activity 101 with a logic delay of one week; this is similar to activity 102.

This activity is part of the bill item A 2.7, and the work will be subcontracted.

104 Temporary access roads

The base of these roads requires rock from the main excavation, so they must await the start and completion of at least some of the excavation work. Consequently this logic relationship cannot be entered until the contractor has decided upon the activity for the rock excavation.

The activity "rock excavation" will generate enough rock in one week to enable activity 104 to begin. Therefore, the precedence is again start-to-start link with a delay of one week.

This activity is provided by the remaining part of the item A 2.7, and will be included in the work of subcontractor E. Mover Ltd.

REFERENCE: Preliminary Activities

Activity Number	Activity descriptions	Duration	Management Code	PRECEDENT ACTIVITIES									Activity Number
				Number	Link	Delay	Number	Link	Delay	Number	Link	Delay	
101.00	Set up site RE s & Contractors offices	2:0	N0000										101.00
102.00	Constr access track Sub-contract,Lufbra Roadworks Ltd	3:0	D0201	101.00	SS	1:0							102.00
103.00	Temporary fencing Sub-contract,Fence & Son.NB Temporary fencing	1:0	D0101	101.00	SS	1:0							103.00
104.00	Temp. access roads Sub-contract,E Mover.Included in excavation price	2:0	D0205	202.00	FS								104.00

Hornet Project Management Systems   Claremont Controls Ltd

401.00 to 402.15 Floor activities

These are planned according to the strategy rules for floors given above, the construction sequence being given by the preceding activities listed.

801 Permanent fencing

This fencing is erected towards the end of the contract, usually after the landscaping has been completed, i.e. it is dependent upon activity 210 being complete. The activity is covered by bill items X 1.2.3 and X 2.3.5.

901 Site overheads

This is for the site supervision and other overheads and is a general charge throughout the contract. It is defined as a hammock activity. It comprises bill items A 3.2 and A 3.7.

1000 Clear site

This activity serves as the "project complete" activity, so it is given a large round number. It is covered by bill items A 2.2 and A 3.1.

Please note that bill items A 4.1 and A 4.2 on p. 148 are for unspecified daywork, so no such activity can represent this work; the costing section, therefore, excludes the sums for these items. The remaining activity data is given without detailed explanation. The activities and logical relationships are listed in the complete activity data listings given in appendix 2, pp. 180–191.

Analysing the project data

Having loaded the activity data, the next step is to use the data to calculate a project schedule. Before this is done, a target start and target finish date has been assigned to three of the activities:

Activity		Target Start	Target Finish
101	Set up site	30-04-90	11-05-90
303	Inlet pipework	18-06-90	20-08-90
304	Outlet pipework	18-06-90	20-08-90

These give examples of the use of this facility. The practical use is demonstrated by the second and third activities, which are to be done by external organizations, on fixed dates.

The overall project duration is just under a year (48 weeks); however this calculation is based on the estimated activity durations, and the logical links defining the sequence of events. No account has been taken of the human, plant and other resources required by the project. This schedule, therefore, is known as a "time-based" schedule and, in order to achieve the

Activity Number	Activity descriptions	Duration	Management Code	PRECEDENT ACTIVITIES						ACTIVITIES			Activity Number
				Number	Link	Delay	Number	Link	Delay	Number	Link	Delay	
401.00	Floor blinding 6 strips 6m wide	2:0	F00B D0106	104.00	FS		302.00	FS					401.00
402.01	Floor reinf panel 01 NW panel, W tank	0:3	F01R D0108	401.00	FS								402.01
402.02	Floor reinf panel 02 N panel, W tank	0:3	F02R D0111	404.01	FS		404.03	FS					402.02
402.03	Floor reinf panel 03 N centre panel, both tanks	0:4	F03R D0308	401.00	FS								402.03
402.04	Floor reinf panel 04 N panel, E tank	0:3	F04R D0311	404.03	FS		404.05	FS					402.04
402.05	Floor reinf panel 05 NE panel, E tank	0:3	F05R D0508	401.00	FS								402.05
402.06	Floor reinf panel 06 W panel, W tank	0:3	F06R D0511	404.05	FS		404.11	FS					402.06
402.07	Floor reinf panel 07 Centre panel, W tank	0:2	F07R D0114	404.02	FS		404.06	FS		404.08	FS		402.07
402.08	Floor reinf panel 08 Centre panel, both tanks	0:4	F08R D0711	404.03	FS		404.13	FS					402.08
402.09	Floor reinf panel 09 Centre panel, E tank	0:2	F09R D0314	404.04	FS		404.08	FS		404.10	FS		402.09
402.10	Floor reinf panel 10 E panel, E tank	0:3	F10R D0911	404.05	FS		404.15	FS					402.10
402.11	Floor reinf panel 11 SW panel, W tank	0:3	F11R D0708	401.00	FS								402.11
402.12	Floor reinf panel 12 S panel, W tank	0:3	F12R D0116	404.07	FS								402.12
402.13	Floor reinf panel 13 S centre panel, both tanks	0:4	F13R D0908	401.00	FS								402.13
402.14	Floor reinf panel 14 S panel, E tank	0:3	F14R D0316	404.09	FS								402.14
402.15	Floor reinf panel 15 SE panel, E tank	0:3	F15R D1108	401.00	FS								402.15

Hornet Project Management Systems

Claremont Controls Ltd

REFERENCE: Overhead Activities

Activity Number	Activity descriptions	Duration	Management Code	PRECEDENT ACTIVITIES									Activity Number
				Number	Link	Delay	Number	Link	Delay	Number	Link	Delay	
801.00	Permanent fencing Sub-contract,Fence & Son	2:0	D1716	210.00	FS								801.00
901.00	Site overheads Insurances,services,site management		N0000	101.00	SS		1000.00	FF					901.00
902.00	Crane hire On site start forms wall panel 13 to pipework en		N0000	502.01	SS		705.00	FF					902.00
1000.00	Clear site Remove RE s & Contractor s offices	0:2	D1717	705.00 801.00	FS FS		615.01	FS		210.00	FS		1000.00

Hornet Project Management Systems

Claremont Controls Ltd

displayed end date, unlimited resources would have to be made available. This is clearly unrealistic, but is a starting point for developing a more cost effective schedule. This will be developed in the second part of the case-study, given in Chapter 8.

Reports

The results of the planning process are illustrated by the following printed reports (which cannot be reproduced at full size for lack of space in this book):

Overall project plan, in the form of a precedence network (figure 49).

Overall project plan, in the form of an activity-on-arrow network (figure 50).

Four drawings showing enlarged details of the activity-on-arrow plan (figures 51–54).

Three drawings showing the plan in the form of a bar-chart (figures 55–57).

Concluding remarks

This case-study illustrates the planning of a construction project, in some detail. The use of a computer-based project planning system is demonstrated. In the next chapter, the resource implications are studied, and the plan is then adjusted ("shaped") to produce the most effective and economical plan for the construction of this reservoir.

Acknowledgements

Claremont Controls Limited
Albert House
Rothbury
Morpeth
Northumberland
NE65 7SR
Telephone: 0669 21081
Fax: 0669 221182

Figure 49. Overall plan (precedence)

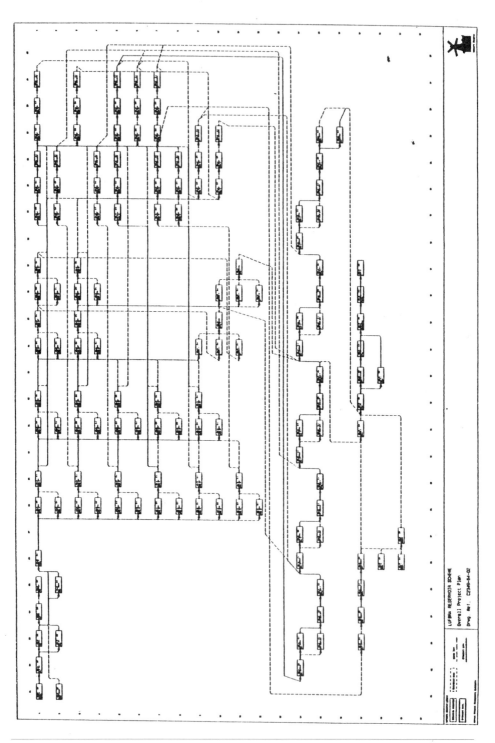

Figure 50. Overall plan (arrows)

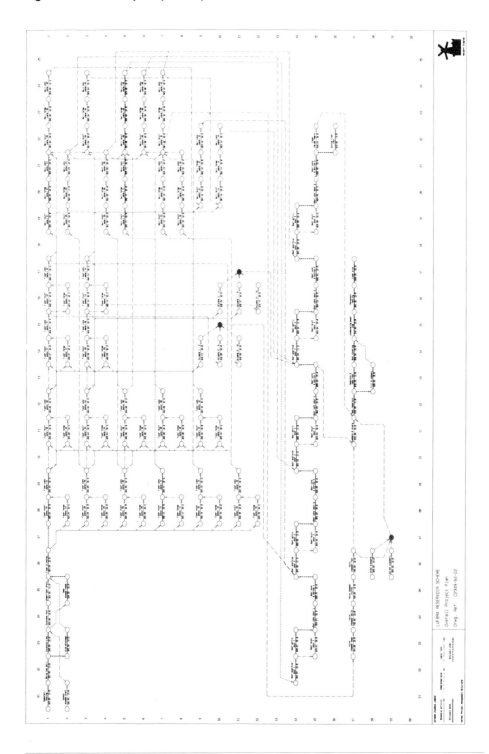

Figure 51. Detailed arrow network, Part 1

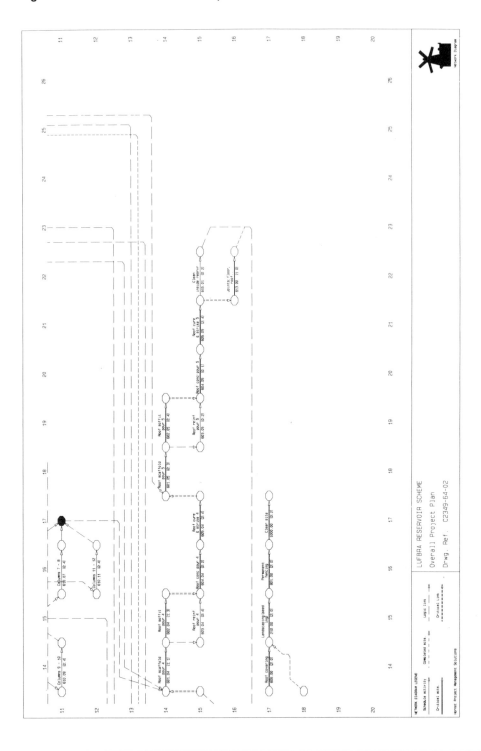

Figure 52. Detailed arrow network, Part 2

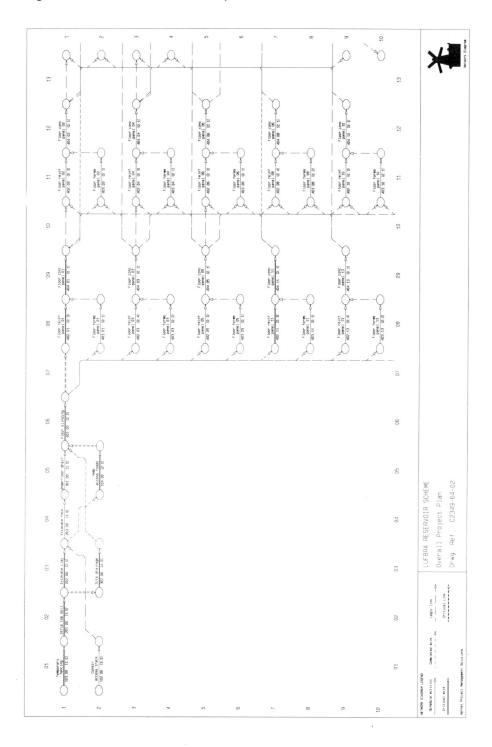

Figure 53. Detailed arrow network, Part 3

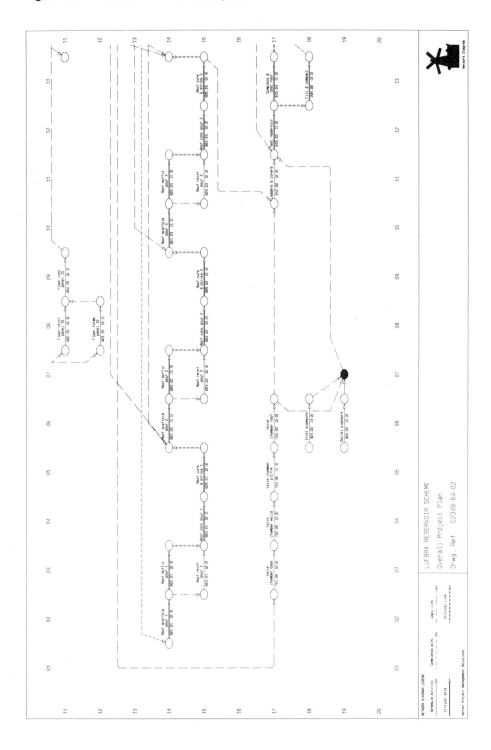

Figure 54. Detailed arrow network, Part 4

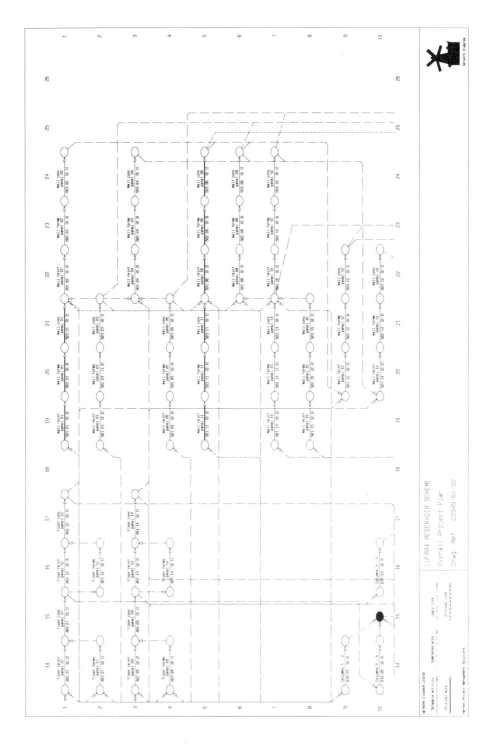

Figure 55. Bar chart, Part 1

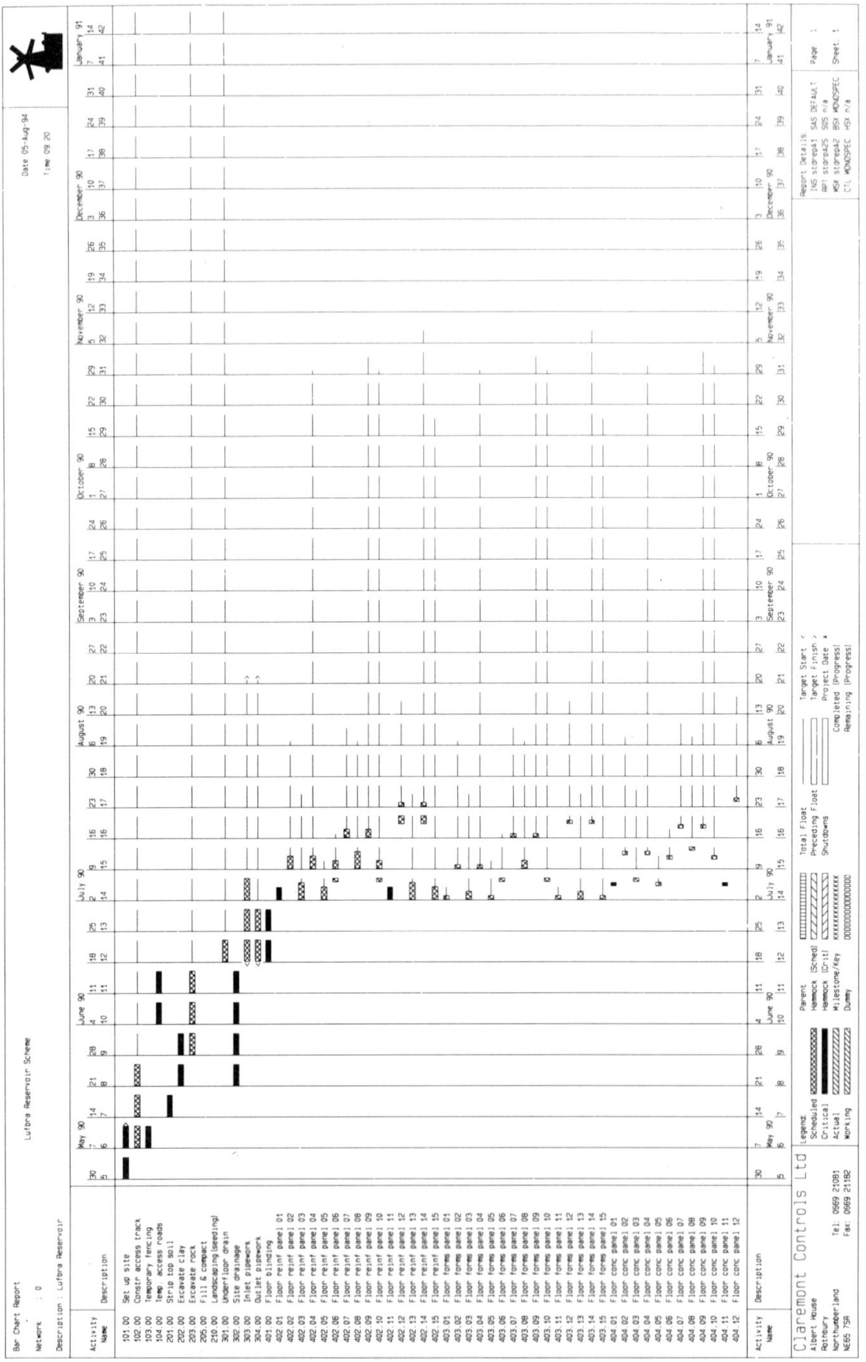

MANAGING INTERNATIONAL CONSTRUCTION PROJECTS: AN OVERVIEW

Figure 56. Bar chart, Part 2

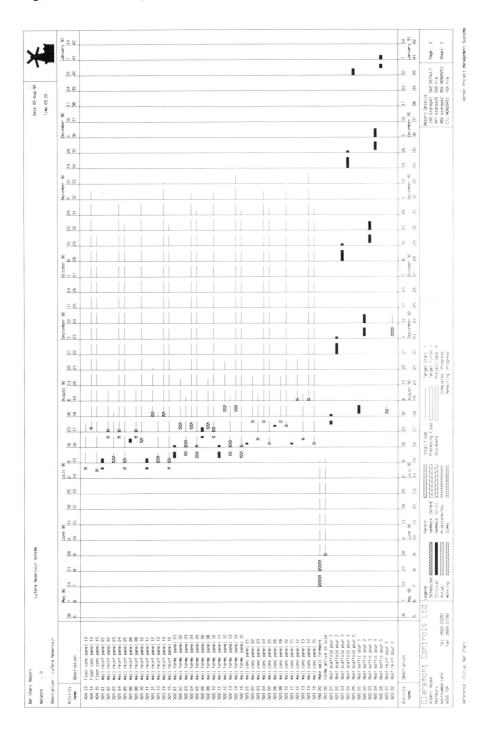

Reference: Initial Bar Chart

Figure 57. Bar chart, Part 3

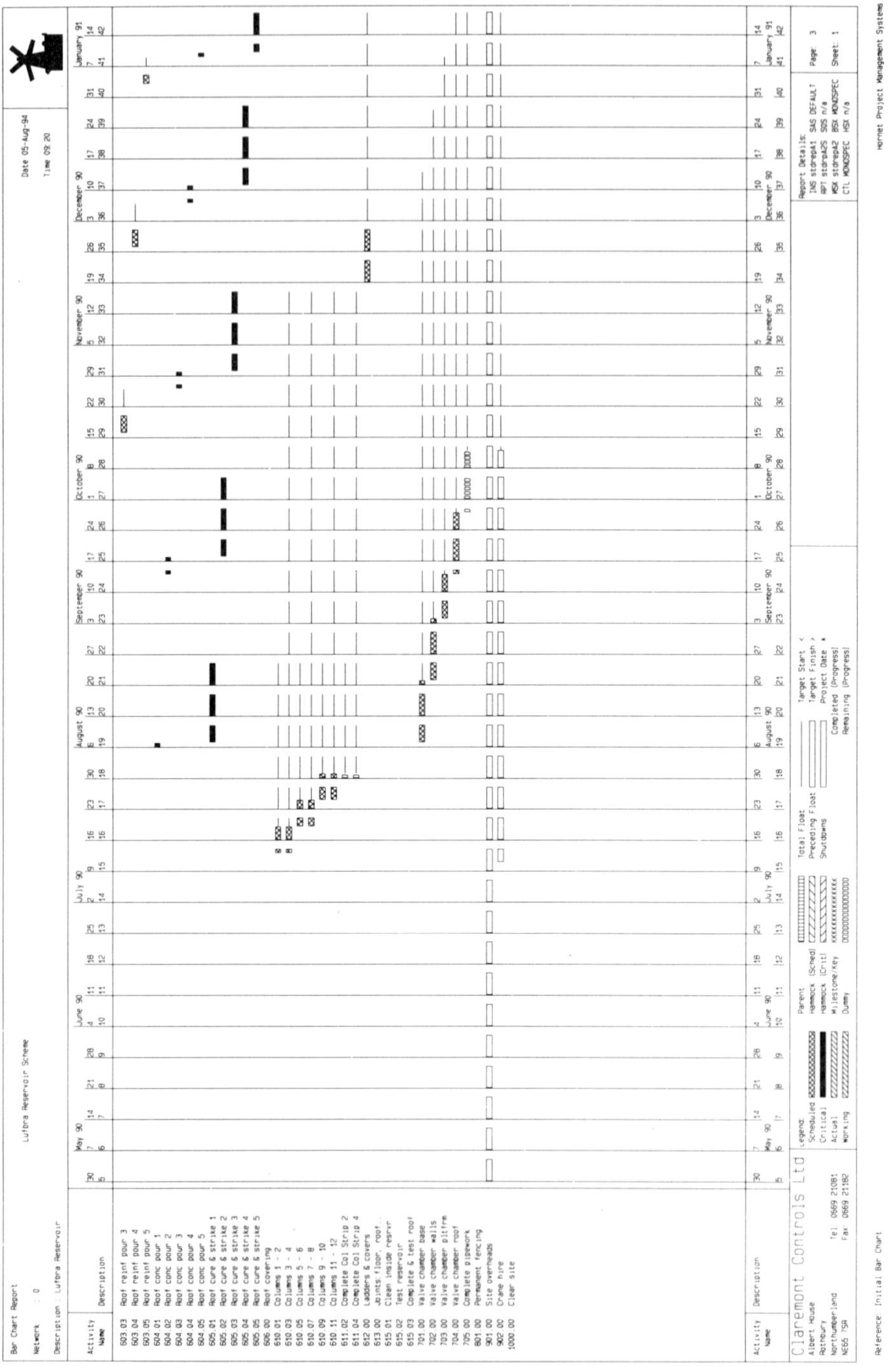

MANAGING INTERNATIONAL CONSTRUCTION PROJECTS: AN OVERVIEW

APPENDIX 1 TO CASE-STUDY F

Examples of input and output screen images of the HORNET computer system

Control parameters and calendar definition

HORNET displays two screens before it creates the new project on the data disk (Screen Images 1 & 2). The first is used to set up the initial information HORNET needs, the second defined the calendar information.

Control parameters:

This is the first screen displayed. Most of the items on the screen can be accepted without change since HORNET adopts an acceptable series of default values. However, most projects are planned in relation to calendar dates, so '1' is entered in the field named "Default Timescale".

Calendar definition:

This is the second screen displayed by HORNET. A number of changes is required, as follows:

a)   the calendar base date should be set to the contract date, using the format "02-04-90";

b)   7 days per week is specified; calendar B will be used for such activities as concrete curing;

c)   calendars A and B are set to give 5-day working on calendar A, for people and machines, and 7-day working on calendar B.

HORNET will proceed to build all necessary data files for the new project, then moves on to the Operation Mode, ready for the user to enter the data.

Examples of input

This section is concerned with entering the basic activity details, the activity numbers, descriptions, durations and precedence logic. From this data it will be possible to schedule the project and get the first estimates of project completion time. The steps needed to enter the activity details for the project are illustrated on the following pages. However, with over 100 activities to enter it is not possible to include displays for all activities. The first half-dozen activities are shown, after which the reader should refer to the activity data listings provided. These are shown on screen images 3–9.

Examples of screen output

Screen image 10 shows part of a bar chart of the project on the screen. The viewer's image can be moved at will to reveal other parts of the bar chart.

Screen image 11 shows the logical relationships for activity 210, as a graphic display. This form of display is very useful for checking logic, and eliminating errors.

SCRN1.IMG

```
HORNET 5000i :              Control Parameters          : LUFBRA  :
                                                            Values loaded
  Project Details
    Project name (directory name)      LUFBRA
    Project title                      <LUFBRA RESERVOIR SCHEME        >

  System Options

    Negative float                     <No >        No/Yes
    Hammock calculation                <Yes>        Yes/No
    Number decimal places              <0>          0 to 4
    Default timescale                  <Calendar>   Calendar/Weeks/Units
    Calendar date format code          <1>          1 to 9      DD MM YY
    Delimiter in calendar dates        <->          Characters / - or space
    Duration display format            <Weeks  >    Weeks/Days

    Starting select and sort file      <DEFAULT >
    Starting bar chart symbols file    <DEFAULT >
    Starting histogram symbols file    <DEFAULT >


  Enter      Shift+F10=Recall              F1=Help           F10=Actions
             F4=Prompt                     F2=Extended help  Esc=Cancel
```

SCRN2.IMG

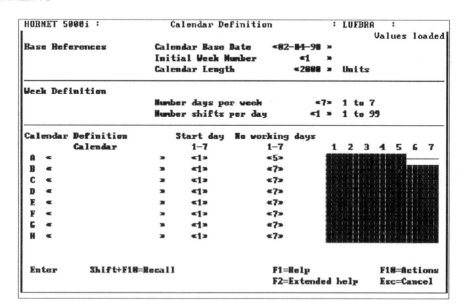

```
HORNET 5000i :              Calendar Definition          : LUFBRA  :
                                                            Values loaded
  Base References            Calendar Base Date    <82-04-90 >
                             Initial Week Number      <1  >
                             Calendar Length       <2000 >  Units

  Week Definition

                             Number days per week        <7>  1 to 7
                             Number shifts per day     <1 >  1 to 99

  Calendar Definition        Start day  No working days
           Calendar            1-7          1-7         1  2  3  4  5  6  7
    A  <                  >    <1>          <5>
    B  <                  >    <1>          <7>
    C  <                  >    <1>          <7>
    D  <                  >    <1>          <7>
    E  <                  >    <1>          <7>
    F  <                  >    <1>          <7>
    G  <                  >    <1>          <7>
    H  <                  >    <1>          <7>


  Enter      Shift+F10=Recall              F1=Help           F10=Actions
                                           F2=Extended help  Esc=Cancel
```

SCRN3.IMG

```
HORNET 5000i :              Data Modification            : LUFBRA  : 0
Activity details 1 - Durations and precedents              Activity loaded
  Activity Number      <  101.00>           Updated  08-Jul-93 13:18

  Descriptions  Short <Set up site          >                  Future
                Long  <RE s & Contractors offices                   >
                Type  <Schedule>
  Management Code      <    H0000   >            WBS Code    <       >

  Durations     Estimated <2:0   >     Target Dates Start <30-04-90 >
                Minimum   <      >               Finish  <11-05-90 >
                Maximum   <      >     Scheduler Priority <0 >

  Calendar      Calendar  <A     >     Shutdown Working  <No >

  Precedents  Network       Activity      Link    Delay       Calendar
      1       <      >   <        >   < >   <        >   <       >  +
      2       <      >   <        >   < >   <        >   <       >  ↑
      3       <      >   <        >   < >   <        >   <       >  |
      4       <      >   <        >   < >   <        >   <       >  |
      5       <      >   <        >   < >   <        >   <       >  ↓
      6       <      >   <        >   < >   <        >   <       >  +
  Enter      F5=Next      F4=Prompt        F1=Help           F10=Actions
  F7=Load    F0=Delete    Shift+F0=Clear     F2=Extended help   Esc=Cancel
```

SCRN4.IMG

```
HORNET 5000i :              Data Modification            : LUFBRA  : 0
Activity details 1 - Durations and precedents              Activity loaded
  Activity Number      <  102.00>           Updated  08-Jul-93 13:18

  Descriptions  Short <Constr access track >                  Future
                Long  <Sub-contract,Lufbra Roadworks Ltd           >
                Type  <Schedule>
  Management Code      <    D0201   >            WBS Code    <       >

  Durations     Estimated <3:0   >     Target Dates Start <         >
                Minimum   <      >               Finish  <         >
                Maximum   <      >     Scheduler Priority <0 >

  Calendar      Calendar  <A     >     Shutdown Working  <No >

  Precedents  Network       Activity      Link    Delay       Calendar
      1       <0     >   < 101.00>   <SS>   <1:0     >   <A     >  +
      2       <      >   <        >   < >   <        >   <       >  ↑
      3       <      >   <        >   < >   <        >   <       >  |
      4       <      >   <        >   < >   <        >   <       >  |
      5       <      >   <        >   < >   <        >   <       >  ↓
      6       <      >   <        >   < >   <        >   <       >  +
  Enter      F5=Next      F4=Prompt        F1=Help           F10=Actions
  F7=Load    F0=Delete    Shift+F0=Clear     F2=Extended help   Esc=Cancel
```

SCRN5.IMG

```
HORNET 5000i :              Data Modification          : LUFBRA   : 0
Activity details 1 - Durations and precedents                Activity loaded
   Activity Number      <  103.00>              Updated  08-Jul-93 13:18

   Descriptions  Short <Temporary fencing    >                     Future
                 Long  <Sub-contract,Fence & Son.NB Temporary fencing onl >
                 Type  <Schedule>
   Management Code      <    D0101      >        WBS Code    <          >

   Durations     Estimated <1:0    >      Target Dates Start <          >
                 Minimum   <       >              Finish    <          >
                 Maximum   <       >      Scheduler Priority <0 >

   Calendar      Calendar  <A      >      Shutdown Working   <No >

   Precedents  Network        Activity       Link    Delay        Calendar
        1      <0      >    <  101.00>     <SS>   <1:0    >    <A       > +
        2      <       >    <       >      < >    <       >    <       > ↑
        3      <       >    <       >      < >    <       >    <       > |
        4      <       >    <       >      < >    <       >    <       > |
        5      <       >    <       >      < >    <       >    <       > ↓
        6      <       >    <       >      < >    <       >    <       > +
   Enter      F5=Next       F4=Prompt        F1=Help           F10=Actions
   F7=Load    F8=Delete     Shift+F8=Clear   F2=Extended help   Esc=Cancel
```

SCRN6.IMG

```
HORNET 5000i :              Data Modification          : LUFBRA   : 0
Activity details 1 - Durations and precedents                Activity loaded
   Activity Number      <  104.00>              Updated  09-Jul-93 12:50

   Descriptions  Short <Temp. access roads  >                     Future
                 Long  <Sub-contract,E Mover.Included in excavation price >
                 Type  <Schedule>
   Management Code      <    D0205      >        WBS Code    <          >

   Durations     Estimated <2:0    >      Target Dates Start <          >
                 Minimum   <       >              Finish    <          >
                 Maximum   <       >      Scheduler Priority <0 >

   Calendar      Calendar  <A      >      Shutdown Working   <No >

   Precedents  Network        Activity       Link    Delay        Calendar
        1      <0      >    <  202.00>     <FS>   <       >    <A       > +
        2      <       >    <       >      < >    <       >    <       > ↑
        3      <       >    <       >      < >    <       >    <       > |
        4      <       >    <       >      < >    <       >    <       > |
        5      <       >    <       >      < >    <       >    <       > ↓
        6      <       >    <       >      < >    <       >    <       > +
   Enter      F5=Next       F4=Prompt        F1=Help           F10=Actions
   F7=Load    F8=Delete     Shift+F8=Clear   F2=Extended help   Esc=Cancel
```

SCRN7.IMG

```
┌────────────────────────────────────────────────────────────────────────────┐
│ HORNET 5000i :              Data Modification           : LUFBRA   : 0      │
│ Activity details 1 - Durations and precedents                 Activity loaded│
│   Activity Number      «  901.00»             Updated  08-Jul-93 13:27      │
│                                                                              │
│   Descriptions   Short «Site overheads      »                      Future   │
│                  Long  «Insurances,services,site management            »    │
│                  Type  «Schedule»                                            │
│   Management Code     «     N0000     »              WBS Code    «      »    │
│                                                                              │
│   Durations      Estimated «      »     Target Dates Start «        »        │
│                  Minimum   «      »             Finish  «        »           │
│                  Maximum   «      »     Scheduler Priority «0 »               │
│                                                                              │
│   Calendar       Calendar  «A     »     Shutdown Working   «No »             │
│                                                                              │
│   Precedents   Network      Activity     Link    Delay        Calendar      │
│        1       «0     »   «  101.00»    «SS»  «       »    «A      »  ↑       │
│        2       «0     »   « 1000.00»    «FF»  «       »    «A      »  ↑       │
│        3       «     »    «        »    «  »  «       »    «       »  │       │
│        4       «     »    «        »    «  »  «       »    «       »  │       │
│        5       «     »    «        »    «  »  «       »    «       »  ↓       │
│        6       «     »    «        »    «  »  «       »    «       »  ↓       │
│   Enter      F5=Next      F4=Prompt        F1=Help          F10=Actions      │
│   F7=Load    F8=Delete    Shift+F8=Clear   F2=Extended help  Esc=Cancel      │
└────────────────────────────────────────────────────────────────────────────┘
```

SCRN8.IMG

```
┌────────────────────────────────────────────────────────────────────────────┐
│ HORNET 5000i :              Data Modification           : LUFBRA   : 0      │
│ Activity details 1 - Durations and precedents                 Activity loaded│
│   Activity Number      «  801.00»             Updated  08-Jul-93 13:27      │
│                                                                              │
│   Descriptions   Short «Permanent fencing   »                      Future   │
│                  Long  «Sub-contract,Fence & Son               »            │
│                  Type  «Schedule»                                            │
│   Management Code     «    D1716     »              WBS Code    «      »     │
│                                                                              │
│   Durations      Estimated «2:0  »     Target Dates Start «        »         │
│                  Minimum   «      »             Finish  «        »           │
│                  Maximum   «      »     Scheduler Priority «0 »               │
│                                                                              │
│   Calendar       Calendar  «A     »     Shutdown Working   «No »             │
│                                                                              │
│   Precedents   Network      Activity     Link    Delay        Calendar      │
│        1       «0     »   «  210.00»    «FS»  «       »    «A      »  ↑       │
│        2       «     »    «        »    «  »  «       »    «       »  ↑       │
│        3       «     »    «        »    «  »  «       »    «       »  │       │
│        4       «     »    «        »    «  »  «       »    «       »  │       │
│        5       «     »    «        »    «  »  «       »    «       »  ↓       │
│        6       «     »    «        »    «  »  «       »    «       »  ↓       │
│   Enter      F5=Next      F4=Prompt        F1=Help          F10=Actions      │
│   F7=Load    F8=Delete    Shift+F8=Clear   F2=Extended help  Esc=Cancel      │
└────────────────────────────────────────────────────────────────────────────┘
```

SCRN9.IMG

```
HORNET 5000i :              Data Modification        : LUFBRA   : 0
Activity details 1 - Durations and precedents          Activity loaded
   Activity Number      « 1000.00»           Updated   09-Jul-93 13:09

   Descriptions  Short «Clear site          »              Future
                 Long  «Remove RE s & Contractor s offices          »
                 Type  «Schedule»
   Management Code    «     D1717    »       WBS Code   «         »

   Durations    Estimated «0:2   »      Target Dates Start «         »
                Minimum   «     »              Finish «         »
                Maximum   «     »      Scheduler Priority «0 »

   Calendar     Calendar  «A    »      Shutdown Working «No »

   Precedents   Network        Activity     Link    Delay       Calendar
        1       «0      »    «  705.00»    «FS»  «      »    «A      »  ♦
        2       «0      »    «  615.01»    «FS»  «      »    «A      »  ↑
        3       «0      »    «  210.00»    «FS»  «      »    «A      »
        4       «0      »    «  801.00»    «FS»  «      »    «A      »
        5       «      »     «        »    «  »  «      »    «      »  ↓
        6       «      »     «        »    «  »  «      »    «      »  ♦
   Enter     F5=Next      F4=Prompt         F1=Help          F10=Actions
   F7=Load   F8=Delete    Shift+F8=Clear    F2=Extended help  Esc=Cancel
```

SCRN10.IMG

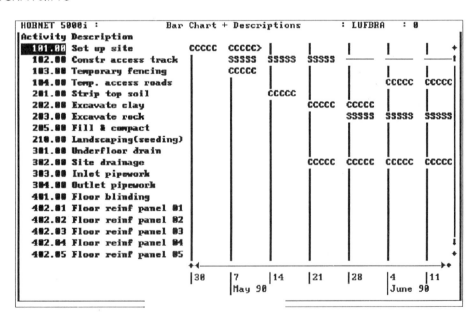

```
HORNET 5000i :           Bar Chart + Descriptions    : LUFBRA   : 0
Activity Description
 101.00 Set up site            CCCCC  CCCCC>                         ♦
 102.00 Constr access track           SSSSS  SSSSS  SSSSS ─────────  ↑
 103.00 Temporary fencing             CCCCC
 104.00 Temp. access roads                              CCCCC  CCCCC
 201.00 Strip top soil                       CCCCC
 202.00 Excavate clay                               CCCCC  CCCCC
 203.00 Excavate rock                               SSSSS  SSSSS  SSSSS
 205.00 Fill & compact
 210.00 Landscaping(seeding)
 301.00 Underfloor drain
 302.00 Site drainage                             CCCCC  CCCCC  CCCCC  CCCCC
 303.00 Inlet pipework
 304.00 Outlet pipework
 401.00 Floor blinding
 402.01 Floor reinf panel 01
 402.02 Floor reinf panel 02
 402.03 Floor reinf panel 03
 402.04 Floor reinf panel 04                                       ↓
 402.05 Floor reinf panel 05                                       ♦
                              |30    |7    |14    |21   |28   |4    |11
                                     May 90                  June 90
```

SCRN11.IMG

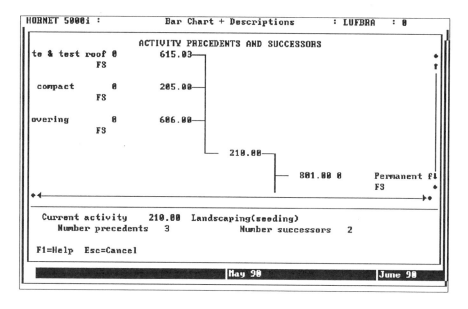

```
HORNET 5000i :        Bar Chart + Descriptions      : LUFBRA  : 0

                   ACTIVITY PRECEDENTS AND SUCCESSORS
te & test roof 0      615.03
          FS                                                        t

 compact       0      205.00
          FS

overing        0      606.00
          FS

                           210.00

                                    801.00 0      Permanent fi
                                                  FS

Current activity   210.00  Landscaping(seeding)
   Number precedents   3          Number successors   2

F1=Help  Esc=Cancel
                                    May 90              June 90
```

APPENDIX 2 to CASE-STUDY F

Activity data listings

REFERENCE: Preliminary Activities

Activity Number	Activity descriptions	Duration	Management Code	PRECEDENT ACTIVITIES									Activity Number
				Number	Link	Delay	Number	Link	Delay	Number	Link	Delay	
101.00	Set up site RE s & Contractors offices	2:0	N0000										101.00
102.00	Constr access track Sub-contract,Lufbra Roadworks Ltd	3:0	D0201	101.00	SS	1:0							102.00
103.00	Temporary fencing Sub-contract,Fence & Son.NB Temporary fencing onl	1:0	D0101	101.00	SS	1:0							103.00
104.00	Temp. access roads Sub-contract,E Mover.Included in excavation price	2:0	D0205	202.00	FS								104.00

Claremont Controls Ltd

Hornet Project Management Systems

REFERENCE: Excavation Activities

Activity Number	Activity descriptions	Duration	Management Code	PRECEDENT ACTIVITIES									Activity Number
				Number	Link	Delay	Number	Link	Delay	Number	Link	Delay	
201.00	Strip top soil Sub-contract,E Mover	1:0	000X D0102	103.00	FS								201.00
202.00	Excavate clay Sub-contract,E Mover	2:0	000X D0103	201.00	FS								202.00
203.00	Excavate rock Sub-contract,E Mover	3:0	000X D0104	102.00	FS								203.00
205.00	Fill & compact Sub-contract,E Mover	3:0	000X D1813	615.02	FS								205.00
210.00	Landscaping(seeding) Sub-contract, Green & Co	2:0	000X D1715	615.03	FS		205.00	FS		606.00	FS		210.00

Claremont Controls Ltd

Hornet Project Management Systems

REFERENCE: Pipework and Drains

Activity Number	Activity descriptions	Duration	Management Code	PRECEDENT ACTIVITIES Number Link Delay	Number Link Delay	Number Link Delay	Activity Number
301.00	Underfloor drain Includes perimeter drain	1:0	D0105	203.00 FS			301.00
302.00	Site drainage Water Board	4:0	D0203	201.00 FS			302.00
303.00	Inlet pipework Water Board.Fixed time (target dates)	3:0	D1806				303.00
304.00	Outlet pipework Water Board.Fixed time (target dates)	2:0	D1906				304.00

Hornet Project Management Systems

Claremont Controls Ltd

REFERENCE: Floor Activities

Activity Number	Activity descriptions	Duration	Management Code	PRECEDENT ACTIVITIES Number	Link	Delay	Number	Link	Delay	Number	Link	Delay	Activity Number
401.00	Floor blinding 6 strips 6m wide	2:0	F00B D0106	104.00	FS		302.00	FS					401.00
402.01	Floor reinf panel 01 NW panel, W tank	0:3	F01R D0108	401.00	FS								402.01
402.02	Floor reinf panel 02 N panel, W tank	0:3	F02R D0111	404.01	FS		404.03	FS					402.02
402.03	Floor reinf panel 03 N centre panel, both tanks	0:4	F03R D0308	401.00	FS								402.03
402.04	Floor reinf panel 04 N panel, E tank	0:3	F04R D0311	404.03	FS		404.05	FS					402.04
402.05	Floor reinf panel 05 NE panel, E tank	0:3	F05R D0508	401.00	FS								402.05
402.06	Floor reinf panel 06 W panel, W tank	0:3	F06R D0511	404.05	FS		404.11	FS					402.06
402.07	Floor reinf panel 07 Centre panel, W tank	0:2	F07R D0114	404.02	FS		404.06	FS		404.08	FS		402.07
402.08	Floor reinf panel 08 Centre panel, both tanks	0:4	F08R D0711	404.03	FS		404.13	FS					402.08
402.09	Floor reinf panel 09 Centre panel, E tank	0:2	F09R D0314	404.04	FS		404.08	FS		404.10	FS		402.09
402.10	Floor reinf panel 10 E panel, E tank	0:3	F10R D0911	404.05	FS		404.15	FS					402.10
402.11	Floor reinf panel 11 SW panel, W tank	0:3	F11R D0708	401.00	FS								402.11
402.12	Floor reinf panel 12 S panel, W tank	0:3	F12R D0116	404.07	FS								402.12
402.13	Floor reinf panel 13 S centre panel, both tanks	0:4	F13R D0908	401.00	FS								402.13
402.14	Floor reinf panel 14 S panel, E tank	0:3	F14R D0316	404.09	FS								402.14
402.15	Floor reinf panel 15 SE panel, E tank	0:3	F15R D1108	401.00	FS								402.15

Claremont Controls Ltd

Hornet Project Management Systems

Activity Number	Activity descriptions	Duration	Management Code	PRECEDENT ACTIVITIES Number	Link	Delay	Number	Link	Delay	Number	Link	Delay	Activity Number
403.01	Floor forms panel 01 NW panel, W tank	0:1	F01F D0208	401.00	FS								403.01
403.02	Floor forms panel 02 N panel, W tank	0:1	F02F D0211	404.01	FS		404.03	FS					403.02
403.03	Floor forms panel 03 N centre panel, both tanks	0:2	F03F D0408	401.00	FS								403.03
403.04	Floor forms panel 04 N panel, E tank	0:1	F04F D0411	404.03	FS		404.05	FS					403.04
403.05	Floor forms panel 05 NE panel, E tank	0:1	F05F D0608	401.00	FS								403.05
403.06	Floor forms panel 06 W panel, W tank	0:1	F06F D0611	404.01	FS		404.11	FS					403.06
403.07	Floor forms panel 07 Centre panel, W tank	0:1	F07F D0214	404.02	FS		404.06	FS		404.08	FS		403.07
403.08	Floor forms panel 08 Centre panel, both tanks	0:2	F08F D0811	404.03	FS		404.13	FS					403.08
403.09	Floor forms panel 09 Centre panel, E tank	0:1	F09F D0414	404.04	FS		404.08	FS		404.10	FS		403.09
403.10	Floor forms panel 10 E panel, E tank	0:1	F10F D1011	404.05	FS		404.15	FS					403.10
403.11	Floor forms panel 11 SW panel, W tank	0:1	F11F D0808	401.00	FS								403.11
403.12	Floor forms panel 12 S panel, W tank	0:1	F12F D0216	404.07	FS								403.12
403.13	Floor forms panel 13 S Centre panel, both tanks	0:2	F13F D1008	401.00	FS								403.13
403.14	Floor forms panel 14 S panel, E tank	0:1	F14F D0416	404.09	FS								403.14
403.15	Floor forms panel 15 SE panel, E tank	0:1	F15F D1208	401.00	FS								403.15
404.01	Floor conc panel 01 NW panel, W tank	0:1	F01C D0109	402.01	FS		403.01	FS					404.01

Hornet Project Management Systems

Claremont Controls Ltd

REFERENCE: **Floor Activities**

Activity Number	Activity descriptions	Duration	Management Code	PRECEDENT ACTIVITIES Number	Link	Delay	ACTIVITIES Number	Link	Delay	Activity Number
404.02	Floor conc panel 02 N panel, W tank	0:1	F02C D0112	402.02	FS		403.02	FS		404.02
404.03	Floor conc panel 03 N centre panel, both tanks	0:1	F03C D0309	402.03	FS		403.03	FS		404.03
404.04	Floor conc panel 04 N panel, E tank	0:1	F04C D0312	402.04	FS		403.04	FS		404.04
404.05	Floor conc panel 05 NE panel, E tank	0:1	F05C D0509	402.05	FS		403.05	FS		404.05
404.06	Floor conc panel 06 W panel, W tank	0:1	F06C D0512	402.06	FS		403.06	FS		404.06
404.07	Floor conc panel 07 Centre panel, W tank	0:1	F07C D0115	402.07	FS		403.07	FS		404.07
404.08	Floor conc panel 08 Centre panel, both tanks	0:1	F08C D0712	402.08	FS		403.08	FS		404.08
404.09	Floor conc panel 09 Centre panel, E tank	0:1	F09C D0315	402.09	FS		403.09	FS		404.09
404.10	Floor conc panel 10 E panel, E tank	0:1	F10C D0912	402.10	FS		403.10	FS		404.10
404.11	Floor conc panel 11 SW panel, W tank	0:1	F11C D0709	402.11	FS		403.11	FS		404.11
404.12	Floor conc panel 12 S panel, W tank	0:1	F12C D0117	402.12	FS		403.12	FS		404.12
404.13	Floor conc panel 13 S centre panel, both tanks	0:1	F13C D0909	402.13	FS		403.13	FS		404.13
404.14	Floor conc panel 14 S panel, E tank	0:1	F14C D0317	402.14	FS		403.14	FS		404.14
404.15	Floor conc panel 15 SE panel, E tank	0:1	F15C D1109	402.15	FS		403.15	FS		404.15

Hornet Project Management Systems

Claremont Controls Ltd

Activity Number	Activity descriptions	Duration	Management Code	PRECEDENT ACTIVITIES Number	Link	Delay	Number	Link	Delay	ACTIVITIES Number	Link	Delay	Activity Number
501.01	Wall reinf panel 01 N W wall, W tank	0:3	W01R D0119	404.01	FS								501.01
501.02	Wall reinf panel 02 N wall, W tank	0:2	W02R D0122	404.02	FS		503.01	FS		503.03	FS		501.02
501.03	Wall reinf panel 03 N tee wall, both tanks	0:3	W03R D0219	404.03	FS								501.03
501.04	Wall reinf panel 04 N wall, E tank	0:2	W04R D0322	404.04	FS		503.03	FS		503.05	FS		501.04
501.05	Wall reinf panel 05 NE wall, E tank	0:3	W05R D0419	404.05	FS								501.05
501.06	Wall reinf panel 06 W wall, W tank	0:2	W06R D0522	404.06	FS		503.01	FS		503.11	FS		501.06
501.08	Wall reinf panel 08 Centre wall, both tanks	0:2	W08R D0622	404.08	FS		503.03	FS		503.13	FS		501.08
501.10	Wall reinf panel 10 E wall, E tank	0:2	W10R D0722	404.10	FS		503.05	FS		503.15	FS		501.10
501.11	Wall reinf panel 11 SW wall, W tank	0:3	W11R D0519	404.11	FS								501.11
501.12	Wall reinf panel 12 S wall, E tank	0:2	W12R D0920	404.12 / 503.08	FS / FS		503.02	FS		503.06	FS		501.12
501.13	Wall reinf panel 13 S tee wall	0:3	W13R D0719	404.13	FS								501.13
501.14	Wall reinf panel 14 S wall, E tank	0:2	W14R D1020	404.14 / 503.10	FS / FS		503.04	FS		503.08	FS		501.14
501.15	Wall reinf panel 15 SE wall, E tank	0:3	W15R D0819	404.15	FS								501.15
502.01	Wall forms panel 01 N W wall, W tank	0:4	W01F D0120	501.01	FS		551.00	FS					502.01
502.02	Wall forms panel 02 N wall, W tank	0:3	W02F D0123	501.02	FS		551.00	FS					502.02
502.03	Wall forms panel 03 N tee wall, both tanks	1:0	W03F D0220	501.03	FS		551.00	FS					502.03

Hornet Project Management Systems

Claremont Controls Ltd

REFERENCE: Wall Activities

Activity Number	Activity descriptions	Duration	Management Code	PRECEDENT ACTIVITIES						ACTIVITIES			Activity Number
				Number	Link	Delay	Number	Link	Delay	Number	Link	Delay	
502.04	Wall forms panel 04 N wall, E tank	0:3	W04F D0323	501.04	FS		551.00	FS					502.04
502.05	Wall forms panel 05 NE wall, E tank	0:4	W05F D0420	501.05	FS		551.00	FS					502.05
502.06	Wall forms panel 06 W wall, W tank	0:3	W06F D0523	501.06	FS		551.00	FS					502.06
502.08	Wall forms panel 08 Centre wall, both tanks	0:3	W08F D0623	501.08	FS		551.00	FS					502.08
502.10	Wall forms panel 10 E wall, E tank	0:3	W10F D0723	501.10	FS		551.00	FS					502.10
502.11	Wall forms panel 11 SW wall, W tank	0:4	W11F D0520	501.11	FS		551.00	FS					502.11
502.12	Wall forms panel 12 S wall, E tank	0:3	W12F D0921	501.12	FS		551.00	FS					502.12
502.13	Wall forms panel 13 S tee wall	1:0	W13F D0720	501.13	FS		551.00	FS					502.13
502.14	Wall forms panel 14 S wall, E tank	0:3	W14F D1021	501.14	FS		551.00	FS					502.14
502.15	Wall forms panel 15 SE wall, E tank	0:4	W15F D0820	501.15	FS		551.00	FS					502.15
503.01	Wall conc panel 01 N W wall, W tank	0:1	W01C D0121	502.01	FS								503.01
503.02	Wall conc panel 02 N wall, W tank	0:1	W02C D0124	502.02	FS								503.02
503.03	Wall conc panel 03 N tee wall, both tanks	0:1	W03C D0221	502.03	FS								503.03
503.04	Wall conc panel 04 N wall, E tank	0:1	W04C D0324	502.04	FS								503.04
503.05	Wall conc panel 05 NE wall, E tank	0:1	W05C D0421	502.05	FS								503.05
503.06	Wall conc panel 06 W wall, W tank	0:1	W06C D0524	502.06	FS								503.06

Hornet Project Management Systems

Claremont Controls Ltd

Activity Number	Activity descriptions	Duration	Management Code	PRECEDENT ACTIVITIES Number	Link	Delay	Number	Link	Delay	Number	Link	Delay	Activity Number
503.08	Wall conc panel 08 Centre wall, both tanks	0:1	W08C D0624	502.08	FS								503.08
503.10	Wall conc panel 10 E wall, E tank	0:1	W10C D0724	502.10	FS								503.10
503.11	Wall conc panel 11 SW wall, W tank	0:1	W11C D0521	502.11	FS								503.11
503.12	Wall conc panel 12 S wall, E tank	0:1	W12C D0922	502.12	FS								503.12
503.13	Wall conc panel 13 S tee wall	0:1	W13C D0721	502.13	FS								503.13
503.14	Wall conc panel 14 S wall, E tank	0:1	W14C D1022	502.14	FS								503.14
503.15	Wall conc panel 15 SE wall, E tank	0:1	W15C D0821	502.15	FS								503.15
550.00	Make wall formwork Made by Windmill Temporary Works Ltd	2:0	N0000	101.00	FS								550.00
551.00	Forms arrive on site	0:1	N0000	550.00	FS								551.00

Hornet Project Management Systems

Claremont Controls Ltd

REFERENCE: **Roof Activities**

Activity Number	Activity descriptions	Duration	Management Code	Precedent Number	Link	Delay	Precedent Number	Link	Delay	Precedent Number	Link	Delay	Activity Number
601.01	Roof scaffold pour 1	0:3	R01S D1402	503.01	FS		503.06	FS		503.11	FS		601.01
601.02	Roof scaffold pour 2	1:1	R02S D1406	605.01 503.12	FS FS		611.02	FS		503.02	FS		601.02
601.03	Roof scaffold pour 3	1:1	R03S D1410	605.02 503.13	FS FS		503.03	FS		503.08	FS		601.03
601.04	Roof scaffold pour 4	1:1	R04S D1414	605.03 611.04	FS FS		503.04	FS		503.14	FS		601.04
601.05	Roof scaffold pour 5	0:3	R05S D1418	605.04 503.15	FS FS		503.05	FS		503.10	FS		601.05
602.01	Roof soffit pour 1	0:4	R01F D1403	601.01	FS								602.01
602.02	Roof soffit pour 2	1:3	R02F D1407	601.02	FS								602.02
602.03	Roof soffit pour 3	1:3	R03F D1411	601.03	FS								602.03
602.04	Roof soffit pour 4	1:3	R04F D1415	601.04	FS								602.04
602.05	Roof soffit pour 5	0:4	R05F D1419	601.05	FS								602.05
603.01	Roof reinf pour 1	0:2	R01R D1503	601.01	FS								603.01
603.02	Roof reinf pour 2	0:4	R02R D1507	601.02	FS								603.02
603.03	Roof reinf pour 3	0:4	R03R D1511	601.03	FS								603.03
603.04	Roof reinf pour 4	0:4	R04R D1515	601.04	FS								603.04
603.05	Roof reinf pour 5	0:2	R05R D1519	601.05	FS								603.05
604.01	Roof conc pour 1	0:1	R01C D1504	603.01	FS		602.01	FS					604.01

Hornet Project Management Systems

Claremont Controls Ltd

REFERENCE: Roof Activities

Activity Number	Activity descriptions	Duration	Management Code	PRECEDENT ACTIVITIES						Link	Delay	Activity Number
				Number	Link	Delay	Number	Link	Delay			
604.02	Roof conc pour 2	0:2	R02C D1508	603.02	FS		602.02	FS				604.02
604.03	Roof conc pour 3	0:2	R03C D1512	603.03	FS		602.03	FS				604.03
604.04	Roof conc pour 4	0:2	R04C D1516	603.04	FS		602.04	FS				604.04
604.05	Roof conc pour 5	0:1	R05C D1520	602.05	FS		603.05	FS				604.05
605.01	Roof cure & strike 1	2:4	R01K D1505	604.01	FS							605.01
605.02	Roof cure & strike 2	2:4	R02K D1509	604.02	FS							605.02
605.03	Roof cure & strike 3	2:4	R03K D1513	604.03	FS							605.03
605.04	Roof cure & strike 4	2:4	R04K D1517	604.04	FS							605.04
605.05	Roof cure & strike 5	2:4	R05K D1521	604.05	FS							605.05
606.00	Roof covering	2:0	D1714	615.03	FS							606.00
610.01	Columns 1 - 2	0:4	C01G D0914	404.02	FS							610.01
610.03	Columns 3 - 4	0:4	C03G D1016	404.04	FS							610.03
610.05	Columns 5 - 6	0:4	C05G D1014	404.07	FS							610.05
610.07	Columns 7 - 8	0:4	C07G D1116	404.09	FS							610.07
610.09	Columns 9 - 10	0:4	C09G D1114	404.12	FS							610.09
610.11	Columns 11 - 12	0:4	C11G D1216	404.14	FS							610.11

Hornet Project Management Systems

Claremont Controls Ltd

REFERENCE: Roof Activities

Activity Number	Activity descriptions	Duration	Management Code	PRECEDENT ACTIVITIES						ACTIVITIES			Activity Number
				Number	Link	Delay	Number	Link	Delay	Number	Link	Delay	
611.02	Complete Col Strip 2 Columns 1,2,5,6,9 and 10		D1015	610.01	FS		610.05	FS		610.09	FS		611.02
611.04	Complete Col Strip 4 Columns 3,4,7,8,11 and 12		D1117	610.03	FS		610.07	FS		610.11	FS		611.04
612.00	Ladders & covers On roof,pour 3	2:0	D1711	605.03	FS		704.00	FS					612.00
613.00	Joints:floor, roof.. Sub-contract, Magic Muck Ltd	1:0	D1622	605.01, 605.04	FS, FS		605.02, 605.05	FS, FS		605.03	FS		613.00
615.01	Clean inside resrvr All roofs cured and struck	0:2	D1522	605.01, 605.04	FS, FS		605.02, 605.05	FS, FS		605.03	FS		615.01
615.02	Test reservoir	1:0	D1712	615.01, 613.00	FS, FS		705.00	FS		612.00	FS		615.02
615.03	Complete & test roof Waterproof membrane and water test	1:0	D1713	615.02	FS								615.03

Hornet Project Management Systems

Claremont Controls Ltd

Activity Number	Activity descriptions	Duration	Management Code	Number	Link	Delay	Number	Link	Delay	Number	Link	Delay	Activity Number
701.00	Valve chamber base	2:0	V01G D1703	503.13	FS		503.12	FS					701.00
702.00	Valve chamber walls Single pour - could be divided if required	2:0	V02G D1704	701.00	FS								702.00
703.00	Valve chamber pltfrm Valve chamber platform for access	1:3	V03G D1705	702.00	FS								703.00
704.00	Valve chamber roof Duration includes slab curing	2:0	V04G D1706	703.00	FS		702.00	FS					704.00
705.00	Complete pipework	2:0	D1907	704.00	FS		303.00	FS		304.00	FS		705.00

Hornet Project Management Systems

Claremont Controls Ltd

Activity Number	Activity descriptions	Duration	Management Code	Number	Link	Delay	Number	Link	Delay	Number	Link	Delay	Activity Number
801.00	Permanent fencing Sub-contract,Fence & Son	2:0	D1716	210.00	FS								801.00
901.00	Site overheads Insurances,services,site management		N0000	101.00	SS		1000.00	FF					901.00
902.00	Crane hire On site start forms wall panel 13 to pipework en		N0000	502.01	SS		705.00	FF					902.00
1000.00	Clear site Remove RE s & Contractor s offices	0:2	D1717	705.00 801.00	FS FS		615.01	FS		210.00	FS		1000.00

Hornet Project Management Systems

Claremont Controls Ltd

Case-study G

BARAJU TUNNEL

A planning case-study for the construction of a tunnel forming part of a hydro-electric project in southern India. It illustrates the practical application of the use of time-chainage charts

Introduction to the project

The Baraju is a turbulent river in southern India. Over one eight-kilometre stretch, immediately after the confluence with a tributary, the river bed falls nearly 65 metres. This fall, and an adequate volume of water, make this a good site for a "run of the river" hydro-electricity generating project.

Figure 58 on page 196 is a diagrammatic plan of the project. The river valley is fairly straight at this point, and both the road and the proposed tunnel run parallel with it. A new dam will divert the water from the river into the tunnel, which will conduct the water nearly eight kilometres to the powerhouse, after which the water will return to the river.

The tunnel is through hard rock and this will be excavated by conventional drill-and-blast excavation techniques. Weak sections of rock will be strengthened by rock bolts where necessary, and the whole tunnel will be lined with concrete.

Contract dates		Start	Completion
Contract 1	Powerhouse	01.01.90	14.08.94
Contract 2	Tunnel	01.01.90	14.08.94
Contract 3	Dam	01.01.91	14.08.94

Construction plan

Such a long tunnel must be excavated at several places at once, and figure 58 shows that there will be a total of six faces. Access will be gained to faces 2–5 by excavating temporary access tunnels – "adits" – from the side of the valley. These will have a slightly smaller diameter than the main tunnel, and because of the topography will be of different lengths. The adits must be securely plugged on completion of the tunnel works.

All work stops during the main monsoon, which is likely to occur from the second week in October to the end of December.

Priority must be given to the completion of the main tunnel from the intake down to adit 2. This section of the tunnel, and adits 1 and 2, will form a temporary tunnel to allow the river to be diverted away from the site of the new dam during the 1991 monsoon. After this, the diversion tunnel for the dam will be complete, and the temporary use of the power tunnel will no longer be required.

The first activity will be to clear the ground, build access tracks, and set up the construction site facilities. This is estimated to take about 10 weeks. Tunnel excavation will then begin at the intake, and excavation will start on adits 1 and 2.

Planning data		
Main tunnel	Nominal excavated diameter	6 800 m
	Finished internal diameter	6 000 m
	Expected "pull" per blast	4 500 m
	Expected average weekly progress	28 000 m
Adits	Nominal internal diameter	5 500 m
	Expected "pull" per blast	5 000 m
	Expected average weekly progress	30 000 m

The tunnel will be lined with concrete. Figure 59 shows that the overt will be formed by a circular form which will be collapsed hydraulically after the concrete has hardened sufficiently. This form will be supported on rails. When the overt has been completed for the whole of a section of tunnel, the tunnel will be cleared and the invert concreted. Finally, any gaps between the lining and the rock, and also any fissures in the rock near the lining, will be sealed with grout.

It is planned to use a total of eight sets of overt forms. Each form will cover 9 m of tunnel, and each section of tunnel will use two pairs of forms, set 27 m apart (see figure 60). The forms will be set up at the mid-point of each section, and will be moved towards the ends. Each form will be used for four pours of 9 m each, then both pairs will be moved forwards, and the pattern repeated for another 72 m. Planning data are as follows:

Overt: Three pours per week per form: i.e. 54 m, per week per set of two forms.

Invert: Planned pour rate of 60 lin. m per week per form, with two forms per section.

Grouting: This is difficult to predict, but it is estimated that one set of equipment and its crew will complete 100 m per week: there will be two sets of equipment per section. This must wait for at least four weeks after the completion of the invert concrete, to allow the concrete to cure.

Finally, the adits will be sealed at the completion of all tunnel works in the adjacent sections. Sealing will take 10 weeks.

Interim calculations for sections 1 and 2 follow in tables 12–16.

Table 11. Project calendar

The working week begins on a Sunday. The dates given are the "week beginning" dates.

Date	Week no.	Comments
1.1.1990	1	Tunnel project start date
	42	Monsoon starts
	52	Monsoon ends
1.1.1991	53	Dam start date
	94	Monsoon starts
	104	Monsoon ends
1.1.1992	105	
	146	Monsoon starts
	156	Monsoon ends
1.1.1993	157	
	198	Monsoon starts
	208	Monsoon ends
1.1.1994	209	
14.8.1994	240	Project completion date
	250	Monsoon starts

Table 12. Adit excavation calculations

Adit no.	Length (m)	Time to complete	Start week	Finish week
1	403	14 weeks	10	24
2	327	11 weeks	10	21

Table 13. Excavation calculations for tunnel sections 1 and 2

Calculations for the meeting point of faces. Note that the excavation for each face may begin at differing times because the adit excavation times are different.

Face no.	Start week	Distance driven before other face starts (m)	Distance of shared drive (m)	Chainage of meeting point
1	10	$(24-10) \times 28 = 392$		
2	24	—	3 217	2 001
3	24	—	3 080	5 149
4	21	$(24-21) \times 28 = 84$		

Calculation of distance driven before the first monsoon, and completion date of excavation for sections 1 and 2 (i.e. when faces meet).

Face no.	Start week	Time to monsoon (weeks)	Distance driven (m)	Chainage at monsoon (m)	Distance at meeting (m)	Time to meeting (weeks)
1	10	32	896	896	1 105	40 (92)
2	24	18	504	3 105	1 104	40 (92)
3	24	18	504	4 133	1 036	37 (89)
4	21	21	588	6 185	1 036	37 (89)

Thus these sections of tunnel should be complete before the second monsoon starts, although there is very little margin for delays.

Table 14. Overt lining calculations for sections 1 and 2 (season 3)

Lining starts from the mid-point of the main tunnel. For section 1, at chainage 0 + 3 609/2 = 1 805 m. For section 2 at chainage 3 600 + (6 773– 609)/2 = 5 191 m.

Section no.	Pair of forms	Distance each pair (m)	Total time (weeks)	Start week	Finish week
1	A	1 805	34	105	138
	B	1 805	34	105	138
2	C	1 582	30	105	134
	D	1 582	30	105	134

Table 15. Invert lining calculations for sections 1 and 2 (season 4)

Section no.	Pair of forms	Time (weeks)	Start week	Finish week
1	A	30	157	186
	B	30	157	186
2	C	26	157	182
	D	26	157	182

Table 16. Grouting calculations for sections 1 and 2 (section 5)

Grouting will begin at the outer ends of each section, and will work towards a meeting point, approximately at the midpoint of the tunnel. This is the reverse direction to that used on previous activities; the rate of progress of the grouting is very unpredictable, and with the machines moving to meet each other, slow progress on one can easily be compensated by increased distance of the other.

Section no.	Rig	Distance for each pair (m)	Total time (weeks)	Start week	Finish week
1	A	1 805	18	209	227
	B	1 805	18	209	227
2	C	1 582	16	209	225
	D	1 582	16	209	225

Table 17. Sealing adits

Adit 1

Start date is latest time of finishing sections 1 and 2 of tunnel grouting, i.e. week 227. This takes 10 weeks, so finish date is 237.

Figure 58.   Diagrammatic plan of Baraju Tunnel Project

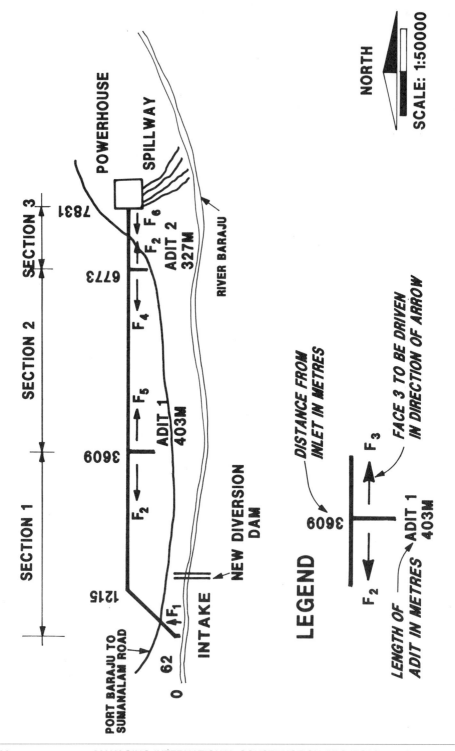

MANAGING INTERNATIONAL CONSTRUCTION PROJECTS: AN OVERVIEW

Figure 59. Section through tunnel showing overt lining formwork

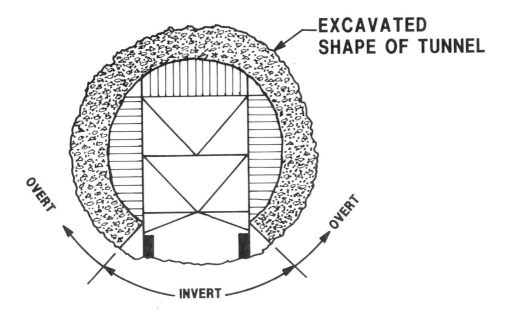

EXCAVATED
SHAPE OF TUNNEL

OVERT

OVERT

INVERT

Figure 60. Lining method

8 SETS OF FORMS, USED IN 4 SETS OF TWO PAIRS
START MIDWAY BETWEEN ADITS

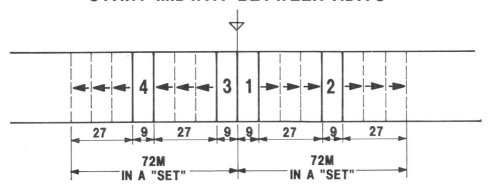

| 27 | 9 | 27 | 9 | 9 | 27 | 9 | 27 |

72M
IN A "SET"

72M
IN A "SET"

PLANNED : 3 POURS PER WEEK PER FORM
54M PER WEEK PER SET

Final calculations

This section gives the calculations for the final part of the tunnel, and the complete Linear Programme diagram.

Table 18: Calculations for tunnel section 3

This is a short section of tunnel, so it is not planned to begin immediately. When resources such as excavation teams and lining equipment become available, they will be moved to start work on this section. The question to be answered is "Will this economical use of resources result in timely completion?"

Excavation meeting of faces

Note that Adit 2 will be complete long before tunnelling starts
(7 831-6 773) /2 + 6 773 = Chainage 7 302 m
Distance to be driven for each face = 529 m
Time required = 529/28 = 19 weeks
Start at beginning of third season, start of week 105
Finish excavation end of week 123

Overt lining

Time required for each half of Section 3 = 529/54 = 10 weeks
Forms are available from Section 2 and the start of week 135
Start week 135
Finish week 144
Monsoon starts week 146, so this is just OK

Invert lining

Time required for each half = 529/60 = 9 weeks
Forms are available from Section 2 at the start of week 183
Start week 183
Finish week 193

Grouting

Time required for each half = 529/100 = 5 weeks
Cannot start until 4 weeks after the completion of the invert concreting, to allow for concrete curing; week 196
Grouting rigs are not available until after week 225
Start week 226
Finish week 230

Seal Adit 2

Start week 231
Finish week 241

Project completion

Thus the project is planned to be completed with the sealing of Adit 2. This is within the required project duration, and also makes economic use of the resources in Section 3. Provision of an extra rig would reduce the project duration.

Figure 61. Linear programme chart

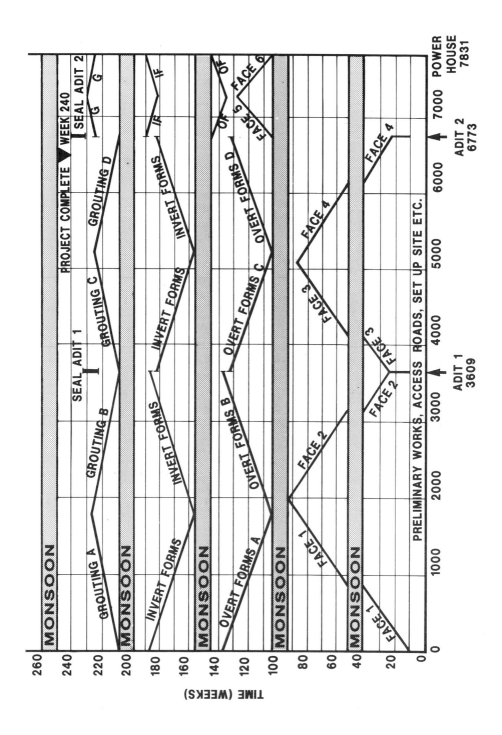

Case-study H

LINE-OF-BALANCE PLANNING BY SPREADSHEET

A simple planning case-study using the line of balance technique, demonstrating the use of computer spreadsheet software

This case-study is based on an article by Richard Neale and Bavindra Raju, published in Building Technology and Management, *Dec. 1988*

Introduction

One of the problems with line-of-balance is the tedium of the calculations. An additional problem is caused by the objective of formulating a work schedule in which all activities are working, more or less, at the same pace, all following on smoothly in harmony. In many cases, this requires a certain amount of trial and error in the calculations, and this adds to the tedium. This is compounded in repetitive construction because the activities for each item follow one behind the other, so a change to the rate of working of one activity often requires adjustments to be made to the schedule of all the succeeding activities.

A spreadsheet program will help with the calculations. By making the calculations easier, it encourages planners to improve and refine their plans, exploring the use of alternative methods and resource levels. With the needs of the industry in mind, this case-study gives a brief description of how a spreadsheet computer system can be used to remove the tedium from line-of-balance calculations. It is important to point out that this has been done without making the spreadsheet application itself too complicated.

Use of standard, general packages

One of the current trends in computing is a move away from writing special software for individual applications, towards increasing use of flexible, general-purpose programs such as spreadsheets and databases. This process is not new; consider, for example, the ICL Prosper program which offered facilities that foreshadowed contemporary spreadsheets. The difference is that the systems available now are much easier to use and the facilities available are now very comprehensive. A further consideration is that through the dominance of IBM-compatibility and MS-DOS, data can be exchanged between the various, standard programs with ease, so a number of standard programs can be brought to bear on an application.

Thus, many applications that used to require specially written software may now be done with standard packages. It is true that a specially written program may often provide a better and more specific solution, but in many cases it so much easier to use standard packages to produce a more limited solution more quickly and with less effort.

It also true that potential users of the application system may first have to acquire some knowledge of the use of the standard package. The counter-argument is that, in the long term, it is more beneficial for users to learn how to use packages of general application (which is not that difficult), than to have to learn how to use a special program for each application. This has the additional benefit of reducing the likelihood that the computer will be misused through lack of understanding of the application.

This approach is also used by software houses; for example, standard packages for graphics, spreadsheets and databases are often found linked to or embedded in project management systems.

A further practical benefit is flexibility. The conventional line-of-balance calculation assumes that the data will be available in a specific form. In practice, of course, data will often be available in a variety of forms (if it exists at all), so planners will have to take what they can get. Then the spreadsheets will be useful to manipulate the data, so that they may be used in the calculation of the line-of-balance schedule.

A line-of-balance example

The line-of-balance technique for planning the construction of a number of similar items is fairly well known. Like all planning techniques, its practical application in construction is not without its problems, but there is no doubt that some firms have found it useful. These are mainly house builders but the authors have also had a very positive report from a civil engineer working in the Sudan. Of course, there are also people who say they have tried it and it doesn't work, but then that is the case for almost all management techniques.

Because line-of-balance is relatively well known (for example reference 1 in the introduction) the technique will be described here in outline only, by means of a simple example. It is usually illustrated by house-building examples, so, just for a change, a bridge has been chosen.

Figure 62 is a diagram of the bridge, shown in much simplified form. In India, such bridges are common, taking railways over rivers. For much of the year the level of these rivers is quite low, because there is very little rain, but during the monsoon the heavy rains cause the river to rise dramatically. Thus all construction work has to be done in the non-monsoon "season", when the river is low.

One consequence of the monsoon floods is that the beds of the lower reaches of many rivers are of deep layers of silt. Therefore, the best way to construct the piers will be constructing the bases as caissons; that is, building them as hollow, concrete shells which sink into the silt under their own weight as they are constructed. This is illustrated by figure 63.

The method is to build an artificial island at the site of each pier, construct and sink the caisson to the required depth and then seal the base with concrete to prevent further settlement when the additional bridge

Figure 62.   Diagrammatic section of bridge

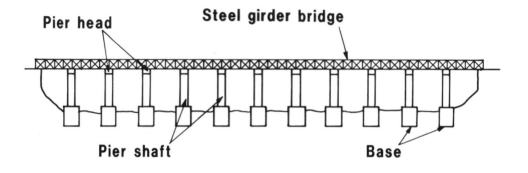

Pier head

Steel girder bridge

Pier shaft

Base

Figure 63.   Base caisson during sinking

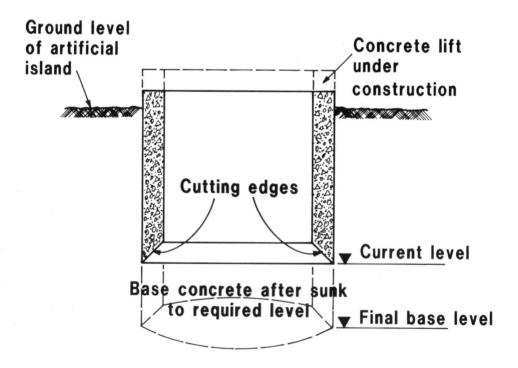

Ground level of artificial island

Concrete lift under construction

Cutting edges

Current level

Base concrete after sunk to required level

Final base level

loads are applied. The caisson is then filled with consolidated silt, and capped. The pier is then built on the cap, and finally the pier head is built ready to receive the bridge beams. Obviously, these activities are sequential. The plan is to build and cap all 11 caissons in one "season" of 42 weeks (the monsoon stops work for about ten weeks); construct all the piers and pier heads in the second season; and complete the bridge in the third season. In this example, we shall only plan the construction of the piers.

The planning data are given in table 19. The accuracy of the estimates of duration is believed to be plus or minus 20 per cent, and the buffers are calculated on this basis (i.e. if the accuracy of estimation is ±20 per cent, then the minimum buffer must be + 20 per cent of activity duration).

The conventional application of the line-of-balance technique is a housing project with a hand-over schedule imposed on the client. The hand-over schedule may be taken to be the planned rate of production, and the line-of-balance chart constructed accordingly. This is convenient, of course, but in many cases only the total project duration is given, so the required planned rate of production is unknown and has to be established by trial and error. This is such a case.

The initial assumption is that only one gang of workers, and one set of equipment and machinery, will be available for each activity. These resources are found to be inadequate to complete the bases in the season, so the spreadsheet is used to experiment with the effects of using additional crews (and sets of equipment and plant) to reduce the construction period.

Table 19. Planning data

Activity		Estimated duration (days)	Estimated buffer* (days)
No.	Description		
1	Construct artificial island	20	4
2	Construct & sink caisson	50	10
3	Construct caisson base	10	2
4	Fill & cap caisson	10	2
5	Construct pier shaft	50	10
6	Construct pier head	20	4

*Note: If accuracy of estimation is ± 20% then minimum buffer must be + 20% of activity duration

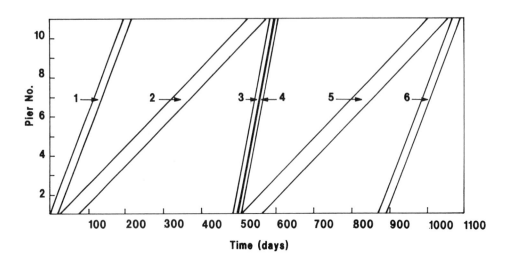

Figure 64 shows the initial line-of-balance chart and table 20(a) gives the supporting calculations. The nomenclature used in the calculations is shown in figure 65. The assumption has been made that the reader has some knowledge of line-of-balance, and that the calculations are self-explanatory. Note, however, that the use of the spreadsheet allows the buffers to be calculated automatically, because in this case they are related to the activity durations.

The method of calculation in the spreadsheet is given by the formulae in table 20(b). The first three columns are input data. The "Time for N-1 units" and the buffer calculations are simple arithmetic. The "type of buffer" is determined by comparing the value of T for the activity with that of the preceding activity. The calculations for the start and end dates depend upon the type of buffer, but are otherwise simple arithmetic.

The scheduled duration is obviously far too long. Given that projects like this work a seven-day week, then a season of 42 weeks is 294 days. In fact, it would be prudent to plan to complete the piers in less time than this, to give some margin of safety.

In the next season, the piers (activities 5 and 6) must be complete within the 294 working days available, i.e. starting at the beginning of the

Table 20(a). Railway bridge example spreadsheet

ACT. NO.	ACTIVITY DESCRIPTION	DURATION t (days)	TIME N-1 UNITS T (days)	BUFFER (days)	TYPE OF BUFFER	START DAY UNIT 1	START DAY UNIT N
1	ISLAND	20.0	200.0			0	200
				4	1		
2	CAISSON	50.0	500.0			24	524
				10	0		
3	BASE TO CAISSON	10.0	100.0			484	584
				2	0		
4	CAISSON CAP	10.0	100.0			496	596
				2	1		
5	PIER	50.0	500.0			508	1008
				10	0		
6	PIER HEAD	20.0	200.0			868	1068
				4	0		
7	PIERS COMPLETE						1092

LEGEND   START BUFFER   1
            END BUFFER   0

Figure 65. Nomenclature used in table 20

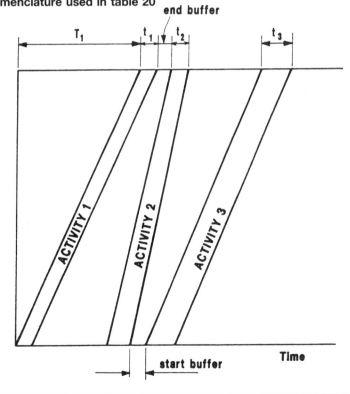

Table 20(b). Railway bridge example spreadsheet

ACT NO.	ACTIVITY DESCRIPTION	DURATION t (days)	TIME N-1 t (days) * UNITS	BUFFER (days)	TYPE OF BUFFER	START DAY UNIT 1	START DAY UNIT N
1	ISLAND	20	(F3-1)*F12			0	+N12+H12
				+F12*0.2	@IF(H14>H12,1,0)	@IF(L13=1,N12+F12+J13,P14-H14)	@IF(L13=1,N14+H14,P12+F12+J13)
2	CAISSON	50	(F3-1)*F14				
				+F14*0.2	@IF(H16>H14,1,0)	@IF(L15=1,N14+F14+J15,P16-H16)	@IF(L15=1,N16+H16,P14+F14+J15)
3	BASE TO CAISSON	10	(F3-1)*F16				
				+F16*0.2	@IF(H18>H16,1,0)	@IF(L17=1,N16+F16+J17,P18-H18)	@IF(L17=1,N18+H18,P16+F16+J17)
4	CAISSON CAP	10	(F3-1)*F18				
				+F18*0.2	@IF(H20>H18,1,0)	@IF(L19=1,N18+F18+J19,P20-H20)	@IF(L19=1,N20+H20,P18+F18+J19)
5	PIER	50	(F3-1)*F20				
				+F20*0.2	@IF(H>22H20,1,0)	@IF(L21=1,N20+F20+J21,P22-H22)	@IF(L21=1,N22+H22,P20+F20+J21)
6	PIER HEAD	20	(F3-1)*F22				
				+F22*0.2	@IF(H24>H22,1,0)		@IF(L23=1,N24+H24,P22+F22+J23)
7	PIERS COMPLETE						

LEGEND START BUFFER 1
END BUFFER 0

second season, day 295, and completed (with a safety margin) before the end of day 588.

From figure 64 it is obvious that something must be done to increase the rate of production of the caissons (activity 2) and pier shafts (activity 5). Given that the duration of each individual activity are those thought most likely to occur using the firm's usual methods, the obvious way to reduce the time required is to double the resources on these two activities. The results of this are shown in table 21. (This is a simple assumption, and ignores the effects on productivity of the learning process.)

A further refinement in table 21 is to impose a target start on the pier construction. Although these activities have a logical dependency on the preceding activities, the basis of the plan is to build the bases in one season and the piers in the next. Thus the formula in the relevant cell has been adjusted to give the latest time of either:

1. that normally calculated by the line-of-balance method; or

2. the imposed target date.

(The project manager may decide that partially built piers will suffer no damage in the monsoon floods, so this may be an unnecessary refinement.)

Unfortunately, table 21 shows that these increased resources still do not give the required completion date. Time may be reduced by changing the method of construction. The original plan was to use one floating batching plant, and to transport and place the concrete entirely by manual methods. The height of lift of the pour was determined by the wish to complete each pour in a reasonable time by these means.

However, the height of the lift of the pours can be increased either by:

1. using two batching plants and two placing crews; or

2. by acquiring a bigger batching plant and pumping the concrete.

By these means, the durations of activities 2 and 5 may be reduced. The final line-of-balance schedule is in table 22.

Further development and re nements

Naturally, this fairly crude application can be refined and developed. The obvious development is to include all the labour-output-related calculations normally associated with line-of-balance. Thus columns would be added to the spreadsheet for: person-hours per unit; theoretical crew size; persons per item of construction; hence, actual crew size by calculation and rounding to an integral number; actual rate per period; etc. These calculations are straightforward in a spreadsheet.

The best approach to this is to create a new spreadsheet for these preliminary calculations, then to transfer the results by linking this spreadsheet to the line-of-balance spreadsheet. Alternatively, if the

Table 21. Railway bridge example with no adjustment

ACT NO.	ACTIVITY DESCRIP-TION	DURA-TION t (days)	No. of GANGS	TIME N-1 UNITS T (days)	BUFFER (days)	TYPE OF BUFFER	START DAY UNIT 1	START DAY UNIT N	END DAY UNIT N	TAR-GET END DAY
1	ISLAND	20	1	200			0	200	224	
					4	1				
2	CAISSON	50	2	250			24	274	334	
					10	0				
3	BASE TO CAISSON	10	1	100			234	334	346	
					2	0				
4	CAISSON CAP	10	1	100			246	346	358	294
					2	1				
5	PIER	50	2	250			294	544	604	
					10	0				
6	PIER HEAD	20	1	200			404	604	624	588
					4					

LEGEND   START BUFFER 1
          END BUFFER 0

productivity data are already stored in a database, then the necessary manipulations may be done within it, and the results transferred to the spreadsheet.

If these data are included, the whole calculation process can be reversed, starting with the planned hand-over rate and men (or other resource) per period as input. The schedule can then be calculated in the conventional line-of-balance way; experimenting with different hand-over schedules would yield the best schedule. Intellectually, this is the more elegant solution, because it is related directly to the basic principle of the technique; that is, that all activities will be planned to proceed as nearly as possible at a common rate of production. This has not been done in this case, for two reasons:

1. The method described in the bridge example given above reflects more closely the way in which project managers actually plan their work – and thus this approach is more likely to be accepted in practice; and

2. The line-of-balance technique is a powerful analytical tool for planning repetitive construction even if a common rate of production is not achieved.

Table 22. Railway bridge example with adjusted duration

ACT NO.	ACTIVITY DESCRIP-TION	DURA-TION t (days)	No. of GANGS	TIME N-1 UNITS T (days)	BUFFER (days)	TYPE OF BUFFER	START DAY UNIT 1	START DAY UNIT N	END DAY UNIT N	TAR-GET END DAY
1	ISLAND	20	1	200			0	200	224	
					4	0				
2	CAISSON	35	2	175			49	224	266	
					7	0				
3	BASE TO CAISSON	10	1	100			166	266	278	
					2	0				
4	CAISSON CAP	10	1	100			178	278	290	294
					2	1				
5	PIER	40	2	200			294	494	542	
					8	0				
6	PIER HEAD	20	1	200			342	542	566	588
					4					

LEGEND   START BUFFER 1
           END BUFFER 0

A further refinement is to introduce activities that run concurrently. This has been done for two concurrent activities. Additional columns have to be included in the spreadsheet, and two additional analyses have to be performed:

1. for the concurrent activities, in relation to their preceding activity; and

2. for the successor of the concurrent activities.

The method of calculation for the first analysis is quite straightforward, because the formulae in the relevant cells are simply adjusted to define a non-sequential, preceding activity. In the second case, two calculations have to be done; to determine which of the two preceding activities has the latest end date, and whether the successor follows with a start or end buffer. This is a complex relationship to express in one spreadsheet cell. It is far easier to create some auxiliary cells, outside the main spreadsheet, to perform some simple intermediate calculations. This is not very elegant, but it has the advantage of clarity.

Conclusions

One of the main purposes of this case-study is to demonstrate that contemporary general-purpose packages can be used in applications that would have required a specific program a few years ago. Spreadsheets, databases and other general packages can be used to solve everyday planning problems, and the planner who masters their use has acquired a powerful, general-purpose planning tool.

The case-study also demonstrates that the application of the technique and the preparation of input data can be integrated and mutually adjusted. In many cases, the data available for planning are quite heterogeneous in form, and planners have to spend some time before manipulating and interpreting them before they become useful for planning. A spreadsheet does this well.

Acknowledgement

The authors are grateful to the Chartered Institute of Building for permission to reproduce this article. The reference is given below:

R. H. Neale and B. Raju: "Line of Balance Calculations by Spreadsheet", in *Building Technology and Management*, Dec. 1988. Published by the Chartered Institute of Building, Englemere, Kings Ride, Ascot, Berkshire, SL5 8BJ, United Kingdom.

COST ANALYSIS CASE-STUDY 8

8.1 Introduction

This is the second part of the case-study given in Chapter 7, and it demonstrates the following aspects of construction project management:

1. Resource analysis at a practical level of detail

2. The application of a project management system to analysis of costs

3. The use of spreadsheet calculations within a project management system

4. Using the system to formulate a cost-effective plan

Research has shown that many "cost control systems" used by construction companies are ineffective in actually controlling costs, for two main reasons:

1. They attempt to collect and analyse data, and to present data in information, in too much detail. As was stated in Chapter 2, construction managers need information of immediate relevance, at a level of detail which is adequate for timely decision-making. Systems which attempt to control cost in detail almost always have to work on a monthly cycle of reporting, because this is the time required to collect and process the data. In most cases, this is far too long, and a simpler but much quicker system is usually far more effective.

2. Most systems report information on historic cost without attempting to forecast future trends. In addition, the style of presentation tends to approximate to that of accounting systems (quite reasonably, in many ways, because they focus on money) and so they rarely present the information in graphical form. Most non-accountants find graphical information easier to assimilate than tables of figures.

Means of overcoming these two problems are illustrated in this case-study, which explains how the resources are analysed, the resulting graphical histograms, and the way in which the duration – and hence overhead costs – are influenced by different resourcing strategies.

The case concludes with suggestions on how such systems may be extended for use in cost control. This is given in Section 8.2, which follows the case-study. The explanation will emphasize how important it is to consider data collection, and control methods, when designing the project plan. This links the case back to its start in Chapter 7, so providing an example of a unified approach to planning and control. It also shows how the system can be used to produce the type of charts shown in figure 9 in Chapter 2, thus linking this case to the principles discussed earlier.

Case-study F, Part 2

LUFBRA RESERVOIR

A planning and resource analysis case-study for a construction project, using a project management computer system

Part 2. Cost analysis

This case-study was compiled by Richard Neale and Simon Barber

Resources and cost information structure

The resources required for the construction of the reservoir were described in the first part of case-study F, Chapter 7. The HORNET computer system contains a spreadsheet for resource analysis which allows for up to 120 different resources. However, in the interests of keeping the system simple, only the following cost categories are used in this case-study:

Site workers	Resource nos. 1—10
Wall formwork	Resource nos. 11—20
Plant	Resource nos. 21—30
Subcontractors	Resource nos. 31—40

These are expanded to identify specific resources, as tabulated below.

Allocation of resources to activities

In general, resources can be allocated to activities in two ways:

1. As a lump sum, where the total of a resource is allocated, to be spread evenly over the duration of the activity. Examples of this type of allocation are work content in person-days (or person-hours), or financial sums.

2. As a "rate", where an allocated value is applied to each week, day or other time unit of the activity duration. Examples of this allocation of resources is where work content is expressed in "persons" (or "crews"), or the requirement of specific items of plant.

Most project management systems will accept both types of input, and convert one to another as required. In this case-study all resources have been allocated as "rates".

Resource no.	Description
1	Labourers (including concreters)
2	Formwork carpenters
11	Formwork—inner straight
12	Formwork—outer straight
13	Formwork—corners
14	Formwork—columns
21	Crawler crane
22	Concrete pump
23	JCB
31	Lufbra Roadworks Ltd
32	Fence & Son
33	E. Mover Ltd.
34	Green & Co
35	Shamrock Ironfighters
36	Magic Muck Ltd
37	Windmill Temporary Works Ltd
38	V. Sloform & Co. Ltd

The following notes describe the resources that have been estimated to be required for this project. The complete allocation of resources is given in the listings which follow.

Operatives. The work required for each of the activities was assessed in Part 1 of case-study F, and this was interpreted to give an activity duration and resource requirement. The number of persons required to complete each task is allocated to the activities as a "rate". An alternative approach would have been to enter the number of man-days work directly as a lump sum; HORNET would then divide this work over the duration of the activity.

An initial estimate has been made that eight unskilled labourers and four formwork carpenters will be required. The validity of this estimate will be examined in the scheduling section, below.

Formwork panels. Initially, only the minimum number of formwork panels will be used in the analysis, because they are quite expensive items to produce. At a later stage, the possible effects on the project duration of making extra panels, will be investigated, allowing a full cost analysis to be made. The number of panels allocated is as follows:

Resource no.	Description	No. allocated
11	Formwork—inner straight	2
12	Formwork—outer straight	2
13	Formwork—corners	2
14	Formwork—colums	2

Note that the two corner forms are not interchangeable; one is a left-hand and the other is a right-hand form.

When allocating the resource, the number required is allocated as a "rate". For example, wall panel 2 requires one inner straight and one outer straight form, resource numbers 11 and 12. Formwork is required for both "Wall forms" (activity 502) and "Wall concrete" (activity 503).

Roof soffit forms. The roof soffit also requires specialized formwork and this will be in limited supply; only enough to undertake one pour at a time will be brought onto the site. It seems appropriate, therefore to apply similar resource limits to this item. However, since this task is subcontracted and there is a strict sequence of events (proceed from west to east), the resource limitations are effectively introduced through the network logic links. (This approach is suitable for the roof structure because of the simple sequence, but cannot be applied readily to the wall panels without tying the project logic up in an enormous knot.)

Plant. Only three items of plant are of interest initially, a general purpose excavator (a "JCB"), a crawler crane for general lifting, and a concrete pump for the roof pours. This is relatively straightforward and there is no need to make the inclusion of these items over-elaborate. The allocations given in the listings simply indicate a requirement of the resource by always allocating a "rate" value of one. This will result in a requirement for two, three or more cranes at certain times; these figures will be meaningless if regarded as absolute values.

It would be possible to assess crane usage by estimating the proportion of the working day each activity actually requires access to the item. For example, erecting the wall formwork would occupy approximately 20 per cent of the day (less for a simple "straight" panel). Concreting the large tee section walls would occupy most of the day, say 80 per cent. By specifying allocation rates of "0.2" and "0.8" respectively, and extending this to cover all activities, it is very easy to produce a histogram of crane usage, and so any periods of excess requirement will be highlighted. Extra cranes could be ordered if thought appropriate.

It is assumed, however, that the contractor has sufficient experience to make a confident judgement that one crane will satisfy his requirements.

Subcontractors. A similar approach is applied to the activities subcontracted to other organizations. Rate allocation values of one are made to all activities that are not performed by the main contractor's own workforce. This technique simply highlights the fact that the activity is subcontracted on all printed resource reports.

Summary of resource allocations

Having defined the resources, the next step is to allocate the values to the activities. This has been done through a link between the resources spreadsheet and the activity data files. The results are summarized in the listings that follow. As in the case of the basic data listing given in Part 1, the activities have been broken down into various sections, such as excavations, floor, walls, etc. Each activity is listed with activity number, short and long descriptions, duration in weeks and days and resource allocation. To save space, the logical relationships are not repeated.

REFERENCE: **Preliminary Activities**

Activity Number	Activity descriptions	Duration	Management Code	RESOURCE Resource	Description	Value	ALLOCATIONS Resource	Description	Link	Value	Activity Number
101.00	Set up site RE s & Contractors offices	2:0	N0000	#1	Labourers	2 0	#2	Formwork Carpenters		2 0	101.00
102.00	Constr access track Sub-contract,Lufbra Roadworks Ltd	3:0	D0201	#31	S/C Lufbra Roadworks	1 0				0 0	102.00
103.00	Temporary fencing Sub-contract,Fence & Son.NB Temporary fencing onl	1:0	D0101	#32	S/C Fence & Son	1 0				0 0	103.00
104.00	Temp. access roads Sub-contract,E Mover.Included in excavation price	2:0	D0205	#33	S/C E Mover Ltd	1 0				0 0	104.00

Hornet Project Management Systems   Claremont Controls Ltd

REFERENCE: **Excavation Activities**

Activity Number	Activity descriptions	Duration	Management Code	RESOURCE Resource	Description	Value	ALLOCATIONS Resource	Description	Link	Value	Activity Number
201.00	Strip top soil Sub-contract,E Mover	1:0	000X D0102	#33	S/C E Mover Ltd	1 0				0 0	201.00
202.00	Excavate clay Sub-contract,E Mover	2:0	000X D0103	#33	S/C E Mover Ltd	1 0				0 0	202.00
203.00	Excavate rock Sub-contract,E Mover	3:0	000X D0104	#33	S/C E Mover Ltd	1 0				0 0	203.00
205.00	Fill & compact Sub-contract,E Mover	3:0	000X D1813	#33	S/C E Mover Ltd	1 0				0 0	205.00
210.00	Landscaping(seeding) Sub-contract, Green & Co	2:0	000X D1715	#34	S/C Green & Co	1 0				0 0	210.00

Hornet Project Management Systems   Claremont Controls Ltd

REFERENCE: Pipework and Drains

Activity Number	Activity descriptions	Duration	Management Code	RESOURCE		ALLOCATIONS				Activity Number
				Resource Description	Value	Resource Description	Link	Value		
301.00	Underfloor drain Includes perimeter drain	1:0	D0105	#1 Labourers	4 0	#23 JCB (hired)		1 0		301.00
302.00	Site drainage Water Board	4:0	D0203		0 0			0 0		302.00
303.00	Inlet pipework Water Board.Fixed time (target dates)	3:0	D1806		0 0			0 0		303.00
304.00	Outlet pipework Water Board.Fixed time (target dates)	2:0	D1906		0 0			0 0		304.00

Claremont Controls Ltd

Hornet Project Management Systems

REFERENCE: Floor Activities

Activity Number	Activity descriptions	Duration	Management Code	Resource	RESOURCE Description	Value	Resource	ALLOCATIONS Description	Link	Value	Activity Number
401.00	Floor blinding 6 strips 6m wide	2:0	F00B D0106	#1	Labourers	40	#2	Formwork Carpenters	2	0	401.00
402.01	Floor reinf panel 01 NW panel, W tank	0:3	F01R D0108	#21	Crawler crane	10	#35	S/C Shamrock Ironfig	1	0	402.01
402.02	Floor reinf panel 02 N panel, W tank	0:3	F02R D0111	#21	Crawler crane	10	#35	S/C Shamrock Ironfig	1	0	402.02
402.03	Floor reinf panel 03 N centre panel, both tanks	0:4	F03R D0308	#35	S/C Shamrock Ironfig	10	#21	Crawler crane	1	0	402.03
402.04	Floor reinf panel 04 N panel, E tank	0:3	F04R D0311	#21	Crawler crane	10	#35	S/C Shamrock Ironfig	1	0	402.04
402.05	Floor reinf panel 05 NE panel, E tank	0:3	F05R D0508	#21	Crawler crane	10	#35	S/C Shamrock Ironfig	1	0	402.05
402.06	Floor reinf panel 06 W panel, W tank	0:3	F06R D0511	#21	Crawler crane	10	#35	S/C Shamrock Ironfig	1	0	402.06
402.07	Floor reinf panel 07 Centre panel, W tank	0:2	F07R D0114	#21	Crawler crane	10	#35	S/C Shamrock Ironfig	1	0	402.07
402.08	Floor reinf panel 08 Centre panel, both tanks	0:4	F08R D0711	#21	Crawler crane	10	#35	S/C Shamrock Ironfig	1	0	402.08
402.09	Floor reinf panel 09 Centre panel, E tank	0:2	F09R D0314	#21	Crawler crane	10	#35	S/C Shamrock Ironfig	1	0	402.09
402.10	Floor reinf panel 10 E panel, E tank	0:3	F10R D0911	#21	Crawler crane	10	#35	S/C Shamrock Ironfig	1	0	402.10
402.11	Floor reinf panel 11 SW panel, W tank	0:3	F11R D0708	#21	Crawler crane	10	#35	S/C Shamrock Ironfig	1	0	402.11
402.12	Floor reinf panel 12 S panel, W tank	0:3	F12R D0116	#21	Crawler crane	10	#35	S/C Shamrock Ironfig	1	0	402.12
402.13	Floor reinf panel 13 S centre panel, both tanks	0:4	F13R D0908	#21	Crawler crane	10	#35	S/C Shamrock Ironfig	1	0	402.13
402.14	Floor reinf panel 14 S panel, E tank	0:3	F14R D0316	#21	Crawler crane	10	#35	S/C Shamrock Ironfig	1	0	402.14
402.15	Floor reinf panel 15 SE panel, E tank	0:3	F15R D1108	#21	Crawler crane	10	#35	S/C Shamrock Ironfig	1	0	402.15

Hornet Project Management Systems

Claremont Controls Ltd

Activity Number	Activity descriptions	Duration	Management Code	RESOURCE Resource	RESOURCE Description	RESOURCE Value	ALLOCATIONS Resource	ALLOCATIONS Description	ALLOCATIONS Link	ALLOCATIONS Value	Activity Number
403.01	Floor forms panel 01 NW panel, W tank	0:1	F01F D0208	#2	Formwork Carpenters	4 0				0 0	403.01
403.02	Floor forms panel 02 N panel, W tank	0:1	F02F D0211	#2	Formwork Carpenters	4 0				0 0	403.02
403.03	Floor forms panel 03 N centre panel, both tanks	0:2	F03F D0408	#2	Formwork Carpenters	4 0				0 0	403.03
403.04	Floor forms panel 04 N panel, E tank	0:1	F04F D0411	#2	Formwork Carpenters	4 0				0 0	403.04
403.05	Floor forms panel 05 NE panel, E tank	0:1	F05F D0608	#2	Formwork Carpenters	4 0				0 0	403.05
403.06	Floor forms panel 06 W panel, W tank	0:1	F06F D0611	#2	Formwork Carpenters	4 0				0 0	403.06
403.07	Floor forms panel 07 Centre panel, W tank	0:1	F07F D0214	#2	Formwork Carpenters	4 0				0 0	403.07
403.08	Floor forms panel 08 Centre panel, both tanks	0:2	F08F D0811	#2	Formwork Carpenters	4 0				0 0	403.08
403.09	Floor forms panel 09 Centre panel, E tank	0:1	F09F D0414	#2	Formwork Carpenters	4 0				0 0	403.09
403.10	Floor forms panel 10 E panel, E tank	0:1	F10F D1011	#2	Formwork Carpenters	4 0				0 0	403.10
403.11	Floor forms panel 11 SW panel, W tank	0:1	F11F D0808	#2	Formwork Carpenters	4 0				0 0	403.11
403.12	Floor forms panel 12 S panel, W tank	0:1	F12F D0216	#2	Formwork Carpenters	4 0				0 0	403.12
403.13	Floor forms panel 13 S Centre panel, both tanks	0:2	F13F D1008	#2	Formwork Carpenters	4 0				0 0	403.13
403.14	Floor forms panel 14 S panel, E tank	0:1	F14F D0416	#2	Formwork Carpenters	4 0				0 0	403.14
403.15	Floor forms panel 15 SE panel, E tank	0:1	F15F D1208	#2	Formwork Carpenters	4 0				0 0	403.15
404.01	Floor conc panel 01 NW panel, W tank	0:1	F01C D0109	#1	Labourers	4 0				0 0	404.01

Hornet Project Management Systems

Claremont Controls Ltd

REFERENCE: Floor Activities

Activity Number	Activity descriptions	Duration	Management Code	RESOURCE Resource	RESOURCE Description	RESOURCE Value	ALLOCATIONS Resource	ALLOCATIONS Description	ALLOCATIONS Link	ALLOCATIONS Value	Activity Number
404.02	Floor conc panel 02 N panel, W tank	0:1	F02C D0112	#1	Labourers	4 0				0 0	404.02
404.03	Floor conc panel 03 N centre panel, both tanks	0:1	F03C D0309	#1	Labourers	4 0				0 0	404.03
404.04	Floor conc panel 04 N panel, E tank	0:1	F04C D0312	#1	Labourers	4 0				0 0	404.04
404.05	Floor conc panel 05 NE panel, E tank	0:1	F05C D0509	#1	Labourers	4 0				0 0	404.05
404.06	Floor conc panel 06 W panel, W tank	0:1	F06C D0512	#1	Labourers	4 0				0 0	404.06
404.07	Floor conc panel 07 Centre panel, W tank	0:1	F07C D0115	#1	Labourers	4 0	#21	Crawler crane		1 0	404.07
404.08	Floor conc panel 08 Centre panel, both tanks	0:1	F08C D0712	#1	Labourers	4 0	#21	Crawler crane		1 0	404.08
404.09	Floor conc panel 09 Centre panel, E tank	0:1	F09C D0315	#1	Labourers	4 0	#21	Crawler crane		1 0	404.09
404.10	Floor conc panel 10 E panel, E tank	0:1	F10C D0912	#1	Labourers	4 0				0 0	404.10
404.11	Floor conc panel 11 SW panel, W tank	0:1	F11C D0709	#1	Labourers	4 0				0 0	404.11
404.12	Floor conc panel 12 S panel, W tank	0:1	F12C D0117	#1	Labourers	4 0	#21	Crawler crane		1 0	404.12
404.13	Floor conc panel 13 S centre panel, both tanks	0:1	F13C D0909	#1	Labourers	4 0				0 0	404.13
404.14	Floor conc panel 14 S panel, E tank	0:1	F14C D0317	#1	Labourers	4 0	#21	Crawler crane		1 0	404.14
404.15	Floor conc panel 15 SE panel, E tank	0:1	F15C D1109	#1	Labourers	4 0				0 0	404.15

Claremont Controls Ltd

Hornet Project Management Systems

Activity Number	Activity descriptions	Duration	Management Code	RESOURCE Resource	RESOURCE Description	RESOURCE Value	ALLOCATIONS Resource	ALLOCATIONS Description	Link Value	Activity Number
501.01	Wall reinf panel 01 / N W wall, W tank	0:3	W01R D0119	#35	S/C Shamrock Ironfig	1 / 0			0 / 0	501.01
501.02	Wall reinf panel 02 / N wall, W tank	0:2	W02R D0122	#35	S/C Shamrock Ironfig	1 / 0			0 / 0	501.02
501.03	Wall reinf panel 03 / N tee wall, both tanks	0:3	W03R D0219	#35	S/C Shamrock Ironfig	1 / 0			0 / 0	501.03
501.04	Wall reinf panel 04 / N wall, E tank	0:2	W04R D0322	#35	S/C Shamrock Ironfig	1 / 0			0 / 0	501.04
501.05	Wall reinf panel 05 / NE wall, E tank	0:3	W05R D0419	#35	S/C Shamrock Ironfig	1 / 0			0 / 0	501.05
501.06	Wall reinf panel 06 / W wall, W tank	0:2	W06R D0522	#35	S/C Shamrock Ironfig	1 / 0			0 / 0	501.06
501.08	Wall reinf panel 08 / Centre wall, both tanks	0:2	W08R D0622	#35	S/C Shamrock Ironfig	1 / 0			0 / 0	501.08
501.10	Wall reinf panel 10 / E wall, E tank	0:2	W10R D0722	#35	S/C Shamrock Ironfig	1 / 0			0 / 0	501.10
501.11	Wall reinf panel 11 / SW wall, W tank	0:3	W11R D0519	#35	S/C Shamrock Ironfig	1 / 0			0 / 0	501.11
501.12	Wall reinf panel 12 / S wall, E tank	0:2	W12R D0920	#35	S/C Shamrock Ironfig	1 / 0			0 / 0	501.12
501.13	Wall reinf panel 13 / S tee wall	0:3	W13R D0719	#35	S/C Shamrock Ironfig	1 / 0			0 / 0	501.13
501.14	Wall reinf panel 14 / S wall, E tank	0:2	W14R D1020	#35	S/C Shamrock Ironfig	1 / 0			0 / 0	501.14
501.15	Wall reinf panel 15 / SE wall, E tank	0:3	W15R D0819	#35	S/C Shamrock Ironfig	1 / 0			0 / 0	501.15
502.01	Wall forms panel 01 / N W wall, W tank	0:4	W01F D0120	#11 / #13	Formwork-inner strai / Formwork-corners	1 / 1	#12 / #2	Formwork-outer strai / Formwork Carpenters	2 / 4	502.01
502.02	Wall forms panel 02 / N wall, W tank	0:3	W02F D0123	#11 / #2	Formwork-inner strai / Formwork Carpenters	1 / 4	#12 / #21	Formwork-outer strai / Crawler crane	1 / 1	502.02
502.03	Wall forms panel 03 / N tee wall, both tanks	1:0	W03F D0220	#11 / #13	Formwork-inner strai / Formwork-corners	2 / 2	#12 / #2	Formwork-outer strai / Formwork Carpenters	1 / 4	502.03

Claremont Controls Ltd

Hornet Project Management Systems

REFERENCE: Wall Activities

Activity Number	Activity descriptions	Duration	Management Code	RESOURCE Resource	RESOURCE Description	RESOURCE Value	ALLOCATIONS Resource	ALLOCATIONS Description	ALLOCATIONS Link Value	Activity Number
502.04	Wall forms panel 04 N wall, E tank	0:3	W04F D0323	#11 #2	Formwork-inner strai Formwork Carpenters	1 4	#12 #21	Formwork-outer strai Crawler crane	1 1	502.04
502.05	Wall forms panel 05 NE wall, E tank	0:4	W05F D0420	#11 #13	Formwork-inner strai Formwork-corners	1 1	#12 #2	Formwork-outer strai Formwork Carpenters	2 4	502.05
502.06	Wall forms panel 06 W wall, W tank	0:3	W06F D0523	#11 #2	Formwork-inner strai Formwork Carpenters	1 4	#12 #21	Formwork-outer strai Crawler crane	1 1	502.06
502.08	Wall forms panel 08 Centre wall, both tanks	0:3	W08F D0623	#11 #21	Formwork-inner strai Crawler crane	2 1	#2	Formwork Carpenters	4 0	502.08
502.10	Wall forms panel 10 E wall, E tank	0:3	W10F D0723	#11 #2	Formwork-inner strai Formwork Carpenters	1 4	#12 #21	Formwork-outer strai Crawler crane	1 1	502.10
502.11	Wall forms panel 11 SW wall, W tank	0:4	W11F D0520	#11 #13	Formwork-inner strai Formwork-corners	1 1	#12 #2	Formwork-outer strai Formwork Carpenters	2 4	502.11
502.12	Wall forms panel 12 S wall, E tank	0:3	W12F D0921	#11 #2	Formwork-inner strai Formwork Carpenters	1 4	#12 #21	Formwork-outer strai Crawler crane	1 1	502.12
502.13	Wall forms panel 13 S tee wall	1:0	W13F D0720	#11 #13	Formwork-inner strai Formwork-corners	2 2	#12 #21	Formwork-outer strai Formwork Carpenters	1 4	502.13
502.14	Wall forms panel 14 S wall, E tank	0:3	W14F D1021	#11 #2	Formwork-inner strai Formwork Carpenters	1 4	#12 #21	Formwork-outer strai Crawler crane	1 1	502.14
502.15	Wall forms panel 15 SE wall, E tank	0:4	W15F D0820	#11 #13	Formwork-inner strai Formwork-corners	1 1	#12 #2	Formwork-outer strai Formwork Carpenters	2 4	502.15
503.01	Wall conc panel 01 N W wall, W tank	0:1	W01C D0121	#1 #11	Labourers Formwork-inner strai	4 1	#21 #12	Crawler crane Formwork-outer strai	1 2	503.01
503.02	Wall conc panel 02 N wall, W tank	0:1	W02C D0124	#1 #11	Labourers Formwork-inner strai	4 1	#21 #12	Crawler crane Formwork-outer strai	1 1	503.02
503.03	Wall conc panel 03 N tee wall, both tanks	0:1	W03C D0221	#1 #11	Labourers Formwork-inner strai	4 2	#21 #12	Crawler crane Formwork-outer strai	1 1	503.03
503.04	Wall conc panel 04 N wall, E tank	0:1	W04C D0324	#1 #11	Labourers Formwork-inner strai	4 1	#21 #12	Crawler crane Formwork-outer strai	1 1	503.04
503.05	Wall conc panel 05 NE wall, E tank	0:1	W05C D0421	#1 #11	Labourers Formwork-inner strai	4 1	#21 #12	Crawler crane Formwork-outer strai	1 2	503.05
503.06	Wall conc panel 06 W wall, W tank	0:1	W06C D0524	#1 #11	Labourers Formwork-inner strai	4 1	#21 #12	Crawler crane Formwork-outer strai	1 1	503.06

Hornet Project Management Systems

Claremont Controls Ltd

REFERENCE: Wall Activities

Activity Number	Activity descriptions	Duration	Management Code	RESOURCE			ALLOCATIONS				Activity Number
				Resource	Description	Value	Resource	Description	Link	Value	
503.08	Wall conc panel 08 Centre wall, both tanks	0:1	W08C D0624	#1 #11	Labourers Formwork-inner strai	4 2	#21	Crawler crane		1 0	503.08
503.10	Wall conc panel 10 E wall, E tank	0:1	W10C D0724	#1 #11	Labourers Formwork-inner strai	4 1	#21 #12	Crawler crane Formwork-outer strai		1 1	503.10
503.11	Wall conc panel 11 SW wall, W tank	0:1	W11C D0521	#1 #11	Labourers Formwork-inner strai	4 1	#21 #12	Crawler crane Formwork-outer strai		1 2	503.11
503.12	Wall conc panel 12 S wall, E tank	0:1	W12C D0922	#1 #11	Labourers Formwork-inner strai	4 1	#21 #12	Crawler crane Formwork-outer strai		1 1	503.12
503.13	Wall conc panel 13 S tee wall	0:1	W13C D0721	#1 #11	Labourers Formwork-inner strai	4 2	#21 #12	Crawler crane Formwork-outer strai		1 1	503.13
503.14	Wall conc panel 14 S wall, E tank	0:1	W14C D1022	#1 #11	Labourers Formwork-inner strai	4 1	#21 #12	Crawler crane Formwork-outer strai		1 1	503.14
503.15	Wall conc panel 15 SE wall, E tank	0:1	W15C D0821	#1 #11	Labourers Formwork-inner strai	4 1	#21 #12	Crawler crane Formwork-outer strai		1 2	503.15
550.00	Make wall formwork Made by Windmill Temporary Works Ltd	2:0	N0000	#37	S/C Windmill Temp Wo	1 0				0 0	550.00
551.00	Forms arrive on site	0:1	N0000			0 0				0 0	551.00

Hornet Project Management Systems

Claremont Controls Ltd

REFERENCE: **Roof Activities**

Activity Number	Activity descriptions	Duration	Management Code	Resource	RESOURCE Description	Value	ALLOCATIONS Resource	Description	Link	Value	Activity Number
601.01	Roof scaffold pour 1	0:3	R01S D1402	#38	S/C Slowform & Co Lt	1 0				0 0	601.01
601.02	Roof scaffold pour 2	1:1	R02S D1406	#38	S/C Slowform & Co Lt	1 0				0 0	601.02
601.03	Roof scaffold pour 3	1:1	R03S D1410	#38	S/C Slowform & Co Lt	1 0				0 0	601.03
601.04	Roof scaffold pour 4	1:1	R04S D1414	#38	S/C Slowform & Co Lt	1 0				0 0	601.04
601.05	Roof scaffold pour 5	0:3	R05S D1418	#38	S/C Slowform & Co Lt	1 0				0 0	601.05
602.01	Roof soffit pour 1	0:4	R01F D1403	#2	Formwork Carpenters	4 0	#21	Crawler crane		1 0	602.01
602.02	Roof soffit pour 2	1:3	R02F D1407	#2	Formwork Carpenters	4 0	#21	Crawler crane		1 0	602.02
602.03	Roof soffit pour 3	1:3	R03F D1411	#2	Formwork Carpenters	4 0	#21	Crawler crane		1 0	602.03
602.04	Roof soffit pour 4	1:3	R04F D1415	#2	Formwork Carpenters	4 0	#21	Crawler crane		1 0	602.04
602.05	Roof soffit pour 5	0:4	R05F D1419	#2	Formwork Carpenters	4 0	#21	Crawler crane		1 0	602.05
603.01	Roof reinf pour 1	0:2	R01R D1503	#35	S/C Shamrock Ironfig	1 0	#21	Crawler crane		1 0	603.01
603.02	Roof reinf pour 2	0:4	R02R D1507	#35	S/C Shamrock Ironfig	1 0	#21	Crawler crane		1 0	603.02
603.03	Roof reinf pour 3	0:4	R03R D1511	#35	S/C Shamrock Ironfig	1 0	#21	Crawler crane		1 0	603.03
603.04	Roof reinf pour 4	0:4	R04R D1515	#35	S/C Shamrock Ironfig	1 0	#21	Crawler crane		1 0	603.04
603.05	Roof reinf pour 5	0:2	R05R D1519	#35	S/C Shamrock Ironfig	1 0	#21	Crawler crane		1 0	603.05
604.01	Roof conc pour 1	0:1	R01C D1504	#1	Labourers	4 0	#22	Concrete pump(hired)		1 0	604.01

Hornet Project Management Systems

Claremont Controls Ltd

Activity Number	Activity descriptions	Duration	Management Code	RESOURCE Resource	Description	Value	ALLOCATIONS Resource	Description	Link	Value	Activity Number
604.02	Roof conc pour 2	0:2	R02C D1508	#1	Labourers	4 / 0	#22	Concrete pump(hired)		1 / 0	604.02
604.03	Roof conc pour 3	0:2	R03C D1512	#1	Labourers	4 / 0	#22	Concrete pump(hired)		1 / 0	604.03
604.04	Roof conc pour 4	0:2	R04C D1516	#1	Labourers	4 / 0	#22	Concrete pump(hired)		1 / 0	604.04
604.05	Roof conc pour 5	0:1	R05C D1520	#1	Labourers	4 / 0	#22	Concrete pump(hired)		1 / 0	604.05
605.01	Roof cure & strike 1	2:4	R01K D1505	#1 #21	Labourers Crawler crane	4 / 1	#2	Formwork Carpenters		4 / 0	605.01
605.02	Roof cure & strike 2	2:4	R02K D1509	#1 #21	Labourers Crawler crane	4 / 1	#2	Formwork Carpenters		4 / 0	605.02
605.03	Roof cure & strike 3	2:4	R03K D1513	#1 #21	Labourers Crawler crane	4 / 1	#2	Formwork Carpenters		2 / 0	605.03
605.04	Roof cure & strike 4	2:4	R04K D1517	#1 #21	Labourers Crawler crane	4 / 1	#2	Formwork Carpenters		4 / 0	605.04
605.05	Roof cure & strike 5	2:4	R05K D1521	#1 #21	Labourers Crawler crane	4 / 1	#2	Formwork Carpenters		4 / 0	605.05
606.00	Roof covering	2:0	D1714	#1	Labourers	4 / 0				0 / 0	606.00
610.01	Columns 1 - 2	0:4	C01G D0914	#14 #2	Column forms Formwork Carpenters	2 / 4	#1 #31	Labourers S/C Lufbra Roadworks		4 / 1	610.01
610.03	Columns 3 - 4	0:4	C03G D1016	#14 #2	Column forms Formwork Carpenters	2 / 4	#1 #21	Labourers Crawler crane		4 / 1	610.03
610.05	Columns 5 - 6	0:4	C05G D1014	#14 #2	Column forms Formwork Carpenters	2 / 4	#1 #21	Labourers Crawler crane		4 / 1	610.05
610.07	Columns 7 - 8	0:4	C07G D1116	#14 #2	Column forms Formwork Carpenters	1 / 4	#1 #21	Labourers Crawler crane		4 / 1	610.07
610.09	Columns 9 - 10	0:4	C09G D1114	#14 #2	Column forms Formwork Carpenters	2 / 4	#1 #21	Labourers Crawler crane		4 / 1	610.09
610.11	Columns 11 - 12	0:4	C11G D1216	#14 #2	Column forms Formwork Carpenters	2 / 4	#1 #21	Labourers Crawler crane		4 / 1	610.11

Claremont Controls Ltd

REFERENCE: Roof Activities

Activity Number	Activity descriptions	Duration	Management Code	Resource	Resource Description	Value	Resource	Description	Link	Value	Activity Number
611.02	Complete Col Strip 2 Columns 1,2,5,6,9 and 10		D1015			0 / 0				0 / 0	611.02
611.04	Complete Col Strip 4 Columns 3,4,7,8,11 and 12		D1117			0 / 0				0 / 0	611.04
612.00	Ladders & covers On roof, pour 3	2:0	D1711	#2	Formwork Carpenters	2 / 0	#21	Crawler crane	1 / 0		612.00
613.00	Joints:floor, roof.. Sub-contract, Magic Muck Ltd	1:0	D1622	#1 / #36	Labourers / S/C Magic Muck Ltd	2 / 1	#21	Crawler crane	1 / 0		613.00
615.01	Clean inside resrvr All roofs cured and struck	0:2	D1522	#1	Labourers	6 / 0	#21	Crawler crane	1 / 0		615.01
615.02	Test reservoir	1:0	D1712	#1	Labourers	2 / 0			0 / 0		615.02
615.03	Complete & test roof Waterproof membrane and water test	1:0	D1713	#1	Labourers	2 / 0			0 / 0		615.03

Activity Number	Activity descriptions	Duration	Management Code	RESOURCE			ALLOCATIONS				Activity Number
				Resource	Description	Value	Resource	Description	Link	Value	
701.00	Valve chamber base	2:0	V01G D1703	#1 #21	Labourers Crawler crane	4 1	#2 #35	Formwork Carpenters S/C Shamrock Ironfig		4 1	701.00
702.00	Valve chamber walls Single pour - could be divided if required	2:0	V02G D1704	#1 #21	Labourers Crawler crane	4 1	#2 #35	Formwork Carpenters S/C Shamrock Ironfig		4 1	702.00
703.00	Valve chamber pltfrm Valve chamber platform for access	1:3	V03G D1705	#1 #21	Labourers Crawler crane	4 1	#2 #35	Formwork Carpenters S/C Shamrock Ironfig		4 1	703.00
704.00	Valve chamber roof Duration includes slab curing	2:0	V04G D1706	#1 #21	Labourers Crawler crane	4 1	#2 #35	Formwork Carpenters S/C Shamrock Ironfig		4 1	704.00
705.00	Complete pipework	2:0	D1907	#1	Labourers	4 0				0 0	705.00

Hornet Project Management Systems

Claremont Controls Ltd

Activity Number	Activity descriptions	Duration	Management Code	RESOURCE			ALLOCATIONS				Activity Number
				Resource	Description	Value	Resource	Description	Link	Value	
801.00	Permanent fencing Sub-contract,Fence & Son	2:0	D1716	#32	S/C Fence & Son	1 0				0 0	801.00
901.00	Site overheads Insurances,services,site management		N0000			0 0				0 0	901.00
902.00	Crane hire On site start forms wall panel 13 to pipework en		N0000	#21	Crawler crane	1 0				0 0	902.00
1000.00	Clear site Remove RE s & Contractor s offices	0:2	D1717	#1	Labourers	2 0	#2	Formwork Carpenters		4 0	1000.00

Hornet Project Management Systems

Claremont Controls Ltd

Scheduling

The project has now been defined and the basic data entered into the system. The analysis of Part 1 of the case-study has given an initial time-scale for the project, based on the time required to complete individual tasks in the logical sequence. The resources required to complete the work within each activity have now been added to these data. The next step is to assess the total resources that must be made available to complete the project in this time, and when they will be required. In addition, if sufficient resources cannot be made available, to assess the consequences on the project duration.

In this case, the labour and formwork resources are of principal interest initially. These are the main resources under the control of the contractor, apart from the plant which, being hired when required, is a far more flexible resource for scheduling purposes. The following analyses assess the implications of making different levels of these two critical resources available. In trying different ideas for resourcing the project, the data have to be re-scheduled several times, with different restrictions on the quantity of the resources to be used. This is a classical application of "what if", or feasibility, planning.

The computer system has a scheduling capability. This undertakes a complex analysis, working through the project, activity-by-activity, time-period-by-time-period, allocating resources to activities. When more resources are required by the activities scheduled for a particular time period than have been made available to the project, the scheduler will delay one or more, according to a set of rules, and so produce a revised, resource-limited schedule. Most project management systems have these facilities, and their use is illustrated in the following sections.

The six reports reproduced on the following pages were obtained by using the user-defined reporting facilities. These allow the user to specify the form and content of the reports, within fairly wide limits, and so obtain exactly the information required. These reports used the system's graphics capability to draw histograms of the resource demands of the project activities, and also to reflect management strategies in resource provision. The histograms are summarized briefly below.

Histogram report 1: preliminary resource profiles. This report shows three histograms, one each for the key resources identified above. The basis of analysis has been the initial planning information, and no limits on the resources available have been assumed. The scheduled project duration is, therefore, the minimum possible: 48 weeks, as stated in the first part of the case-study F, in Chapter 7. The following peaks in resource demand are identified:

Resource no.	Description	Proposed limit (no.)	Maximum demand (no.)
1	Labourers	8	24
2	Formwork carpenters	4	40
11	Formwork—inner straight	2	8
12	Formwork—corners	2	10
13	Formwork—inner straight	2	8

Clearly the project cannot be expected to require the peaks of input indicated on the resource profiles, indeed a glance at the profiles shows great fluctuations with areas of gross underuse as well as high peaks in demand. The next step is to turn to the resource schedulers in the system to see what this facility has to offer.

Resource sensitivity analysis. The resource scheduler has produced a new schedule for the project, in which the dates for the activities are not only based on durations and logical relationships, but also ensure that some specified resource limits are not exceeded. Therefore, in theory at least, all that is required is to apply the limits indicated above (they should in fact already be in the data) run the resource scheduler and print off the new bar chart for the project.

The calculating takes only a minute or two to complete, and the resulting resource profiles will confirm that at no point in the project are the specified limits exceeded Clearly to perform this task on even this simplified case-study would be extremely time-consuming by hand and there would be very little chance of having a number of trial runs.

The strategy adopted in this case-study is to explore the effects of limiting each resource, or combinations of resources, in turn, rather than to simply apply all the limits at once. This form of analysis enables the planner to develop insights into the way in which each individual resource affects the project schedule, which is much more meaningful than simply relying upon the automatic scheduler. This is known as "resource sensitivity analysis" because it reveals just how sensitive the project duration is to variations in the level of each resource. It is one of the most powerful tolls of management, and illustrates the contribution that information technology may make to project management.

There is a number of ways of approaching the task, but a fairly obvious first step is to study the use of the wall formwork panels. These are known to be expensive items to make and the contractor will only make extra panels if a very significant saving in time is achieved. The time

Histogram report no. 1

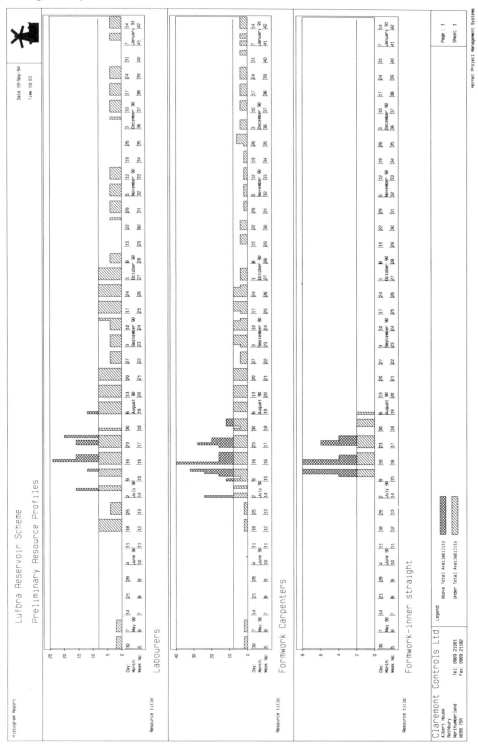

analysis gives a 48-week project duration with a large number of panels. That is the impact of making only the minimum number of two of each type.

Histogram reports 2 and 3: resource profiles with formwork limited. The reports on the previous two pages show the project schedule when the formwork has been limited to the construction manager's original allocation. The first report, with three histograms, shows this clearly. This restriction has resulted in an extension of the project duration from 48 weeks to 51 weeks. The conclusion is obvious: the contractor needs only a minimum of panels, since the making of extra panels will not be cost effective.

The second report shows that this extension has also been of benefit to the demands for labour, with both the peak demands for labourers and carpenters being reduced (labourers from 24 to 16, and formwork carpenters from 40 to 24).

Histogram report 4: resource profiles with all resources limited. The result of running the resource scheduler again, with the main resources limited in availability, is to obtain schedules in which excess resource requirement is prevented. By limiting all the resources at once, the planner produces a "worst-case schedule", giving an upper limit on the likely project duration. The result is a schedule where the project duration is increased from 51 weeks to 69 weeks and four days. In doing the calculation no indication is given of which resources are actually limiting progress on the project. However, since the planner now knows what are the effects of limiting all resources, and formwork only, then further analyses can be performed to investigate the effects of the other resources, within this "envelope".

Histogram reports 5 and 6: resource profiles with "best practical" levels of resources. The two profile reports given on the following pages show the final schedule, after making a number of analyses with different resource levels.

The calculations so far have taken the basic project model and derived different schedules based on different constraints. Further considerations would require a few policy decisions to be made. This is a summary of the conclusions so far:

1. Only a minimum number of wall formwork panels are required, the extra cost of making more panels will not result in significant savings in time.

2. A general labour force of eight men does not constrain the overall duration of the project.

3. Restricting the maximum number of formwork carpenters to eight does not constrain the overall duration of the project; however,

Histogram report no. 2

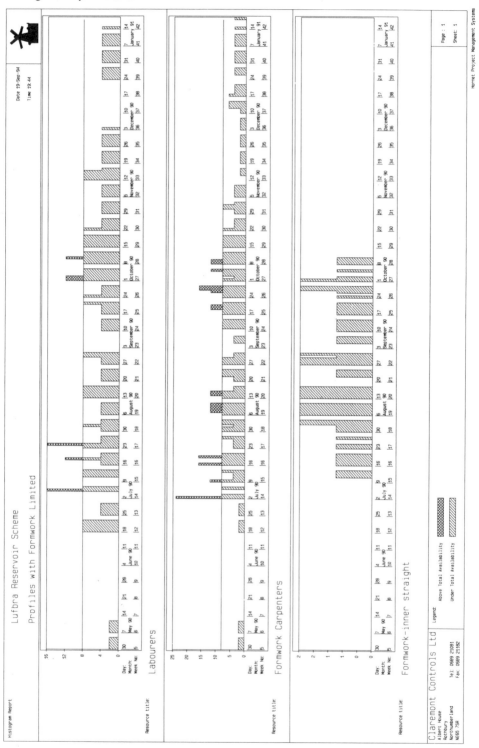

Histogram report no. 3

Histogram report no. 4

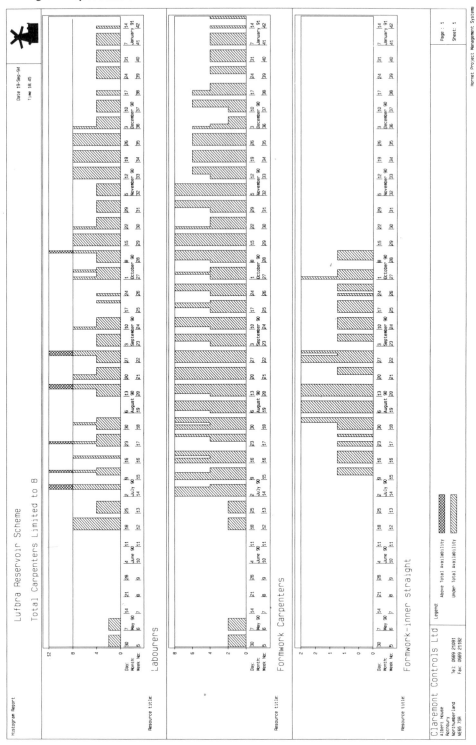

Histogram report no. 5

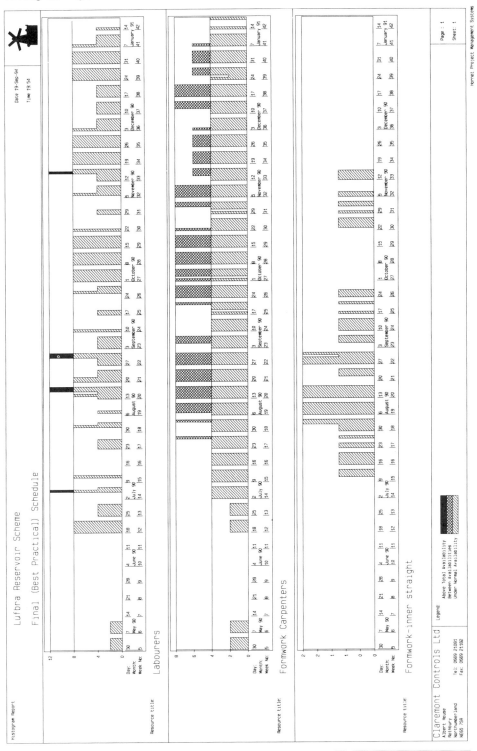

Histogram report no. 6

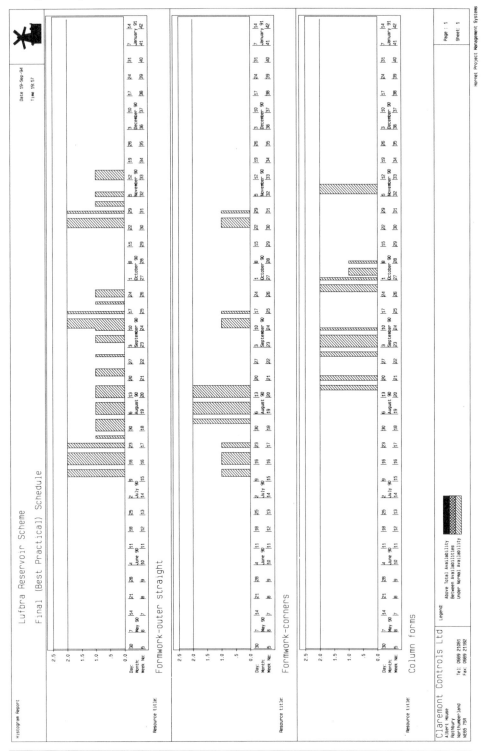

MANAGING INTERNATIONAL CONSTRUCTION PROJECTS: AN OVERVIEW

imposing a lower limit of four men increases the completion time by 14 weeks, from mid-March to the end of July 1991.

In summary, the project has been scheduled with a sensible number of formwork panels, carpenters are scheduled with a base level of 4 persons and a maximum level of 8 persons. This maximum is for a short duration, and since the construction manager will have considerable warning of this problem, it is anticipated that measures can be taken to overcome it. The alternative would be a serious extension to the project duration, which is uneconomic. This is where scheduling theory stops, and the practice of management starts! Similarly, the requirements for labourers only exceeds eight men on a few occasions, so it is proposed not to let the computer "level" this requirement, but to consider these isolated cases manually and, if necessary, revise the project strategy accordingly. This is not an "optimum schedule" in textbook terms, but the "best practical schedule".

8.2 Use of project management systems in the control of time and cost

The use of simple control charts was discussed in Chapter 2, and figure 9 showed an example. The chart on page 239 is based on the Lufbra Reservoir plan produced earlier in this chapter, and demonstrates how these types of charts may be easily produced by the HORNET and similar systems, using the planning and resources data already in the system. These charts can be made simply by requesting the standard output format, or users can access another part of the system and design their own charts. Multiple lines can be produced, so comparisons are possible.

This case-study has given the full data needed to plan such a project. One purpose has been to explain realistically and comprehensively how projects may be planned using modern computing systems, but a second purpose is that readers have sufficient information to experiment with their own systems, developing solutions to suit their own working practices. This subject will not, therefore, be pursued further in this book.

8.3 A practical approach to the control of time and cost

This case-study illustrates how data structures may be designed to provide a simple and straightforward basis for control. Although detailed plans may be made, and excellent graphical representations produced, control relies on the provision of realistic feedback on the progress of work as the job proceeds; this is the basis on which decisions are made. However, the timely capture of performance data is notoriously difficult, mainly because the people involved are usually preoccupied with the day-to-day challenge managing the physical construction work, and are not highly motivated to measure and report in great detail. Thus, a system of data capture and reporting must be devised that is simple to operate, produces information quickly, and yet is sufficiently accurate to influence decision-making.

This type of structure is illustrated in this case-study. Consider, for example, wall formwork. The original information provided by the client is unhelpful as a control tool. The information provided in the bill of quantities is:

Item G1 Formwork Rough Finish
Item Number G 1.4.5 Vertical Reservoir Walls   440 square metres

Item G 2 Formwork Fair Finish
Item Number G 2.3.5 Battered to walls and
chamber   654 square metres

If this were to form the basis for control, then at the end of each control period (week or month), the site staff would have to measure progress on the basis of square metres complete, and compare this to that which was planned.

In the data used for the planning case-study, the planner has converted this information so that it matches exactly the planned construction method. For example, the following is taken from the Resource Allocation data for Wall Activities:

Activity Number 502.02: Wall forms panel 0 N wall W tank

Duration: 3 days

Resources: 1 formwork inner straight, 1 formwork outer straight, 4 formwork carpenters, 1 crawler crane

Thus, in one succinct, measurable item the work to be done, the time allowed and the budgeted resources are defined. When assessing progress, it is very easy to assess whether this work is complete, because it is defined as a self-contained item of work, which is visually very obvious. The resources allocated may then be claimed against the budget, and the information used to compare actual expenditure. If the work is partially complete, it is relatively easy to assess a percentage completion with, say, 10 per cent accuracy.

It is, clearly, unrealistic to make comparisons between budget and actual for each item of formwork. The cost of collecting this data would be high, and the time required to do so would probably rob the reporting system of its timeliness. However, carpenters and cranes would be likely to work on a number of items of wall formwork during a day, so allocating their time to a simple heading such as "wall formwork" could be done quite accurately. It is, therefore, practical to make reasonably accurate and timely comparisons between planned and actual at a broad level of activity definition. This can then be plotted as a control curve (see Histogram Report No. 7, p.239), future trends predicted, and action taken.

Histogram report no. 7 (line graph)

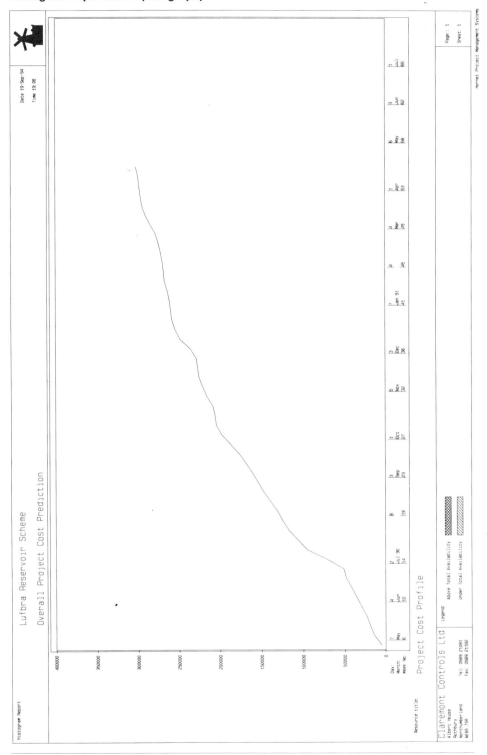